Leviné

Leviné
the Spartacist

ROSA LEVINÉ-MEYER

With an introduction by E. J. Hobsbawm

GORDON & CREMONESI

© 1973 Rosa Leviné-Meyer *first published in abbreviated German translation, 1972.*

This edition first published 1978

ISBN 0-86033-062-1

Printed in Great Britain by Robert MacLehose & Co Ltd
The University Press, Glasgow

Gordon & Cremonesi,
London & New York,
New River House,
34 Seymour Road,
London N8 0BE

Contents

Introduction

by E. I. Hobsbawm

On the 29th of October 1918 the German navy received the order to sail out for a last, desperate – and since Germany had visibly lost the war – pointless attack on the British. The sailors mutinied, took over the naval base, garrison and city of Kiel, and elected a workers' and soldiers' council. Within a few days the news, often spread by travelling sailors, swept across a warweary and rebellious Germany. The German Revolution had begun, and on the 9th of November Kaiser William II abdicated, handing over government to a moderate and respectable ex-saddler, Friedrich Ebert, leader of the Social Democratic Party. The apparatus of German imperial rule abdicated with the emperor. Ebert, who was to be the first president of the German Republic, did not want a republic, but another, more realistic Social Democratic leader proclaimed one. The former imperial administration, the army itself, transferred its loyalty without the slightest resistance to the new regime, but on conditions. General Groener, speaking for the army, telephoned Ebert on the 10th of November that he would put the armed forces at his disposal but 'expected' the new government to fight Bolshevism and support the officer-corps in maintaining army discipline. The Kaiser went, the generals remained. Such was the inauspicious start of the Weimar Republic.

The Social Democratic Party, the child of Karl Marx and Frederick Engels themselves, had long ceased to be the dangerous revolutionary movement that its supporters and opponents thought it to be before 1914. The war revealed it to be a moderate, respectable patriotic organisation which loyally supported the imperial war and its aims – so loyally that its more radical elements had seceded from it. Numerically the most important of these was the Independent Social Democratic Party, which had for some time supported a 'peace without annexations and indemnities.' The main body of working class activists in and out of uniform, from the shop-stewards of the Berlin engineering works to the revolutionary sailors, supported it. It took a half-share in the new Berlin government, but its leaders who were uncertain about what to do, in effect allowed the anti-revolutionary Majority Social-Democrats a free hand and soon resigned from the government. What was worse, they also left the leadership of the Central Council, elected by the workers' and soldiers' councils which had sprung up all over Germany, to the Majority Social Democrats, who profoundly distrusted these forms of grass-roots democracy as potentially Bolshevik. It cannot be stated to often and too clearly that, whatever the differences between the army and the Majority Social-Democrats, which were substantial, both were totally at one in their horror of revolution and their determination to restore 'order.'

This was not easy. The new government operated in a temporary vacuum. The army was unreliable: its leaders preferred to demobilise the revolutionary rankers as quickly as possible and to rely for the time being on volunteer 'Free Corps' of ultra-reactionary complexion. De facto power was or could have been in the hands of the councils, but the councils got no central leadership and had no clear idea of what to do. In fact, this powerful but uncoordinated movement subsided, and with it the hopes of the German revolution. The army concentrated its forces in Berlin, insisted on a return to constitutional government. A National Assembly was elected in January 1919 and the Weimar Republic was in being.

The hero of Mrs Leviné-Meyer's book belonged to the smallest and (with some localised groups) most radical organisation of the left, the Spartacus League, which formed the German Communist Party at the end of December 1918. Its leaders were extremely able, and some of them – notably Karl Liebknecht and the brilliant Rosa Luxemburg – were also well-known. Most of them were to be murdered or executed in 1919. The Spartacus League, though at this time relatively uninfluential, was not unrealistic. It recognised that Germany was by no means ready for an immediate 'October Revolution' or proletarian seizure of power. But it was exposed on the right because of the prominence of Liebknecht and Luxemburg and its associations with the Bolsheviks, while on the left it was vulnerable to the mood of ultra-left utopianism which, understandably enough, gripped the revolutionary militants, including some of the Independents. (A large body of the Independents was eventually to merge with the new Communist Party, providing it with its mass basis.) A brief and ill-judged rising in Berlin in early Januari – not so much an attempt to seize power as to counter the growing offensive of the army – failed and cost the party its most eminent leaders.

In this gloomy picture there was one apparent and unexpected exception. In Bavaria, hardly a stronghold of the labour movement, the revolution under the leadership of the Independent Social Democrat Kurt Eisner and a peasant leader, each representing quite small organisations, had demonstrated what it might have achieved in Germany. Eisner became prime minister of a Bavarian Republic, supported by all sections of the left, and attemped a sort of combination of a democratic constitution with a republic of the councels. This left-wing régime survived the collapse of the revolution in Berlin and most other parts of the country, but Eisner was assassinated in February 1919 by an ultra-reactionary, Count Arco. To this part of Germany the Communist Party sent Eugen Leviné. Here he participated in, and attempted to introduce some element of serious organisation and effectiveness into, the Bavarian Soviet Republic of April 1919.

It is possible, though perhaps not very likely, that Bavaria could have maintained itself as an autonomous and relatively left-wing regime, based on the unity of its labour movement and the proverbial dislike of Bavarians for going the way of the rest of Germany. At all events Berlin hesitated to intervene against it. But a Soviet Republic was doomed. Leviné himself was opposed to it. After the proclamation of the Hungarian Soviet Republic on March 21, 1919, however a wave of utopian hope swept across the Bavarian movement. If they gave another signal, would not Austria also rise and a central European soviet zone come into existence? A Soviet Republic was proclaimed in Munich and enthusiastically joined by the numerous, often anarchist and semi-anarchist writers and intellectuals of what was Germany's most celebrated Latin Quarter. Leviné, a lucid, sceptical, efficient professional of revolution among noble amateurs living out the dream of liberation and confused militants, knew that it was lost, but also that it had to fight. Though not lacking in at least passive support among the Munich workers, the Soviet Republic horrified the conservative and Catholic peasantry and the notably reactionary middle class of Bavaria to the point where they welcomed the joint invasion of government troops and Free Corps from all over Germany (including a Bavarian Free Corps). The Soviet Republic ended on May 1 and was drowned in blood. Eugen Leviné its ablest leader, was one of the victims.

He died comparatively young, and it is impossible to say what this impressive Russian, a figure closer by origin and sympathy to Lenin's Bolsheviks than to most German revolutionaries of the time, would have achieved had he lived. There is little point in speculating about it. We can only welcome this most valuable memoir in which his widow has made him live again for us, and incidentally provided a notable addition to our knowledge of the German tragedy of 1918–19, and to our understanding of the revolutionaries and revolutions of our century.

London April 1973

I

I first met Leviné in Heidelberg in the spring of 1910 at a literary party given by Olgin, a socialist and well-known Jewish journalist.

For me it was love at first sight.

Heidelberg abounded with revolutionaries. They included the two handsome Steinberg brothers – the elder was for a while Minister of Justice in Lenin's first Bolshevik Left Social-Revolutionary Government – and another very prominent member of that party, Kamkov. But the legend of the town was Leviné.

I had come to Heidelberg to learn German. I hoped that the knowledge of a second language would enable me to earn a living in Russia as a governess or by teaching German privately.

My father, a rabbi in Grodek, a small town near Bialystok, died when I was not yet fifteen. A married sister who lived in Vilno took me in with her.

With the necessary books I prepared myself externally for the state examination for the O-level certificate which could be taken at any Russian high-school. Such a certificate did not, however, suffice to earn a living in the big city and it was altogether almost impossible for a woman to enter a profession in the Russian provinces.

I learned of Heidelberg through Russian literature. The greatest attraction though was for me the name, Alt-Heidelberg (Old-Heidelberg). I thought it an escape into an old, romantic world.

The atmosphere in Russia after the failure of the '05 revolution did not appeal to me. Everybody wanted to be original, different, a superman, and the Jewish ghetto was no exception to this craving.

I remember an incident when a young girl committed suicide because she thought herself too ordinary. This feeling was expressed in a very popular Jewish song: 'If the bird cannot soar, kill it on the spot.'

These were her last words.

There was much talk of free love. A book appeared, *Sanin* by Arzybashev, which dared to deal openly with naked sex, and it was so unusual that it produced a storm of protests headed by the wife of Leo Tolstoy. It became very difficult for a 'progressive girl' to refuse advances without long explanations. The provincial lads were not very demanding, simple kisses were enough, but the university students from the capital who often spent their holidays in our area were not so modest and could not easily be turned down. 'Are you that old-fashioned, Fräulein?' And who wanted to be old-fashioned?

Another reason for my choice was Olgin, a man of great erudition and a leader of the Bund, a party with Jewish nationalist and Menshevik orientations.[1] He was twenty-two years older than I and I thought he could help me in my search for the meaning of life and further my sparse education.

In the large Russian colony with very few girls I was rather a sought-after person.

But Olgin teased me, 'You need not be proud about your admirers. There is one man who is worth conquering but he is beyond your reach.'

He told me of the man who scorned wealth and position to serve the people, and showed me the large mansion where he lived with his mother.

I abhorred party politics. I had my own ideas about world problems. Of course conditions must change – I hated poverty and injustice – but what had tedious parties and ignorant workers to do with it?

'The world will grow weary of pain, will choke with blood and will turn its tormented mind to eternal love,' prophesied my beloved poet Nadson.

The awakening of the oppressed, 'the people', came into it, it sounded beautiful in songs, but the task, I was convinced, would be performed by a set of heroic idealists, men like Leviné. He was one of the great heroes and I was overwhelmed with admiration.

We met once in the street and he invited me for a walk. On a bench at the romantic Heidelberg Castle he kissed me fleetingly and, to play fair, told me a story of a weary wanderer and a young blossoming tree: the wanderer wanted to rest for a while in its shade. It was his duty to continue his life of wandering. The part reserved for me in the parable – I was not even twenty yet – was chilly and rather pitiful. Not even a word of love would the wanderer carry away with him, and preferably for the rest of his life.

I could not accept this and he was convinced it was all he could offer.

He was still suffering from the results of his prison treatment. Above all he believed that it would be unfair to marry or even to get seriously attached to another person and expose her to the uncertain destinies of a revolutionary. He decided to avoid me. But he was too young, only twenty-seven.

At the Russian gatherings he would come to greet me and always asked: 'May I speak to you afterwards?' But he never did. Once or twice we had longer conversations, though, but they hardly brought us closer. On one occasion he described the deplorable social position of Russian women who could find no outlet for their gifts and energy.

'But they could go to Germany or another country,' was my quick remedy.

It earned me an angry rebuke and a lecture on financial and many other unsurmountable obstacles. This was lost on me. I had come to Germany on the very little money I had earned as a private teacher in my small home town. But I did not wish to give away my secret. It would amount to boasting.

My savings were dwindling away and Heidelberg was not the place to look for work. Leviné advised me to move to Berlin.

He supplied me with innumerable addresses and with many letters of introduction. I owed it to him alone that I found a job – a combination of governess and nanny to two German-Russian children – within a fortnight of my arrival in Berlin.

I thanked him in a short note. Attempts at long letters always revealed my real feelings and I wished to keep them to myself. Unlike his wanderer, I, for one, carried with me that 'eternal love' and I left with the firm resolution to see him again.

My newly acquired German enabled me to eke out a meagre living, but I did not know what to do with myself. I felt lonely, forlorn.

In 1912 I unexpectedly met Olgin in Vilno. His beautiful mistress had left him and I was to take her place. I did not love him but he introduced me to a new world, to the socialist elite of the town, whom I had always admired from afar. He brought into my life a sense of security and stability.

It is not true that one sells oneself only for money. What

Olgin gave me was more than enough to become his mistress. It was, however, an unhappy alliance. Haunted by the police, Olgin fled to Vienna and I refused to follow him.

But this was not the end. I went to Vienna after all as a member of the first set of the Habima, the world-famous Hebrew theatre whose first performance was to take place in Vienna in honour of the Zionist World Congress.

Even before I arrived in Vienna, Olgin had 'discovered' me and sent an emissary to persuade me to go on the stage.

I must 'follow my real vocation'. He would give me any help to achieve this aim. He called it 'a good investment.'

Fearing another unhappy entanglement, I kept quiet. But I met him immediately upon my arrival. He had found out the address of our group and was waiting for me. Once again he introduced me to a world of prominent revolutionaries, including the renowned Menshevik Abramovitz. I even shook hands with Trotsky.

This time Olgin was able to do much more for me. His Vienna friends were well connected with the theatre world. I was introduced to Dr Rundt, the manager of two Vienna theatres, the Volksbühne and, I believe, the Neue Wiener Bühne. He prophesied a great future for me and promised to engage me as soon as I could reasonably overcome the language and other technical difficulties.

He himself had chosen for me the right teacher and allowed me to attend the daily rehearsals. My dream of becoming an actress became a reality. How could I reward Olgin, express my gratitude to him? I again became his mistress.

The approaching war caught Olgin and me on holiday in a Bavarian village near the fashionable spa Reichenhall. Overnight we became suspected spies to the friendly villagers. A kind local factory owner came one day to advise us to move to Reichenhall. He overheard his workers plotting to raid our cottage. We would be better protected among our many Russian compatriots.

On our short twenty-minute train journey it suddenly struck me that should a war really break out, this might be my last chance to see Leviné.

To Olgin I said, 'What shall we do in the expensive Reichenhall? Let's go to Heidelberg. You have many friends there and I an old devoted landlady.'

This was reasonable and Olgin praised my common sense.

A clever man once said, 'Every man is always both rational

and passionate. We must search out man's passions behind his reasoning and man's reasoning behind his passions.'

I was well aware by what I was driven.

Olgin counted the money; it was just enough for two tickets.

We arrived in Heidelberg on the first day of the Great War and on the last train to carry civilian passengers.

Olgin told me that Leviné had gone the way of other young dreamers of his social standing. He had made peace with his society and was embarking on a scientific career.

The shining image received a considerable crack. I was very sad. But my resolution to have another look at him was as strong as ever. I saw Leviné on the morning of my arrival. He came to invite me to his home for lunch.

He had changed almost beyond recognition and was altogether not 'my type'. Instead of his former 'Russian' beard which, in my eyes, gave him an air of distinction, he was wearing a goatee, making him look to me conventional and bourgeois. I was above all very disappointed that he seemed to like me. I suffered greatly from my relationship with Olgin and was at that time at great odds with myself. How could he approve of me?

Steeped in the Russian classics, I often expressed myself in the language borrowed from my favourite heroines. Now I was quoting to myself Tatyana's bitter reproach:

Onegin, I was younger then,
And also prettier, I believe.... .

But my feelings for him had not changed. I did not even ask myself whether I was in love. I simply belonged to him.

Later in the day he produced a card, dated April 1911. He had tried to contact me and was officially informed that I had left for Russia. He kept the card because it carried my name, he said.

Yet he appeared to be in pursuit of just another casual girlfriend and I again refused to play the part. This time he was adamant. I was no longer the teenager of the old days and he could not understand my behaviour. He accused me of playing with him and was very angry. We argued, but we also took walks every day for long hours, hand in hand, mute with emotion.

In the meantime he had undergone the routine military inspection and could be conscripted any day. I was about to go to Berlin to resume my studies. The whole atmosphere was charged with the urge to snatch from life what happiness one could. It was the time of quick marriages as well as quick love affairs. I succumbed in the end and agreed to spend three weeks with him in Berlin. Nothing was said about the future. He made no promises. The wanderer would continue on his way. But I had my declaration of love. On the eve of our departure, a rainy night in late October, he asked me:

'Do I have to say "those words"?'

He had to.... He had never said them before and found it strangely difficult.

Eugen Leviné was born on the 10th May, 1883, in St Petersburg of wealthy Jewish parents.

His father, Julius Leviné, was a self-made man who had amassed a large fortune without ready capital, through his abilities and great initiative.

Julius Leviné had received a good education, had a perfect knowledge of German and very good manners – qualities rather rare for the society in which he moved. Coupled with his scrupulous honesty, they made him generally popular and largely contributed to his financial successes.

Leviné's mother, Rosalia, was a woman of great beauty and charm, intelligent and determined, the perfect hostess in an elegant and cultured home. She had been educated in a German public school in Koenigsberg and became, thereafter, completely obsessed with everything German.

After her marriage, she set up house in St Petersburg, but her admiration for the German way of life made her move almost exclusively in German circles. The language spoken in her house was German.

This atmosphere of wealth and general respect created in the family a feeling of exclusiveness and superiority. It was even increased when, for business reasons, Julius Leviné acquired Italian nationality and changed his name from Levin to Leviné. It sounded foreign and exotic – qualities much appreciated in Russia and particularly in his milieu.

At the climax of his success and personal happiness, Julius Leviné suddenly died of smallpox.

Eugen Leviné was then only three years old, the same age as his own child at the time of his early death.

His mother was only twenty-seven years old. She had hardly started to live. But her code of morals, coloured by the exclusive atmosphere of Koenigsberg, the town of the venerated philosopher Kant, demanded that a true and loving wife should remain faithful to her husband until death. She submitted to that severe command.

Her sacrifice only deepened her feeling of grandeur. She 'devoted herself entirely to the upbringing of her children,' the three-year-old Genja and her six-year-old daughter Sonja. It goes without saying that the practical part of the task was left to well-trained governesses, teachers and servants. Her own role was confined to that of a supervisor, administering all-merciful and all-terrible justice.

Here too she was guided by the traditions of Germany, where the upbringing of children was very strict and the 'justice' rather harsh. In her own way a passionately devoted mother, she thought it her duty to replace the absent father, again according to German traditions a very severe figure.

Her educational scheme was simple enough. She sent her children to a German private school; for music lessons she engaged the best musicians in St Petersburg; for dancing lessons a ballet teacher from the famous Maryinsky Theatre. The most expensive was the best and the best was just good enough for 'her' children.

Meanwhile, the financial position of the family lagged far behind those standards. In the first few years of her widowhood, her relatives succeeded in squandering nearly all her fortune. When she became aware of it and took matters into her own hands she discovered that all she was left with was outstanding debts which her family found difficult to call in.

There was, however, enough left to secure for her what she used to define as a carefree existence. She could still maintain her luxurious flat in St Petersburg; she could later on rent a villa in Heidelberg, was able to travel and to visit watering places. But she had to dispense with her carriage and other costly amenities to which she was accustomed. And often when the children spent small sums of money for purposes of which she did not approve, she would complain that she had no money.

The unhealthy atmosphere created by a woman who, full of vitality and energy, had condemned herself to a life of seclusion and idleness and was guided by a ready-made code of morals, permeated her environment and weighed heavily on the very sensitive little Genja. In great need of simple human affection and sympathy, he made the discovery that this could be best found among persons confined to the back door of his fine home and referred to as – 'the people.' At the age of seven, upset by some 'injustice,' he tried to run away from their summer resort to Sasha, the family cook, who had remained in St Petersburg. At a very early age the word 'people' penetrated his mind as a contrast to all he felt to be unfair and hypocritical in his own environment. As a boy of twelve he declared, to the great amusement of his family, that he was going to be an elementary school teacher, in German 'a people's teacher.' Everywhere, at home, on walks, at games, and on his frequent journeys he made comparisons between his friends and 'the people,' and they were never to the advantage of the former.

This idolising of the people grew in time into a desire to protect and assist them. As a boy of fourteen he wrote his first revolutionary verses:

Endure no longer your servitude, oh people
Tear off the slavish bonds
Put on you with impudent arrogance
By rich and aristocratic snobs.

A year later, when he was barely fifteen, he wrote in his diary:

I should like to serve the people but not in the way I intended before. Not by sham but by genuine service, not by offering them crumbs like the councillors of Rome to gain the sympathy of the masses, but by sincere work for their welfare.... I wish to denounce the enemies of the people from the council tribunals, to protect the oppressed and to help them to establish their rights. And if I am not rewarded by eager acclamations, I shall yet know that I fulfilled my obligations in serving their cause. That is my aim. That is what I vow to fulfil.

Excessive luxury combined with the necessity to deprive himself of many things enjoyed by other boys of his age and background produced great confusion in his young mind. This feeling was to become stronger when he was sent to an exclusive boarding school in Wiesbaden. He found himself in the company of sons of millionaires and senior civil servants, with whom he could hardly compete socially. At the same time, the shallowness, lack of interests and ideals which were characteristic of German boys of that class could not but repel a boy like Genja, well read and, like many other Russian boys, preoccupied with 'world problems.' The gulf between him and his social set grew wider. He felt lonely and depressed. He longed for the friends he knew were to be found in St Petersburg and who could help him with his problems. His letters to his mother were melancholy and full of ardent requests to take him home. But she believed that he was longing only for her, his mother, and came to visit him in Wiesbaden. He implored her to take him away. Again her educational principles overruled her immediate sympathy for her boy. He had to remain in the school he detested and in the pretentious milieu of a fashionable German watering place.

It was a very dangerous period in his development. Unable to find a channel, let alone an application for his ideals, he might easily have become absorbed in fruitless day-dreaming and idle resignation. But his healthy nature rebelled against this. He decided to adjust himself to his surroundings and to accept the little pleasures this life could offer. He would play the young gentleman and be just a trifle smarter and more original to compensate for some privileges closed to him.

With a consistency worthy of better aspirations, Leviné devoted himself to this Plan. His collars were higher, his hands better cared for; a touch of mystery and wistfulness in his looks and a calculated eloquence completed the artificially created image.

Carried away by his game, he went so far as to fight a duel – an expression of high distinction in the German drawing-room society. He challenged some idle lout who had made an anti-Semitic remark. To the end of his life he was to carry, as a relic of that strange phase, a scar above his right eyebrow.

It was in Heidelberg, in 1903, at the age of twenty, that Leviné for the first time in his life came into contact with Russian intellectuals, and became acquainted with revolutionary ideas. They found a powerful response in his restless mind, and no distractions or attempts at reconciliation with his society were ever able to stifle them.

He received his first revolutionary ideas from the Social Revolutionaries whose programme included acts of individual terror.[2] They believed that by assassinating certain dignitaries of state, above all the Czar, they could shatter the foundation of the existing system and bring about socialism. This programme called for a great deal of individual gallantry and self-sacrifice. It was only too natural that the young and inexperienced Leviné should be fascinated by its heroic aspects. To correct injustice, to give his life for the oppressed – had this not been his dream since childhood? He became an enthusiastic member of that party.

It was all very well to join a revolutionary party in Heidelberg, but a hard struggle lay ahead. He had to go to Russia, which meant a break with his customary life, his friends, his family, his mother. His mother threw into the balance all the egoism and unconscious cruelty of a lonely woman of delicate health, who had renounced personal happiness for the sake of her children and especially for his sake. His own pity and grief at having to cause her pain were mixed with resentment at this uncalled for, unnecessary sacrifice for which he was presented the bill.

The Russo-Japanese war and the revolutionary situation in Russia made him forget all personal considerations. He broke with his mother, who made a last attempt to curb him by cutting off his allowance.

Without a penny, his only source of subsistence a vague promise from the *Frankfurter Volksstimme* to employ him as a freelance correspondent, Leviné went back to Russia. He was twenty-two years old.

It was not an easy decision. He was torn between two loyalties: his mother and his ideals. And he was not a man who would wish to hurt.

In 1906, after his first imprisonment, which lasted six months, he wrote to his mother from St Petersburg:

...If you try to keep me with you for a longer period or try again to persuade me to give up my way of life, my visit will be quite senseless. The result would only be bitterness and misunderstanding. Only if you are really reconciled to realities, if you have given up hope of changing me, could I come...

Dear Mother, I know very well that you are not strong, that you would find peace if I stayed with you. But I cannot, I have no right to do it. If you had only tried not to see in me your son but a human being and understand me, you would have perhaps realised that I cannot act otherwise and that it is better this way.

This conflict with his mother affected him so strongly that – brutally tortured by the Czarist jailers, wounded and gravely ill – he wrote to her:

...if prison and all I have gone through here will bring about your understanding, it has not been in vain.....

It is true that this letter was written in the first flush of exaltation when he was informed that his mother intended to come to see him. It was never actually despatched.

Leviné did not like to talk of his revolutionary activity, and the Social-Revolutionary Party which he had joined, being more or less a party of leaders without an organised mass basis, suffered so ruthlessly in the years 1905–1908, that it was impossible to gather correct information about the work of its members.

We have to rely on some letters and on the evidence of his friends.

It is known that Leviné very soon gained the confidence of the St Petersburg organisation which entrusted him with very responsible tasks, including the distribution of arms.

He would skilfully attach rifles and other weapons to the inside of his magnificent fur coat – a relic of his affluent past – and deliver them to their destination.

To kill time between appointments he used to visit friends who lived in luxurious hotels, and he described with great humour the battles he waged with eager servants who would try to help him out of his coat, unaware of its dangerous cargo.

It is characteristic of Leviné that, contrary to his Party, he very soon grasped the necessity of establishing a basis among the workers. He joined the Union of the Petersburg Bakers, disregarding the mockery of his comrades who considered his activities childish play.

His great rhetorical gift soon attracted general attention and his Party started sending him from meeting to meeting. At the beginning of 1906 he was arrested in Petersburg. He conducted his defence skilfully and after six months was aquitted for lack of evidence. But he could not remain in Petersburg without endangering his friends and was sent to the provinces. As an orator he covered a great part of West Russia, Vitebsk, Smolensk, Bryansk and Minsk districts. Constantly on the move and on the alert, his work required great endurance. He wrote to his sister:

> I am now in Bryansk province Orlov, one of the most important economic centres. It has a strong organisation but I am the only 'intellectual'. And since the factories are scattered between forests and swamps hundreds of miles apart, I am always 'on the move'.

In another letter to her he wrote:

> I spent six weeks in Bryansk. I was travelling to and fro under

the most exacting working conditions. Among other things, I caught swamp fever [malaria]. Without a place of my own I could not afford to rest more than two days. I continued my wanderings in spite of the fever and in this way overcame the disease.

In the Vitebsk district, he contracted an eye infection; for a long time he was unable to distinguish colours. There was no question of treatment; he had to carry on. He invented his own method of combating this affliction. He argued: 'After all, I know that leaves are green and not pink or blue. So why should I rely on such imperfect organs as my eyes?' For the rest he decided to just ignore his illness. It was all he could do.

Disregarding difficulties, hardship and illness, the refined and pampered Leviné went, sometimes on foot and often hungry, from town to town, from village to village, to waken, to enlighten, to sow the seeds of socialism among the workers and peasants. For the first time in his life, he experienced real satisfaction and even happiness. Describing this period he wrote in prison to a friend:

You are walking at my side and talking of Venice, you are describing how well one can rest there, rest and enjoy oneself. And I feel that the time for rest has not come yet and I visualise the years ahead of me. Hunted by the police. In constant danger of losing freedom and even life. And yet I am happy.

...In streaming rain, on frosty, wet nights they are gathering in hundreds from all the villages, listening, seeking the truth, learning to fight for the truth.

What is truth?

Nowhere has such sacred earnestness been put into this question. For nowhere else is the answer to be paid for with your life.

While I am writing to you our friends in Kronstadt are being executed. Among them are young girls and boys who have hardly started to live and are forsaking their lives because they cared more for others than themselves.

At the end of 1907, Leviné was betrayed by a spy, arrested and brutally beaten.

The St Petersburg correspondent of the liberal *Frankfurter Zeitung* wrote: [3]

Eugen Leviné, the correspondent of the *Frankfurter Volk-*

stimme was arrested in Minsk. During a promenade in the prison courtyard, he noticed an unlocked door. He slipped into the adjoining garden, then into the street. He found a cab in which he tried to escape. Three policemen rushed out and caught him. He was unarmed, and surrendered without any resistance. The policemen, however, knocked him down, started kicking him with their boots, and beat him brutally with their fists and rifles across his face and head. It was all done in the presence of a huge crowd and in spite of protests against the cruelty.

Back in prison the beatings went on until a woman prisoner who witnessed the scene burst into violent hysterics. The paper further reported:

As a result of the beatings Leviné was for a long while dangerously ill, yet he was left in his prison cell without any care, even his wounds were not attended to.

Leviné himself wrote to his sister three months later: 'True, it was not a trifling matter. However, mentally I have already recovered and feel well. As to the physical condition – I shall receive medical treatment in a couple of days.'

Leviné's mother learnt of his fate from the newspapers and hurried to his rescue. She was resolved to get him out on bail for treatment abroad and went about her task with unparalleled devotion and energy. She flooded the prison with food – she knew her son and realised that she had to provide for a number of his comrades if she was to make him eat. She lavished presents on the warders and excessive bribes on officials, including those in higher ranks – to each according to his importance . . . .

Her efforts were undoubtedly helped by her great charm. All doors were opened to her and soon she could visit her son and the various offices as often as she thought fit.

She spared nothing, least of all herself. The prison was swarming with vermin, rats and cockroaches. Bugs and lice were eating the convicts alive. It did not deter her from visiting her son. But back in her hotel she had to make minute inspections of her clothes. The results often filled her with horror. She could not suppress her revulsion when telling me of this procedure many years later.

After many consultations, the local authorities declared themselves unable to release Leviné in a relatively small town such as Minsk. It would arouse too much suspicion; rumours of bribery had already become very disturbing. They advised her to transfer Leviné to St Petersburg and afforded her generous help and advice in this manoeuvre.

More bribes. More struggles. She spent a small fortune but achieved her aim; she got Leviné out on bail and carried him off to Heidelberg.

Leviné returned a very sick man, partially deaf in one ear. It took a long time and great effort on the part of his devoted, resourceful mother to nurse him back to health, and for several years he had to live the life of a semi-invalid.

He was not altogether idle. He felt more than ever committed to his cause and was preparing for a further struggle.

He changed over from the faculty of law to that of politics and economics, and devoted much of his time to acquainting himself with the German working-class movement.

He also wrote short stories about his gruesome experiences in the Czarist prisons. In 'The End Of a Revolutionary' he wrote:

> Some, indifferent and cool as always, take the coffin. The four prisoners stand erect and bare-headed in the icy cold wind. The black iron gate opens with a creak. A unit of soldiers with their lieutenant come out. They draw up facing the prisoners. From one window comes the subdued sound of the funeral march of the Russian revolutionaries: 'You have fallen a victim in the fatal struggle.' The coffin slowly sways towards the black gateway. The four are still bareheaded in the yard. The Lieutenant shouts 'Away from the windows, I'm going to shoot. Fire! The shots ring out. We draw back into the damp cells. Outside, behind the bars, the dusk falls. From far, far away we can hear the hearse rumbling down the street. Rest in peace, comrades. Now you are free.

Another, entitled 'Comrade, I Cannot Take Your Letter', is a true story. A revolutionary was facing execution. His prison friends tried to smuggle a farewell letter to him through his cell window but he could not take it. His arms had been broken by the jailers.

This story became a classic with the German workers.

Leviné actively participated in the life of the Russian colony, many of whose members were revolutionaries and very poor. He organised collections and literary discussions, often lecturing himself on literature and art.

Fjodor Stepun writes:
By his faith he was a humanitarian atheist; in his appearance a typical Jew, with an almost aristocratic long face, beautiful melancholy eyes, moving with a slightly protruded shoulder, resembling an Egyptian relief.

During our friendship he was an uncommonly soft, even sentimental young man who wrote poems about the autumn rain drumming on the roofs of the workers. His socialism, not enlivened by any personal experience and devoid of any fanaticism and dogmatism, was clearly marked by ethical and pedagogical features.

For a time Leviné was closely connected with a German association, Ethos, and lectured on their behalf in various towns. Once we travelled together. He spoke about Maxim Gorky, I read extracts from his works. Here is the most expressive example of Leviné's emotional appeal.

On one of my visits to Leviné's grave I met an elderly peasant woman. She crossed herself several times and laid down flowers.

She could not be a communist and I asked: "Did you know him?"—"No, but I know my Bible. He too died for us. He was like our Christ only much closer to us. It is a long way from our village but I always find time to come. It is my loveliest walk. But you are a communist, aren't you?"

"I was his wife."

She startled, took both my hands and her eyes filled with tears. She opened her mouth, gulped, but could not speak and walked slowly away. I let her go.

We had no need for words. I knew: we shall never forget each other.

As soon as he felt fit he tried to join the Social-Democratic Party, and later on he liked to recall the snobbishness of those 'labour' leaders. The recommendations of his well-known Russian Party friends and German comrades were completely overlooked. He then decided to seek the help of his university professors, and the letters of Gothein and Alfred Weber duly broke the ice and opened the doors of the Party sanctuaries.

As before in Russia, Leviné was chiefly employed as a propagandist. Under his mother's maiden name, Goldberg, he lectured on the Russian revolution of 1905 and its lessons. He also devoted much time to studying the workers themselves, believing that he could serve them best if he understood their mentality, their strengths and their limitations.

It is worth noting that he adopted here the methods of the best Bolshevik leaders who, following Lenin's example, started their revolutionary careers on a thorough acquaintance with the life of the workers.

The near-by city of Mannheim, with its large industrial proletariat, offered abundant opportunity for the purpose. With the aid of personal friends and socialist organisations Leviné had circulated elaborate questionnaires among the workers, 1,500 in all. A considerable proportion, over 500, filled in the lists. (He used the material for his degree thesis *Types and stages in the development of trade-union workers*.) This enabled Leviné to make many personal contacts, to visit the workers' homes and study their habits. He joined numerous organised excursions to inspect conditions in the mining districts. To complete his observations, he worked in Mannheim as an unskilled labourer first in a small factory and then in a large plant of 3,000 workers.

Leviné had returned to Germany damaged in health but as a fully developed and determined personality. Having found his goal he set out to forge the instrument for its fulfilment – himself. Essentially a romantic dreamer, sensitive and highly introspective, he was well aware of the difficulties facing him. He consciously set aside all that might distract him from his primary task – to serve the revolution. He suppressed his considerable literary gifts and all artistic aspects of his personality. 'Not now, later on, it is not important,' he used to say when urged to concentrate on a scientific or literary career.

He no longer idealised 'the people.' He saw in them the powerful force, destined to transform the hated social order, but he was not blind to their shortcomings, suburban outlook and indolence. He was particularly critical of the so-called workers' aristocracy, their snobbishness and contempt for less fortunate workers, whom they regarded as 'simpletons' unable like themselves to push their way up.

In the German labour movement Leviné worked side by side with the left wing of the Party represented by Karl Liebknecht, Rosa Luxemburg and Franz Mehring. But he was a foreigner, and this put great limitations on his activities.

There was no question of going back to Russia and facing trial. He was, above all, aware that he had acquired during his convalescence, a far better knowledge of the German movement than he had ever had of the Russian. He decided to obtain German nationality and settle down in that country.

His social position facilitated the task. His socialist activities under an assumed name were unknown to the authorities. He was considered the son of a wealthy family with good connections in the scientific world.

However, although an independent state, Baden as a matter of routine sought information from Prussia and referred Leviné's application to Berlin. It was well known that Prussia collaborated with the Czarist Police, whose report would hardly further Leviné's cause.

He was helped out of the predicament by his sense of humour and insight into human frailty: what could be more effective than playing on the patriotism of the Baden authorities? He insinuated, in an interview, that referring the matter to Berlin was nothing short of servility and lack of independence. It worked.

No, the authorities protested, Baden would not be bullied by anyone.

Leviné was granted naturalisation papers without further delay.

At last he was able to cast off all the bonds and work without hindrance. Copies of his letters to various organisations offering his services as a lecturer bear witness to his wide range of knowledge and his hopeful anticipation of a new life.

It was, however, autumn 1913, and the Great War was to cut short his well-laid plans. War caught Leviné in Heidelberg. The small university town was soon submerged in a wave of hysterical patriotism. Things were no better in industrial Mannheim, where Leviné rushed in search of associates.

He was knocking at closed doors. The Party, including the Left, was carried away by the slogan 'War Against Czarism':

'And you, after all you have suffered in Russia, are not among the fighters?' asked his bewildered friends.

The example was set by the leader of the Mannheim socialists, the fiery and brilliant Ludwig Frank, who volunteered for the Army and soon died an infamous death in the service of his capitalist fatherland.

The attitude of the German Social Democrats, the strongest party in the world with a million members, was a great blow to all who cherished the ideas of international workers' solidarity. Rosa Luxemburg cried bitterly and unashamedly at the news of the acceptance of the war-credits by the Socialist section of the Reichstag.

Leviné was no less shaken. He anticipated a struggle against a new wave of national prejudice and chauvinism which in his own environment seemed a relic of the past. He also reckoned with a long war: 'At least eighteen months or two years,' he said in his mother's and my presence, and we were both very angry with him. Perish such a cynical and cruel thought! *Everybody* knew that the war would end by Christmas....

He had foreseen that the war would be accompanied by a severe world crisis and revolutionary shocks, and he occasionally spoke to me of his views. But world crisis and revolutionary shocks were meaningless words to me and I was indifferent to his predictions.

In Berlin Leviné soon found associates on the extreme Left of the Party – the Spartacus League[6] – and among his own personal friends, workers and employees.

He was one of the very few German socialists who cultivated friendly relations outside the Party intelligentsia. I thus came into contact with the socialist rank and file and found them exceedingly dull and ignorant. I could not understand why Leviné wasted so much time on them. An office girl explained at great length how careful she was to save her money. She was so prudent, I could not see where socialism came into it.

'A young Socialist worrying about savings,' I exclaimed with contempt when she had left, Leviné gave me a long lecture on the life of a wage-earner with no other resources to fall back on but his own labour: If loses his job, he pawns all he can, down to his last respectable suit; he can not even apply for new employment; he sinks and become a beggar for life. Savings were thus elevated to a symbol of dignity and independence – this had nothing to do with money and the primitive lust for it.

As to the revolutionary value of such prudent people, Leviné explained, they were carrying forth revolutionary ideas and preparing the ground for the oncoming battles.

'It is easier to convert thousands of workers than one single well-meaning intellectual,' he said.

Due to his greater experience in illegal propaganda methods, Leviné was soon able to spread anti-war ideas on a larger scale. In a series of lectures on 'War Lyrics in Ancient and Modern Times' he demonstrated that people had always abhorred war.

It was a masterly selection of evidence based on Roman,

Indian, Chinese and Russian epics, plays, poems, songs and sayings.

He also quetioned Homer's description of Tersithes's ugliness: 'the ugliest of men,' 'squint-eyed,' 'lame,' 'hunchbacked,' 'bald.'

'The entire hatred of the ruling class breaks through here,' he commented.

Beauty is in the eye of the beholder. Why not ugliness? During the war even the looks of Karl Liebknecht were described in not exactly flattering terms in the bourgeois Press. And Toller, carried away by his wild hatred, described Leviné as 'a haggard man, whose hooked, fleshy nose stuck conspicuously out of an emaciated face.' And that was in 1933!

In his lectures Leviné explained who profited from wars, dispelled the legend that Germany had been attacked, and awakened the suppressed feelings of international solidarity. The innocent-sounding title of the lectures averted the vigilance not only of the Kaiser's censors but also of the Social-Democratic top brass, who would hardly have tolerated such heresy without its subtle disguise.

Leviné later used these lectures for a Russian book *People's Voices on War*, intended for the Russian war prisoners. It was published in Russia only after the war and later translated in German.

Leviné and I remained together in Berlin until he was called up in the following April for military service. Nothing seemed to change in his relationship with me. He often spoke of his future while I searched in vain for my place in his life.

He told me of his sex life. It had differed in no respect from the life of other German students. But most students tended to keep their pick-up girls, typists, shop-girls and preferably the daughters of their landladies, their 'Student-Liebchens,' for the duration of their studies, whereas Leviné, true to his convictions, carefully avoided long-term relationships.

This attitude was new to me. Free-love associations, almost as binding as marriage, were regarded in Russian socialist circles as the highest degree of 'permissiveness.'

I was bewildered, but he explained that he could not endure celibacy for any length of time.

I wanted to know how long.

'About, three, four weeks.'

Any lengthy separation would therefore put an end to our relationship, for I would have never 'taken him back.'

It was disturbing but somehow did not seem to matter. Perhaps 'true love' should not be measured by months and years but by the rare moments of fulfilment, by the process of getting to know each other, by the blissful hours we spent sitting together, unravelling our deepest emotions, our darkest thoughts, and regaining our original purity.

It could not last, I thought. Sometimes I woke up in the early morning and waited in anguish for his first look. His grey-blue eyes could be cold and steely. One day he would look at me with such eyes and all would be over.

I knew I would never be the same again, but he too was no longer the same. Returning home he would sometimes speak of his changed attitude to women. Now they aroused in him only protective, brotherly feelings.

'I want to warn them, even against myself,' he said once cheerfully. 'Women are bound to be hurt in this kind of relationship.'

Yet he was unaware of his changed mood and, I am convinced, would still insist on his 'chastity limits.'

I soon discovered that he was almost organically incapable of stating anything he had not verified by direct experience. His honesty sometimes bordered on the grotesque and we both used to laugh at his 'I don't know', when he could easily disped my anxieties and doubts in a few words. It was laughable indeed, but those little oddities somehow manifested hidden traits, incomprehensible but delicate and infinitely moving. Not even the rough conditions of the last phase of his life, not even the stormy Munich days, could obliterate these characteristics.

After one of those interminable governmental sessions he had spent the rest of the night in the Wittelsbach Palace on one of those tricky sofas which abound in such places and make one wonder why kings should surround themselves with such discomfort.

I was ill and he offered to take me to the doctor, as he intended to sound the mood of the town.

When I came to fetch him he could hardly open his eyes, and we drove in silence. He was looking wearily through the windows and seemed so far away. Craving for some communication I said, in the typical female way, 'You don't love me any more, do you?'

'How should I know?' was his reply.

How indeed! How could he say anything that even for a moment would not be true! Enchanted, I squeezed his arm and laughed. He seemed to know then.

The knowledge of the true nature of our relationship was brought to him by an accident. I lost my identification papers and was taken into 'protective custody,' a form of imprisonment widely practised in Germany during the war. This could be the end of our relationship, I thought in despair. Thanks to his intervention my internment lasted only twelve days in December. We were reunited and Leviné listened with surprise to my anxieties: what would happen if I were detained for a longer period?

Of course he would wait for me for ever, and of course on my terms. Had he ever felt differently?

But he 'knew' then. We were married as soon as I could procure the required papers, the following May, 1915.

For a blissful moment the joy of personal fulfilment was so powerful that Leviné, the committed revolutionary, seemed to regard it as the sole purpose of his life.

We were celebrating the New Year of 1915 and went on to the balcony to listen to the church bells and cheering.

'Let us die now,' he said. 'We have reached a degree of happiness which will never be surpassed.'

This feeling is expressed in the following letter:

> Everything seems to attain sense and meaning. I wake up with you, I walk with you all day long, I lie down and my right arm waits for you with joy and tenderness.
>
> When I find time I shall go one of these evenings to the Neckar. But I shall first write to you and you will be with me. And I shall thank you for making me young again, for teaching me to love so deeply, to glow and to love; and for loving me, for the gift of your tender, delicate-passionate love.
>
> I kiss you, my child, my wife, my Oslik, my Issele, my only one, my all.
>
> I am all, all yours. I embrace you.
>
> Your husband. Your Tjulen
>
> Dear, sweet Oslik. I kiss you again and put all my soul in this kiss.

In the early spring Leviné was called up and appointed as an interpreter in a camp for high-ranking allied prisoners of war, situated on the outskirts of Heidelberg.

It was an easy assignment. He was allowed to live out and report for duty like any other civilian. Yet he soon came to hate his work. His obligations included the censorship of the incoming and outgoing letters, which made him an involuntary participant in the intimate life of the camp inmates. He felt like an intruder and when he had to deliver particularly sad or emotional letters could not look the recipient in the eye. They were class-enemies, military men who in a given situation would shoot him – or he them for that matter. But he always knew where to draw the line between revolutionary necessity and his innate humanitarian feelings, and never refused anybody help or sympathy in his private life.

Life in such a large group was not devoid of lighthearted and funny episodes. Leviné was very popular with the Russian prisoners who, less bound by conventions, confided in him all their troubles. An elderly colonel told him of his bellicose wife whose favourite target happened to be his beard. He had had to shave it off. Now he was proudly wearing a luxuriant ginger beard again and seemed to prefer captivity to his domestic bliss.

A young officer bitterly complained of his mother who did not quite comply with his demands.

He wrote to her, 'Now I wish to know: who am I? A bastard or the son and legitimate heir of a rich land-owner?'

Leviné recorded his experiences at the camp in a long story entitled 'Letters I Was Obliged To Read.' But the censors refused to allow publication. Leviné explained it to me as a token of the class-solidarity which was alive even among war enemies.

It was after all an officers' camp. Soon afterwards a series of soldiers' letters appeared in print which even bore their real names.

Leviné's life at the camp did not last long. An overzealous woman-comrade denounced him as a security risk: he could use his post for intelligence service for his own fatherland. He was immediately subjected to close scrutiny which revealed not so much his allegiance to 'his country' as, to the embarrassment of his superiors, his revolutionary ideas. He was dismissed on the spot.

In mischievous anticipation of a good joke, which he could never resist, Leviné asked for an explanation.

'You see,' said the kind old colonel, 'We learned of your revolutionary past, which makes it impossible to keep you on this post.'

'Why? We are living under a political truce. The Kaiser himself declared that "he knew no parties, only Germans".

'I know, but there are socialists and socialists. Some are only concerned with the happiness of their own country and are keen contributors to our war effort. But you are a "world benefactor." You are striving for the happiness of the whole of mankind. This is very dangerous.'

A rather complex political issue was thus presented in a nut-shell. Leviné's sense of humour was rewarded.

The informer was an old friend of the family whom Leviné converted to socialism, and she knew a good deal about the true nature of his relations with the Czarist Fatherland. Yet she openly boasted of her 'vigilance' and it was characteristic of the German attitude that only one of her confidants took exception to her betrayal of an old friend.

It was a great blow to us. The camp had given Leviné a great deal of freedom and time for writing and earning a living, and this flimsy security was all our marriage had been built on.

My first visit to Leviné in Heidelberg was in no way a happy occasion. Unknown to us, our correspondence had been submitted to censorship and my letters and a telegram announcing my arrival were not delivered in time.

There was no one waiting for me at the station. I found Leviné at our new home, peacefully writing a letter to me. It was a very tearful and altogether not a happy start.

Once again, though in a different way, he became a victim of his ideas. But this time he did not have a devoted mother at his side. On the contrary, she had been against our marriage and had tried to prevent it with a determination only comparable to that which she had shown in her fight for her son's freedom.

As a last resort, she had declared, 'I cannot prevent this perilous marriage but I warn you, if you bring your wife to Heidelberg, I shall break with you for good.'

She actually used a German expression which sounded even more distasteful: '*Das Tischtuch ist dann zwischen uns zerschnitten.*'

She rejected me ostensibly on 'moral grounds.' Leviné did not deny my relations with Olgin, which made me a fallen woman. And contrary to the generally accepted rules, *my* marriage did not suffice to restore my 'honour.' My mother-in-law forbade all her relatives and friends to receive me, which made me practically an outcast in such a small town. The very violence of her behaviour made me appear a sinister figure.

Yet when she had been told of our forthcoming marriage she had accepted the news with only a legitimate motherly warning of the difficulties involved.

On April the 3rd of 1915, Leviné sent me a telegram: 'Yesterday informed mother. Everything will turn out all right.' But then she made a painful discovery. Her son could write letters and did so daily. Their own communication was chiefly carried on by telephone and telegraph. No pleading – later on even my own – no remonstrations helped.

'I just cannot write letters,' was his excuse.

She tried to believe him but it remained a festering sore. He could write letters; it was just that he did not love her sufficiently. She could not bear the thought.

Her attempt to enforce an indefinite separation on a young husband and his wife was indeed a measure of her ravings, and Leviné saw in it only a demonstration of an obsessive craving for domination.

Yet the crude ultimatum was perhaps no more than an expression of a desire for some concessions to her, for a certain sacrifice to prove his affection.

She was herself a slave of stale and rigid ideals, and moulding children to fit accepted patterns was quite common in her time and environment. Her exceptional position as a rich widow and the idol of a large family whom she generously supported (even those members who nearly ruined her when they needed help) could not but foster her undoubtedly strong inclinations to dominate.

And in her case it was not, as with other families, a matter of trivial adjustments, but a struggle between two opposite basic conceptions of life. She had on her hands an impassioned revolutionary.

Fundamentally, she might have even been in favour of the marriage. She was fond of me and treated me as a member of the family. She was not mercenary and realistic enough to know that a wealthy wife would hardly have fitted into her son's life. And she was aware of my genuine affection for her. I had lost my mother at the age of sixteen and transferred to her all my unspent love. We parted very friendly.

A few soothing words from Leviné could easily have brought his mother to her senses, but he could not find them. He was blinded by a lifelong struggle.

The feud had started at a very early age. The gentle child had been incensed by her overbearing manner and had found a peculiar way of fighting back. Ordered in a majestic voice to leave the room, he would retaliate by moving with such deliberate slowness that she would run after him and give him a good smacking. The smacks? He apparently thought it was worth it... .

It did not occur to her to look into the reason for his reaction. He clearly 'misbehaved' and had to be punished. The scene was periodically played out in the same pattern.

She found it, however, only very amusing and laughed when she heard him muttering to himself, 'If I were the mother and she were my daughter, I would have thrown her out of the window.' Intentions expressed in inoffensive language were not punishable.

Leviné's refusal to wake up in the mornings might be another expression of defiance, but here she was not immediately involved and displayed great indulgence. The governess would dress the boy, still half asleep, and send him off to school. He and his sister were allowed money for a cab, but he often had to pay for the coachman with his own pocket-money, being too slow for his sister to wait for him.

His mother saw no cause for alarm and was rather amused when told that he occasionally succeeded in overtaking his sister in their race to school.

One day, the seven-year-old boy must have felt that he had reached the limit of his endurance and decided to run away. The Levinés were then living in a summer resort and he went to the family coachman and asked to be taken to St Petersburg to the cook Sasha. His mother did nothing to calm the child or prevent his going. Instead, the coachman was instructed to pretend that he was doing as he asked, to drive him around for a while and then bring him back home.

The frustrated boy suddenly found himself facing his mother and she was cruel enough to punish him severely.

She herself told me of the incident at great length, including the last sequence. She was convinced that she was only doing her duty by him and had nothing to hide.... My involuntary gasp of horror was, I believe, the first crack in our friendship.

The atmosphere of the elegant home was charged with barely hidden irritation. A frequent guest at their table, I often witnessed puzzling exchanges.

'May I offer you something, Genja?' his mother would ask in a very amiable voice, and would receive a calculated, chilling, 'Thank you, Mother.'

It seemed so unnatural and was so disturbing that I decided to speak up. With all the appropriate apologies ('I know that I have no right to interfere in your affairs' and so on) I asked once, 'Please tell me what is the connection between a friendly offer and such a resentful "thank you"?'

I got my deserved rap on the knuckles.

'Yes, Rosa Nissanovna, you have no right to interfere in other people's affairs.'

Later, when my rights were established, I received my answer:

'She kindly offered me things at the table I could very well help myself to. It vexed me to compare it with her angry remonstrations for picking a few flowers or fruit from her "garden."

Once she was expecting a visitor and described her to me: 'She is a teacher, but not really a teacher.'

Both her 'children' immediately pounced on her.

'How can one be a teacher and not a teacher?' they sneered. They just wouldn't miss an opportunity to fight her.

The proud, self-assured woman lost all her composure. She had not anticipated the turn. It was 'illogical' and she was vainly trying to explain herself. She was stammering and so pitiful that I interfered.

'One can be a teacher by profession and at the same time be different by social and cultural standards,' I explained to the valiant attackers.

It brought the controversy to a halt. But it doesn't take much imagination to assess what bitterness it left in the mother's heart and the seed it sowed for new encounters. It just kept the fire burning.

It was all very well for an outsider to take a judicious attitude, but the struggle for his most elementary rights badly obscured Leviné's judgement.

In the course of the struggle he lost all sense of proportion. Neither his character nor even simple dignity could justify some of his reactions.

He said once, 'Suppose I was eating an orange and she threatened: "If you won't stop eating I'll jump out of the window." What would you do?'

It was apparently a fair illustration of her possessiveness and he was appalled at my answer: 'I would throw the wretched thing away.'

'You mean I have no right to eat an orange?'

'But if it irritates her so much, an orange is only a small concession.'

This parable became a kind of staple food, dished up again and again. Leviné lost. But it took him years of separation from his mother to see things in their true perspective.

She practised corporal punishment until as a tall youth of seventeen he decided to put an end to it. He caught her hands and declared:

'I will not let go until you promise to put a stop to this.'

Her beautiful face became contorted with rage and she screamed'. 'Has it come to this? Beating your own mother?'

Leviné told me that the ugly scene of which every minute seemed an eternity lasted for some half-hour. She broke down at the end and started sobbing. He knew then that she had given in and he did not insist on promises. The incident did not leave him unscathed. Even after so many years his description retained a dramatic flavour.

She tried to model him after the image of his father, but her praise for the care his father took of his clothes resulted in Leviné treating his own with almost childish negligence.

As a child he was often clad in white silk and the constant 'Genja, be careful!' made him detest both colour and material. He would, he joked, consider dressing our future children in white as the number one reason for divorce.

In spite of her heroic efforts to rescue him, Leviné was convinced that his mother had never loved him and he was literally starved of affection.

He started conditioning me very early to accept joyfully his exacting habits.

'Be gentle, tender, affectionate,' the Russian *laskovaja* ran like a thread through his letters. The requests always disturbed me, even when presented in extravagant, flattering settings:

'... And so you have only learned from Lucie M. that you are pretty. Dear, when you are kind and gentle you are the prettiest, most beautiful, glorious and enchanting. Be only always kind and gentle, Oslik.'

He seemed quite obsessed with the idea. Here is another exhibit:

'I shall be back in a few days and we start again or rather continue a "gentle life." But it will be "only gentle," "exclusively gentle."

He wrote this at a time when there could not be much room for 'gentleness' in the normal sense. 'White roses cannot survive a day in this atmosphere', he used to joke, and he stopped buying them.

It was the more puzzling since he simultaneously delighted in my 'gentleness.'

To make me accept the unflattering name of 'Oslik' – it means 'little donkey' – he dug out a number of pictures and quotations to prove my similarity to that 'smooth' and 'kind' animal.

I only later understood what inhuman effort: 'Be always kind and gentle' implied....

It might be nearer the truth to say that Leviné's mother did not *like* him. He had none of the qualities which appealed to her. She expected him to restore the family fortunes and regarded his revolutionary ideas as a personal affront.

'So the *moujik* is more important to you than your own mother,' she would complain bitterly.

He, in his turn, was also convinced that he did not love his mother.

'You must not be sorry for me,' he reassured me after her breach with him. 'I don't love her and I am none the worse for the loss. I am repelled by her rudeness.'

Unfortunately, filial love does not depend on a mother's perfection nor, for that matter, is hatred necessarily caused by her moral deficiencies. He was much more attached to her than he knew and her influence made itself felt the moment I became 'home and family.' He even adopted some of her ways which he detested.

The artistic child was fascinated by the beauty of his mother. Once at the sight of her dressed in black velvet with a long train he exclaimed: 'How beautiful you are, Mutti, like a real queen.' Apparently out of a desire to be 'with it' he added, 'May I drive on your train?'

I am far from attempting to poach on complicated preserves but I wonder what a Freud would have made of this.

'Her children' whom she proudly exhibited and praised to the skies in public were submitted to harsh scrutiny and merciless censorship whenever they returned home from a party. They both dreaded this sad finale and the more sensitive Genja came to hate the parties themselves.

When I was entering into 'society,' into the so-called academic circles, I was very eager to learn something about the code of behaviour. I had mostly moved among the Russian socialist intelligentsia, notorious for their unconventional manners.

But Leviné soon went beyond tips on proprieties and did exactly the same as his mother. Every word, every movement, was mercilessly examined. He seemed to be urged on by a power beyond his control.

Invisibly his mother played a great part in our life. I had to support myself and, having no qualifications, the available jobs ranged between office-worker, cashier and shop-assistant. None of these would provide a living wage. The only job with sufficient pay, and much more congenial to me, was that of a bus conductress. But that was barred to me: it would scandalise Leviné's mother. Other reasons were advanced: bad weather, late hours, probable approaches by male passengers. I knew I could cope with such problems but I had to comply with my mother-in-law's bourgeois prejudices and I gave in.

Nor was Leviné able to shed habits typical of his hated environment. For example, he insisted on keeping everything under lock and key, which was not only out of character for a man who never cared for possessions but futile in a household which had not much property to lose.

All our landladies were treated as potential thieves.

'She has stolen that, too,' was his immediate reaction each time he mislaid some object.

'You wronged her and must certainly apologise,' I once suggested when the 'stolen property' was found.

He smiled, he was embarrassed and very sorry but the 'stolen that, too' would periodically turn up.

During his illness his mother did her utmost to restore his health. She invented special dishes and often went to the kitchen to prepare them herself. Her nose, she told me, with the implication that it was 'an aristocratic nose,' rebelled and turned red. She was very proud of her sacrifice. She would sit for hours at his bedside and describe at length her culinary achievements. No wonder then that he considered himself an expert on the subject and was eager to impart his knowledge to me. Unfortunately, we lacked the material conditions in which to apply her golden rules.

Besides, I had my own idea of my relations with my husband and they did not include long talks on a kitchen-sink level; nor was it compatible with his own views. He deplored the lack of what he beautifully called 'serene deference' in marital relations, which obviously excluded petty squabbles.

Once I thought I had stumbled on a very convincing argument:

'The yearly loss from my mismanagement could hardly exceed 100 to 150 marks. Regard the loss as a present to me and stop the debates.'

He was terribly moved. He felt quite guilty for not being able to make me presents and never failed to buy me flowers, even if sometimes he could only afford one 'for the buttonhole.' Here was an offer on very favourable 'instalment terms' and the imaginary gift would be a great contribution to our happiness. But he was too entangled in the old habits.

'I cannot promise, my darling,' he answered sadly.

His chivalry did not allow me to handle his discarded linen and he insisted on dealing with his laundry himself. But he continued to treat his clothes with the accustomed negligence. Pleading with him was dangerous. it would remind him of his mother; occasional reasoning that hard brushing to remove stains hardly did his last suit any good and there was no way to replace it under war conditions brought his most embarrassed, most charming, guilty smiles but no results.

He had assimilated the specific technique of quarrelling, of hurling about unjust, wounding words and of carrying on long after what started the dispute was forgotten. Yet I never saw him spiteful or really angry. He took me once to a church to show me old paintings, mass-garments and ornaments. Suddenly he seized my hand and dragged me to the door. He could not bear the organ-music: "threats, vengeance, punishment! that is their God."

Leviné was due at any time to be transferred to another town and he needed some of the documents and papers he had left at his mother's house. His sister Sonja got busy making arrangements: to avoid an unpleasant clash, the mother was to be informed and given the chance to leave the house.

I was convinced that she would try to make up with her son and asked him to make it easy for her.

'Oh, you don't know our mother,' he and Sonja asserted. 'She will never do such a thing.'

Characteristically, they immediately focused their attention on her: both were so embittered that they could not credit her with any human impulse.

'If she will not approach you, the situation will not arise, but please be kind to her if she does.'

Both brother and sister were very embarrassed to be proved in the wrong.

It was a very promising start. Everybody heaved a sigh of relief; but the relaxation was not to last.

Though his mother made it up with him when he went to the house, I myself remained anathematised. Leviné then pondered whether it was proper to communicate with his mother when he could not as much as mention my name to her.

He was particularly vexed that he could not introduce me to his grandmother; he was very devoted to her and was naturally sure of her approval.

His sister visited us in secret, which Leviné thought cowardly and despicable, and this was another source of bitterness. And bitterness is not very conducive to a harmonious life.... .

I was desperate to set his mind at ease. Could not his mother be persuaded to remove the ban if I promised not to make use of it and stayed away?

I met her one morning in the street and decided to submit the idea to her.

'What do you want of me?' she shrieked dramatically when I asked her to spare me a few minutes.

It was an encounter in the best Russian tradition of a Dostoyevsky. It lasted some three hours, during which she avidly poured out reproaches and indictments. She seemed to be in a trance and hardly knew what she was doing. I had expected a short Yes or No and had not anticipated a vulgar, distasteful scene. I was trembling all over.

Passing a bench I said, 'Please let us sit down.'

'How dare you! Sit on the same bench with you!' And immediately she was sitting at my side.... .

I listened in morbid fascination to a flow of abuse between tales she created of an imaginary world:

'How we three lived together before you came and poisoned his mind.'

I was told that I had wormed my way into their harmonious life, attributing to me a skill which would have done credit to a Mata-Hari. The image she created of me was so fantastic and in such contrast to my very appearance that I ventured an interruption.

'Look at me carefully. Am I the person you are speaking of?'

She looked at me with the eyes of a sleep-walker and quickly turned away.... .

Oh, she always knew when he was her true son and when he was soaked in my vicious influence. She gave me an example.

'When he came to collect his belongings, no one could of course foresee that I would speak to him. Free of your influence he was for a while my affectionate boy craving to see more of me. He asked very shyly, very humbly' "Mother, will you permit me to come again?"'

Could I tell a mother that she owed the reconciliation to her hated enemy?

'Don't turn him against me and we shall see,' she kept on saying. There was nothing then for me to do but wait for a miracle.

It was of course inevitable that she should accuse me of marrying her son for money. My question: 'Has he no other attractions?' did not put her out.

'My son towers high above you. Could you ever have expected to marry such a man. Tell me, could you?'

This was meant as another indictment and it was rather hard to speak of my feelings in that context, but I hoped that my answer might appease her, the mother: 'No, I could never have dreamt of it.'

'You see,' she said, as if she had caught me red-handed at some crime. She was not a mother but a rival, competing for the same man.

'Go on, replace everything and everybody for him,' she challenged me.

When I at last succeeded in submitting my request, she shouted, 'I cannot trust you. It is just a trick to sneak yourself into the home of *my mother*.'

I used to speak to her of my father and she knew that I worshipped him.

'I swear by the memory of my father that I shall keep my promise. Remove the ban for your son's sake.'

It appeared that I had given her another weapon to hunt me.

'If your father knew what kind of a person you are, he would today, on Yom Kippur, turn in his grave.'

To involve my father in such an ugly scene was sacrilege to me, and I winced with pain. She noticed the effect and repeated the words again and again with the relish a sadist might feel in inflicting physical blows. She only stopped when she realised that I had frozen up and she could not hurt me any more.

This time she had overdone it. The sanctity of Yom Kippur had been added for good measure, to frighten me. It was not at all in keeping with a sophisticated lady to refer to it and speaking yiddish words was to her almost equivalent to using bad language. The lapse must have tormented her. (Four years later she told me in an amicable conversation how amazed she was to hear her son speak of 'Yom Kippur.' But of course she knew exactly from whom he had learned it ... .')

Propriety meant a great deal to her. I suggested that she should give me a chance – I might not be that bad after all.

She exploded. 'You expect me to take advice from you, a whore – pardon me?'

Her apology was not for the insult but for the obscene word, she, the lady, had to use. I almost laughed.

Her vocabulary of abuse was then exhausted – what could she add?

We parted to meet again at the funeral of her son.

I suddenly understood the parable of the biblical woman who consented to have the child cut in two rather than to give it up. And with it Solomon's verdict that she could not be *the mother*... .

She must have felt uneasy for she sent me a quite generous sum of money. Of course she was unaware that it was another insult to imagine that I would accept it.

Shortly afterwards Leviné was transferred to Karlsruhe for regular military training. He no longer belonged to the Home Guards *Landsturm* category and the prospect of front line service became very real.

All my plans for earning a living came to nothing. I found myself pregnant and was immediately afflicted with very tiring side-effects.

I moved into my old boarding house, it was cheaper and the proprietress was ready to wait for payment as long as we wished. But it was only a breathing space. The house was no place to accommodate a baby.

Incapable of working and without a place of our own, abortion seemed to be the only solution.

The wartime edict – 'the Kaiser needs babies' – made an abortion in our small town well-nigh impossible and Leviné was terrified at the very thought of it.

Undoubtedly, his background played its part in his light-hearted attitude to practical problems. Money, when needed, was always forthcoming. It was available and though he would never think of claiming his due share, he was never too fastidious to accept it. But I was and I could have thought of no greater humiliation than living on his mother's grace.

Of course Leviné was far from consciously considering this solution and never mentioned it. But he was unable to offer any workable plan, any basis for raising a family.

We quarrelled bitterly. I saw no way out and decided to go to Berlin and have an abortion.

Leviné had not given up. He wrote to me:

...I must beg of you, from the bottom of my heart, to give up the terrible thing you have set out to do. The last night and day showed both of us that in spite of all misunderstandings and distress, we are so close to each other that much happiness is yet in store for us. The sooner you give up your plan, the sooner those feelings will take over and your journey will only be a recovery from the painful days.

He threw into the balance all the eloquence of his love:

...I was happy...and I have tears in my eyes when I remember how I was waiting for you at the station, and the long, long hours we were sitting together on our chair seat.... I see every-thing so vividly, our awakening in the morning, our evenings, our days and our nights.... Yes, I know the distressing hours and days before your departure were a bad omen, just the same we were happy....

He followed me to Berlin.

He was granted a longish furlough, made arrangements with Press agencies and newspapers for publication of his articles and short stories. Things were looking up. I gave in.

Routine military service was not very conducive to literary work. Leviné was, in addition, employed as an interpreter at war-prisoners' courts. The offences varied from petty thefts and disobedience to more serious, sexual assaults. The predominantly illiterate convicts were often not even able to state their case, and much skill was needed to unravel the actual proceedings.

This work was originally designed to prevent Leviné from making closer contacts with his unit and hence from spreading revolutionary propaganda. But he became very popular at the courts and was continuously whisked from place to place. His sparse free time he spent in military offices obtaining travel permits and on slow military trains to visit me for a few hours. He sometimes arrived late in the evening and rushed off in the middle of the night to catch an early train back. There was hardly room for concentrated work, particularly since he was facing the danger of being sent to the front.

In March 1916, three months before my confinement, Leviné wrote to a niece: 'The day after tomorrow I go to Belgium. I have a slender hope that the University will apply for an exemption, otherwise I shall, sooner or later, be sent to the front.'

It was a pathetic letter in which he asked the girl, who was completely enslaved by her grandmother and two aunts with whom she was living in Wiesbaden, to stand by me as 'a friend and a sister.' The letter was never sent. He was too realistic to rely on illusions and he knew precisely what he could expect from any person. The letter only reflects his despair.

To me he wrote: '...I have been thinking of you these days incessantly, uninterruptedly and it pains me, pains me indescribably to know that you suffer in such loneliness.'

He was spared by a stroke of luck, he happened to be 'supernumerary.' Following an application from the University, he was soon transferred to Heidelberg as a lecturer in Russian. But he was still not exempt from military service, and the lessons were not lucrative enough to provide us with a living.

Money in the end did come, and in the accustomed way. An emissary turned up to tell us how tormented Leviné's mother was at the thought that her son was in difficulties. She offered a monthly allowance or, if he preferred, a sum of money to last for the duration of the war. In he end she insisted on a monthly allowance, but her son's visits in no way improved their relationship. They were brief and restrained.

In the same aloof manner, Leviné informed her of the birth of our child:

University Hospital, 21st June 1916.
Dear Mother,

> My wife has just borne me a child. I am writing to you because I think you might wish to know it after all.
> Best love,
> Genja.

However, he made an attempt at reconciliation and went to see her.

'Mother, my wife has borne me a child.'
Silence.
'Don't you wish to congratulate me?'
'A child has been born.'
'...Not necessarily yours' was the cruel insinuation.

I knew nothing of the visit. Overwhelmed with the miracle of motherhood, I had pleaded, 'Go to her, be kind to her, whatever she does. Nothing matters. She is your mother and I know now what it means.'

He covered his face, he kissed my hands – I believed in repentance for wronging his mother – he was on the brink of crying and I was terribly moved and choking with happy tears: the joy of 'converting a sinner' is truly immeasurable. I only much later learned of the visit and why he was so shaken.

The flat we had found was infested with fleas. We could not stay. One of those rare charitable women I met by chance took pity on me and agreed to give us temporary shelter. And temporariness was to become with us a natural condition for the rest of our married life. By the time the baby was four weeks old, we had moved twice.

Finding lodgings was one of our main problems. The difficulties of sharing a kitchen under wartime conditions, with restricted gas hours, lack of coal and other shortages, soon made themselves felt. As a rule we had to move every two months: and in the end we stopped unpacking the heavy cases of books, manuscripts, press-cuttings and all the accessories of a politician, a writer or any educated man.

Our greatest difficulties were caused by Leviné's inability to cope with the tiresome daily routine. Habits he might have acquired as a means of protest had their repercussions; getting up in the morning presented a serious problem, and he was generally unable to adapt himself to new conditions.

And those mornings! He would set the alarm clock long before the time and I waited in anguish – one, two or more hours – for him to take the final plunge. He could reset the clock and sleep in between. I could not. Our days were spoilt from the start.

We sometimes woke up together gay and happy.

'Don't get up, stay with me a little longer. I promise to jump out of bed and dress like an acrobat.'

It was the only promise I knew him to make and very rarely, if at all, to keep.

In the early days of our marriage, weary of his endlessly drawn-out undressing, I said once that such habits might even affect our love life.

He was truly shocked. From now on he would dress and undress 'like an acrobat.'

He tried hard next morning. He made rapid and funny 'acrobatic' movements. It was very amusing and we laughed a lot.

I believe that this indulgence of mine played its part in his love for me. For the first time his tiresome ways were accepted in love and not in irritation. He was strangely moved when I imitated his awkward movements and called him tenderly 'Tjulen,' Russian for seal.

His last note to me before his execution was signed 'Yours T.'

In a way, I failed him. He could not change and he reproached me for being 'like my mother' – the greatest abuse he ever hurled at me.

Nor had he ever learnt to keep regular working hours. Yet somehow he could always get away with it. His university colleagues would relate with a certain amusement that he alone was spared the customary rebuff of foot-shuffling meted out to other late-comers.

More astonishing was the indulgence of the camp authorities. He was allowed the privilege of living outside the camp and could report for duty shortly before the arrival of his immediate superior.

He failed to comply even with this modest demand. On the contrary, he was always the last to appear and sometimes collided with the commandant, an old colonel, with no fixed working hours at all. Yet no one thought of punishment or of the most obvious reprisal, the withdrawal of his privileges. This non-commissioned soldier was allowed exceptional status. The colonel himself might have been surprised at his unheard of leniency and tried to rationalise it: 'I could not take a step which would upset your poor wife.'

When he started his Russian seminar, his students, mostly middle-aged people, some of considerable distinction, were often submitted to the same treatment. They exercised the same patient indulgence. On occasion, particularly prior to my confinement, he even failed to notify them in advance of his absence, and they waited in vain for his appearance.

I thought it presumptuous to expect them to enrole for further lectures, but they all appeared again and in even greater numbers. Some wrote personal letters of thanks for the pleasure of attending his lectures. He laughed when I read out the imaginary letters I would have written but, after all, people queue for good theatre performances, why not for good lectures?

On being invalided out of the Army, he worked in one of the war ministries. True to himself he never kept office hours, though everyone groaned under the inconvenience his absence sometimes caused.

'He cannot be treated like other people,' sighed his victims.

'He must not be treated like other people,' I once heard a young worker say in desperation. It happened in Munich, at one of the last council meetings when Leviné's policy was roughly attacked by the anti-Communists.

The young worker did not know who I was – I had no access

to such meetings, but would steal in to see my husband. He would never tolerate my transgressions and I would hide in the far corner of the hall.

He was 'different.' People, particularly the simple and unsophisticated, used to feel this.

Leviné got used to this special treatment and felt no compulsion to change his habits. It had not mattered too much in his former life. When these habits proved destructive he was thirty-two years old. Admonitions were futile. I must not be angry with him, not even just displeased.

'It paralyses my energy and working capacity,' he would claim, which under the circumstances amounted to a sort of blackmail.

His birthday was approaching, the first we could celebrate together, and I was anxious to make it a big occasion. I pulled all strings to get unobtainable luxuries like shirts, underwear and socks. The latter was the most important item. His uncommonly delicate skin would not adjust itself to the overdarned socks, which was another hindrance to getting up in the morning.

Under the surveillance of our landlady I managed to bake my first cake. Everything was set for the big celebration. I even suggested a day off for the event. No, it could not be done, he had very important papers to attend to. But we could get up early in the morning and have a stroll through the Tiergarten and Unter den Linden on his way to the office. It was spring, the 10th of May, 1917.

I got up first to nurse the baby and prepare the festive breakfast table.

'You must not leave the room until everything is ready. Wait until I fetch you.'

He laughed at my excitement and was very touched and amused when, breaking the ritual, I solemnly handed over to him in advance a pair of socks.

'Your feet must not suffer today.'

I got ready, decked out the table, baby and myself and, beaming with anticipation, opened the door.... He was sitting on the edge of the bed, undressed, one of the precious socks in his hand, lost in thought.

I laugh whenever I recapture the scene. But then I thought it a mockery of my efforts and felt utterly humiliated. I burst into tears but was suddenly seized with a morbid desire for 'retaliation.' My own birthday was only a week ahead, I would spoil it for him just as he had spoilt his for me.

I exploded, 'I don't want any celebration of my birthday. Don't try or I'll leave the house.'

If he had only said one sensible word! The damage could easily be mended by a compromise, allowing for some short celebration. But he insisted on being on time on that particular morning.

He did not leave the house at all, not that day or the next. I cannot remember how long the agony lasted.

The blame was put on me. I should not be angry whatever his behaviour. He could not bear it, it paralysed his energy and working capacity, was the steady refrain.

A deep-seated horror of anything resembling reproach or mere disapproval, aggravated by shattered nerves, made him lose his head.

He made up for everything on my birthday: for his selfish disregard, for my disappointment and the torment of the following days. He planned every hour, he overwhelmed me with gifts – unobtrusively, since I had refused 'celebrations' – with expressions of love so tender and imaginative that the day was forever incised in my memory.

Oh, I could bake cakes and procure unobtainable socks, but I felt humble and clumsy compared with his delicacy and tact. I had so much to learn and was ready to carry any burden.

Characteristically, Leviné's craving for unconditional acceptance was exclusively confined to his family life. I have never known anyone to accept criticism and corrections with such natural grace.

He had written many stories about workers' lives. I found many of them too sugary and, later on, when the Party was anxious to publish every scrap of paper carrying his name, I waged a real war against both the Party and Leviné's sister to prevent the turning of a great revolutionary into a second-rate writer.

During his lifetime, I sometimes parodied over-sentimental passages and recited them in a bombastic histrionic manner to him. It used to cause much merriment, never a shadow of resentment.

Neither was he set on acclaim and popularity. He had no need to be. He was highly sought after and, as far as I know, he was the only man in Heidelberg to break down the barriers of its hierarchic academic society.

II

The breath of the Russian revolution had an immediate effect on our personal life. It opened new perspectives and magically swept away our squabbles.

During his convalescence, after his imprisonment in Russia, Leviné had written a book on Czar *Nicholas II*. Designed for the wealthy Russian visitors abroad, it was written in Russian and was adjusted to the style and manner of the readers. To whet their appetites, the chapters were adorned with screaming headlines such as: 'The Honeymoon' or 'Under the Enchantment of Waltzing Tunes' and so on.

In fact he described the abrupt end of an expected liberalisation of the regime and exposed the notorious Khodinka affair – when society danced while ten thousand Czarist subjects were crushed to death in a disastrous stampede for trifling gifts, coronation mementoes. The sugar coating helped the reader to swallow some home truths about Czarist rule. The book was a tremendous success and ran into seven editions in less than two years.

The socialist publishing house was only too eager to issue an anti-Czarist book which Leviné promised to deliver within a few months. He was not to be hoodwinked again: the conditions were favourable enough to free us of all our worries and to enable him to devote all his time to the problems of the anticipated great events.

It was not to be. He worked out an exact plan: so many chapters, so many pages, so many hours. He engaged a stenographer. To find additional data, I ransacked the libraries for newspapers and periodicals.

Unfortunately, he underestimated the task of adding twelve years of Czarist rule to his book, and overrated his physical capacity – he was, after all, invalided out of the Army. Nor, I suppose, should his lack of self-discipline be discounted. He kept on postponing the delivery, and when this became too embarrassing left his publishers without any information at all.

This time his charm did not work. When I rang up to apologise for the delay, I was rudely told that the deal was off for good.

'Your husband should be glad to be let off so lightly. We are prepared to abstain from suing him for breach of agreement. That is all.'

There was, however, a very serious reason for the sternness of the publishers which Leviné had not foreseen. They had found out more about his activities and were anxious not to publicise his name or his interpretations which, they rightly suspected, would have clashed with their own ideas. They thus welcomed the opportunity to annul the contract.

The rosy prospects dissolved into a trail of new burdens. The secretary threatened us with legal proceedings and there were more urgent debts to pay. For a long time, the unpublished manuscript gave me the impression of a monster sucking the life blood out of us.

The manuscript got lost during our long wanderings. It was apparently destroyed, together with other important documents, by one of our landladies when she found out, after the 'Spartacus Week' that her tenant was a wanted man.

I found myself a job in a book-keeping department, even though it took me quite a time to distinguish between the meanings of debit and credit.

In those days people sympathised with 'ladies' (I was a 'Frau Doctor') who had to go out to work, and my employer reassured me: 'There are plenty of well-trained girls in the department. I shall ask them to help you.'

We were forced to put the child into a children's home – our first separation from him. I felt trapped, a stranger in a different world, and for the first time separated from my child. I worked long hours and rushed straight to the nursery to catch a glimpse of him. For the benefit of the staff, the children were put to bed long before the normal bedtime. I was heartbroken.

There was still one bright spot in our life. Leviné gallantly accompanied me every morning to my office, two hours ahead of his own working time. For the first time in his life he was sitting regularly at his desk and that long before his colleagues. For the first time getting up ceased to be an exacting problem.

Our mornings were gay, spiced with his jokes about his heroic behaviour. He seemed cured of his former habits.

His chivalry also had its material reward: his salary was considerably raised. We were able to pay off some debts and the future looked less bleak.

A silly incident ended it all. A heavy object fell on my head. Covered with blood I was brought home and for a long time could not resume work.

Leviné was not cured after all. He was late for work again the very next morning. The increasing complaints from his office were of no avail, and in the end he lost his job.

A friend promised me a loan, and a family in Hamburg was prepared to put me up with the child. I did not hesitate to go, and Leviné did not attempt to stop me.

The plan did not materialise. My friend had second thoughts about the loan and the landlady about the flat. I had to go back to Berlin to look for a job. The child had to be put into a home again.

Leviné found a job on a newspaper in Solingen. Our marriage seemed to be on the rocks.

I wrote to him, 'And so you are going to Solingen. There is no question of me coming with you. You must remember this when you look for a home for the child. It will have to be for a long time.'

We could not part. He gave up his plan to go to Solingen and we struggled on. The sensitive child was ailing.

By a stroke of luck, I found a flat on the outskirts of Berlin, and a girl to look after the child.

We moved in.

It was spring 1918, and it was again the Russian revolution which brightened our life.

The first Russian Embassy arrived in Berlin and engaged us both; Leviné as the Ambassador's adviser on German affairs, and myself as a Russian-German interpreter.

Congenial work in a familiar atmosphere had a miraculous effect on Leviné's health and greatly improved his working habits. That is to say, having more freedom of manoevre, he was always on time. But more often than not he rushed off without breakfast and our neighbours would remark on the speed with which he ran to catch the train... .

Leviné entered the Embassy ostensibly as a member of the Social-Revolutionary Party, at least that is what he still thought he was. Its cloak and dagger programme, demanding great personal heroism, suited the young idealist.

Deeply disturbed by the idea of living with a prospective 'murderer' I questioned him again and again: 'Could you really commit murder? How could you justify it?'

He tried to make the idea acceptable by working on my great affection for my younger sister:

'Would you expect me to idly watch her being raped and not to shoot the criminal?'

'No, of course not,' I thought in confusion.

Thus Leviné, an erudite Marxist and for many years an active participant in the socialist movement, tried to justify the errors of his youth.

Living in far away Germany he might have seen no point in reconsidering his Party allegiance: the underestimation of the agrarian question by West European socialists might have been another reason for him to cling to the Social-Revolutionary Party which put this problem in the forefront of its programme.

The February revolution of 1917 put his Party in a very strong position.

Kerensky's speeches, though highly histrionic, seemed reassuring.

Leviné grew apprehensive when the Minister of Agriculture, Chernov – his friend and teacher – seemed in no hurry to transfer the land to the peasants – the essential part of the programme. He soon learned, however, that his Party had split and that its left wing was actively collaborating with the Bolsheviks. This released him again from the necessity of seriously assessing his political allegiance.

The Embassy was to include representatives of the left wing of the Social Revolutionaries and Leviné was offered the post. An incident followed which is worth recalling, for it makes the political evasions of a man of Leviné's clear-mindedness even more unaccountable.

A second appointee was Fanny Yezerska, a resident of Berlin and also a member of the Social Revolutionaries. Leviné immediately raised the question: 'Who will be the head?'

This produced great astonishment. The old veteran, Natanson, shook his head disapprovingly.

'We are all comrades,' he said. 'Such petty problems should not exist in our midst.'

I remember that I was also surprised, for it was not in keeping with Leviné's nature and tact to try, as it seemed, to assert his superiority.

'I would not have raised the question in a body of three members,' he said. 'But what if Comrade Yezerska and I disagree? Who will be responsible for our work? for possible errors?'

It had escaped us that his question did not imply any attempt at superiority, and he shamed everybody by adding: 'I am quite willing to take orders from Comrade Fanny. I only insist on a clear division of functions.'

Leviné finally broke with his Party after it had staged a putsch to reverse the Brest-Litovsk Treaty and unseat the Bolshevik Government.

This entire evolution was of a rather abstract nature. Leviné's true allegiance belonged to the Bolsheviks from the start. In his discussions with the Mensheviks and the German Independents, (USPD) he defended their policy, however distorted by the flood of anti-Bolshevik propaganda. But he was still listed as a Social-Revolutionary and he did not try to openly declare his breach.

Work at the Embassy was highly coveted by the Russian emigrants in Berlin and he thought it the wrong moment to declare himself on the side of the rulers. The maturing German upheaval would offer a better opportunity to prove his loyalty to both the Russian and the German revolution.

The personnel of the Embassy were not exactly the best advertisement for the new regime. Favouritism and greed ruled supreme. I was growing anti-Bolshevist with the same speed with which Leviné was shedding all vestiges of disagreement with them.

I was particularly outraged by the case of my predecessor, the younger brother of the Ambassador's future wife, a revolting semi-literate youth.

The department was dealing with the repatriation of prisoners-of-war. Many were unable to fill in the application forms and neither was the youth.

He left behind a chaotic mess which I worked hard to put in order. But my white dress made me a bourgeois suspect and I was subjected to strict surveillance lest I sabotaged my work.

When I found out that the youth had received at least twice my salary, I complained. Some German employees supported me. The case was brought into the open. Ledebour himself, the prominent leader of the Independent Social-Democratic Party, arrived to placate us and appealed to our class solidarity.

We laughed. Solidarity! There was a big difference between us and the Russian comrades scurrying along with an air of importance and often dressed to kill.

The corruption was even more serious because it came from the top. The boy, for instance, was obviously employed to please his pretty sister.

Quick to generalise – a sin of many ignorant people – I argued, 'The entire staff! Thirty people! Their behaviour cannot be accidental. There must be something rotten in a system represented by such people!'

Leviné did not discount these sorry facts but made nonsense my conclusions.

His smile put me on my guard. I knew I was in for a good thrashing.

'The entire staff?' he asked. 'How many of them do you really know? They are not representative of the regime. On the contrary, they are the dregs of the revolution. The best, the devoted elements, could not be dispensed with, and they would not wish to leave. This staff, or many of them, are typical "revolutionary-profiteers" and, naturally, good at pulling strings. The Embassy needed a certain number of people. What could be more desirable than going abroad? They hurriedly flocked to fill the demands.'

This was an accurate picture of what really happened; Leviné did not have to be present to see it. Neither did I need the confirmation which I later obtained. It was crystal clear: it could not have been otherwise.

It was another demonstration of Leviné's visionary mind, of his capacity to unravel the truth however intricate it was. From him I learnt that imagination is no less essential for politicians than for poets and artists, long before I discovered this truth in Lenin's works.

Leviné used to astonish Russian visitors with his minute knowledge of Russian life and problems. He coined the word 'factory-patriotism' and anticipated the dangerous tendency of comrades to keep unprofitable works going instead of using the spare raw material for better distribution. He very soon realised the significance of the Soviet system for the German revolution and he was incessantly grappling with that problem.

Out of the few scraps of available information, he constructed in his mind the whole complicated edifice. When a highly erudite comrade with the reputation of being an expert on the soviet system visited the Embassy, Leviné proposed to him: 'Let me tell you how I visualise the structure and the functions of the soviets, and correct me where I am wrong.'

There were no corrections at all, only vigorous nods of confirmation and an astonished 'How do you know?' at the end. He assured Leviné that there were not many leaders in Russia with such a clear knowledge of the subject. I was present, and later on put the same question to Leviné: 'How can you know?'

He was always embarrassed when he had to credit himself with his own accomplishments, and I recognised his faint, almost guilty smile.

'This is the way I thought they should be organised,' he said. 'I worked it out myself.'

He did not convert me though and he treated my absurd talk with exceptional tolerance. Once or twice he exclaimed, 'And my wife says such things.'

I reminded him that I was a human being in my own right and he apologised. Not once had he lapsed into the self-righteous persistence with which he was trying to impose his expertise in domestic matters on me. I thought later on that he was too tolerant and I myself too aggressive.

I remember with shame, I was once nursing the child and defiantly singing a Russian revolutionary song – 'The time will come and the people will awake' – implying, of course, to replace the impostors now in power.

It was a direct challenge and he looked at me sadly but would not be provoked.

Was it force of habit? In this case I was not 'family' but a 'political opponent' and he always treated 'opponents' with exceptional tolerance.

Our main problems remained unresolved. Like many others, I did not believe in the stability of the Soviet government and consequently in the permanence of our jobs. I feared we might be faced again with the anxieties which had already nearly wrecked our marriage. To save it, I must never depend on Leviné for a living.

World events seemed to favour me. Germany occupied the Ukraine and needed interpreters. They paid well, but a greater attraction was the additional lavish daily expenses. I calculated that in six months I could earn enough to provide for myself and for my child for a long time and at last achieve my own ambitions.

The job in an occupied country involved some risk, but the employees were heavily insured. I decided that the child would be better off with a sum of money than with a mother who was incapable of looking after him, and I applied for the job.

Leviné left no stone unturned to prevent me from going. He first appealed to my loyalty: the Ukraine was a festering sore on the Soviet body-politic. I was making myself an accessory to plundering a prostrate country and therefore rendering his position at the Embassy untenable.[1]

It was evidently true, and I nearly gave up. But despair is inventive. I secured an audience with Joffe, the Russian Ambassador, and explained that I knew nothing of politics and was fighting my own battle. He listened attentively, watching me with his black piercing eyes. He was a psychiatrist by profession and saw that nothing could hold me back. He gave me his blessing.

Leviné then resorted to threats: it would break up our marriage and he would not feel obliged to remain faithful to me. We fought daily, hourly, and pasted unreconciled.

This was my fault. Even a momentary reconciliation would have frustrated my plan.

We got up weary after a sleepless night. Leviné saw me off, but we parted in complete silence.

Life in Kiev was more expensive than I had expected, and that particularly for newcomers. As might have been expected, the extra allowances were well justified. But I would not be defeated.

The shops were overflowing with rare food and other precious things unobtainable in Germany. I turned a blind eye to the tempting windows; nothing should upset my scheme.

My job consisted chiefly in collecting information about the harvest and everything connected with food supplies. It was one thing to be told angrily that I would help to 'plunder the country', and another to realise that I was doing exactly that. The Germans behaved like arrogant masters, not as the invited allies they were supposed to be. Voices were heard to say that 'the Germans are even worse than the Bolsheviks.' It was not very edifying to be associated with them.

'Even worse than the Bolsheviks,' however, did not in any way imply a desire for their return. The population as a whole was very politically conscious; and no wonder with the battles at their very doorsteps.

Everybody, or rather the society in which I moved, talked politics, and their verdict was unanimous: Bolshevik rule was a nightmare and must be brought to an end. I heard socialists declare that they would at any time take up their rifles to unseat those 'infamous impostors.' An old and trusted friend, a left-wing socialist whom I met by chance, warned me that collaboration with the Bolsheviks would compromise my husband for life.... Barely a year later, that same man, Goralsky, joined the Bolsheviks and played a great, if pernicious, part in the Comintern, particularly in its German section. But at that time his opinion seemed conclusive. He had 'first hand information.' How could I doubt his word?

I could not write to Leviné about politics and we both avoided writing about our personal life. Our letters were icy.

Like a prisoner I was counting the days to my release. Two months, a third of the time, lay behind me. My release came sooner than I expected.

Ironically, I suddenly became a security risk. One of the employees had seen me at the Soviet Embassy in Berlin and had denounced me as a Bolshevik. I was immediately discharged and ordered to leave the country. I was back where I started. Leviné met me at the station with a huge bunch of flowers... .

We were reunited and for a while all was forgotten. But it did not last. He was down to his last shirt, his shoes and clothes were dilapidated. Wartime conditions, the difficulty of finding a laundry and similar facilities were too much for him. It was high time for me to return.

When I had finished with him, he created quite a stir among his staff; they discovered that he was not only the venerated, beloved comrade, but that he was also a very good-looking man.

But he resented my efforts to 'clean up.' I should take him as he was. Besides, a man of his chivalry could not bear to see me working longer hours than he did, particularly doing manual work which was much despised in Russia – a country of cheap labour. It made him feel guilty and he tried to stop me. We quarrelled.

Leviné no longer worked at the Embassy. With the creation of Rosta, the predecessor of the Soviet News Agency Tass, he was appointed head of its Russian section. He was very short of staff, particularly of people he could implicitly trust. All his assistants were Mensheviks – the best that could be found in Berlin. When I returned from the Ukraine, he offered me the post of his private secretary.

This was the start of my political awakening. My job consisted in correcting the Russian translations. Willy-nilly I had to deal with matters which had never interested me before and to absorb daily a great deal of knowledge of what was going on around me.

When Leviné instructed me to pay as much attention to the text as to the style of the translations, I attributed his suspicions of inaccuracy to the strife between the Bolsheviks and the Mensheviks. Certainly people who like myself rejected the Bolsheviks ostensibly on moral grounds, could not commit breaches of confidence! All anti-Bolsheviks whom I met were oozing with moral superiority and I was so taken in that I truly believed I could detect party allegiance by peoples' looks and manners.

To my astonishment, Leviné was right again. I discovered in the Menshevik translations many subtle distortions to suit their own views which, at times, amounted to overt anti-Bolshevik propaganda.

I took some of the burdens off my greatly overworked husband. But I was not a smooth collaborator. Outraged by some anti-Bolshevik story, I would passionately declare that I could not work for 'such people.' After my experience in the Ukraine, I was very sensitive about my working associates.

In short talks, Leviné would often leave me with a feeling of shame at my flippancy and an awareness of the flimsiness of so-called public opinion. I became very careful and timid in expressing views on 'reliable information' concerning Russian affairs.

But I could not doubt a story of 'Bolshevik atrocities' when it came from the wife of Karl Liebknecht. She in her turn learnt it from Marchlevsky, a Polish Communist leader, second only to Rosa Luxemburg.

In a Russian town, actors refused to play as a protest against Bolshevik rule. They were summoned and curtly told: 'Russia cannot

live without theatre. You will either keep it alive or you will be put
against the wall.'
　　'To shoot people for refusing to act!' she said. 'Terror
used to be justified by issues of vital necessity. But theatre! Brutality
must have reached the limits if a man like Marchlevsky thought nothing
of telling of the incident himself – and with marked approval.'
　　We worked ourselves to a pitch and I rushed to Leviné to
tell him that this time I was quitting for good. I told him the story. He
listened attentively.
　　'And were they?' he asked.
　　'Were they what?'
　　'Shot?'
　　This was my last 'resignation.' Frau Liebknecht and I prided
ourselves on having minds of our own. We, of all the 'socialist ladies,'
were the only two who did not blindly follow our husbands. We considered ourselves critical and objective. Yet we did not escape the
prevailing mood of anti-Bolshevism and did not distinguish between a
threat and an *act*.
　　I realised that much more than personal honesty was required
for correct political judgement.
　　Rosta became my school of politics with Leviné as my patient
teacher. He taught me to read between the lines, to judge events and
human behaviour from an entirely new angle. He had tried it
before, but I needed some of my newly acquired knowledge to follow
him. Besides, I was too suspicious of anything which smacked of
Party 'Marxism' which, of course, was the basis of his approach. Even
our literary conversations usually ended in a clash. The word Dostoyevsky was as explosive as a bomb and led to heated arguments.
My job brought me face to face with new problems and forced me to
look at them seriously.
　　Before long I asked, not without reproach: 'How could you
have lived with such a wife? It is in a way insulting. It means that you
never took me seriously.'
　　'You see,' he said chivalrously, 'I knew you better and could
therefore wait.'
　　He might have credited me with fair play: whatever my
political ignorance, I never tried to interfere with his revolutionary
work. And whatever our ugly quarrels, I never lost sight of his integrity.... I had too much respect for his ideas – for ideals as such – to
dare to tread on such sacred ground. That was the man I loved, and I

tried my best not to hinder his preserving himself in all his purity. He was naturally worried and often looked to me for reassurance. Once when he was leaving for a clandestine meeting, he asked me, 'What will you do if I am arrested?'

'The same as soldiers' wives or widows do.'

I did not fail him on this ground.

Our harmonious work did not last. The German government found the presence of the Russians too hot for safety and decided to send both the Embassy and Rosta packing. The expulsion was covered up with a trick which became known as the 'exploding trunk' incident.

The Embassy was accused of abusing diplomatic immunity when a case conveniently burst open and allegedly revealed dangerous Bolshevik propaganda literature.

Soon an army of police officers invaded our building in search of incriminating evidence. I had deposited in the office a suitcase of food which I was allowed to take from the Ukraine. This produced a great stir.

'Aha!' exclaimed a detective triumphantly and demanded to have it opened. He was very rude and Leviné repaid him in his own way. He took on the air of a conspirator in a detective thriller, and his faked reluctance to produce the key heightened the tension.

When sausages and tins rolled out of the case, the policemen could hardly suppress their laughter. They lost all the self-confidence with which they had started their mission and were embarrassed and subdued. Leviné became master of the situation with hardly a murmur of protest from anyone. During the search he held the police under ostentatiously strict surveillance, keeping an eye on every movement.

'You treat us as though we were thieves,' complained the commissar meekly. 'Are you afraid we might steal your papers?'

'Oh, no, Sir, on the contrary,' Leviné answered with studied politeness. 'I fear you might add some of your own.'

They left hurriedly. Ridicule is also a propaganda weapon. Authority was defeated and Leviné's wit and presence of mind were an encouragement to everybody.

It certainly helped to take my mind off my worries, and I described the incident to Frau Liebknecht with such relish that she became quite angry.

'Don't play with me. I know what you have been through and what losing the job means to you.'

It brought me to my senses but not for long. There was something in the air, and unknown me to I was being carried along by a new, indefinable feeling. I had heard that an approaching revolution is preceded by a mysterious wave which affects people like an epidemic and transforms them suddenly. I was convinced that it was an invention of Party theorists and existed only in the pages of socialist literature.

I was wrong – how could I otherwise explain this excitement, this joyful anticipation of great events?

My growing understanding of Leviné's work and ideas had no reflection in our personal relationship. For his own personality seemed to run in two separate directions.

I watched him working fairly well on a job which really interested him, so that neither I nor our child seemed incentive enough. I resented such an 'aristocratic' attitude to work. I was growing bitter and even a little jealous. Our relationship was progressively deteriorating.

We were facing new predicaments. Our landlady needed the rooms; we had to move and she refused to keep the baby. And the quarrels, senseless, unaccountable, went on mercilessly.

Our last quarrel was just as senseless, but it was really the last one.

In those faraway days the Soviet Embassy was not afraid openly to associate itself with Communists. Liebknecht's release from prison was celebrated with a lavish reception and Leviné and I were among the guests.

The occasion was also memorable for food and drink and healthy, uncrippled men – another rarity in the last year of the war. Banqueting, with a flow of fiery speeches, lasted until late into the night.

There was no transport home and Leviné and I had to spend the night in a hotel. The hotelier insisted on separate rooms: we did not look like a married couple, he said.

Our Russian friend who lived in the hotel had to vouch for our 'legitimacy'!

'You treat your wife too nicely,' he remarked.

We went to work late, cheered and happy.

Later in the day I asked Leviné to send our messenger boy to fetch me some food. I was in great pain and could not go to the restaurant.

'No,' he said, rather emphatically. 'The boy must not be ordered about.'

His answer and tone were in such contrast to our mood, it felt like a cold shower. I was outraged.

He later explained: he only wanted to compel me to have a 'proper warm meal.' Pain or not, I had to comply with his ideas of what was good for me. I would not be easily appeased... . He was a past master of triggering off a quarrel, I of taking it the hard way.

He told me that he really wanted to marry a dumb little blonde, but it was hard to see how she would function in the given circumstances. If only one could have it both ways.

On the eve of the revolution, we were actually separated, this time I thought for good. I was too weary of the continuous ups and downs and Leviné too busy to be concerned with his private life.

I moved from the outskirts, our temporary refuge, back to Berlin where it was easier to find foster parents for the baby. I was put up by my friend, Lucie Mannheim, a prominent German actress. Leviné took quarters somewhere in town. I did not even know his address.

He suddenly sent me a message to fetch the baby at once. At any moment communications might be brought to a standstill and I might be separated from my child indefinitely.

It was the 9th November, 1918. The great day of the revolution was thus spent in trams, railway stations and trains, in feverish haste and agonising fear of getting marooned with the baby *en route*. I was shut off from the outside world and saw and heard nothing. I could not recall the faintest impression, not a single episode.

As far as I could see, nothing had changed. The bits of gossip the maid brought from her shopping expeditions contained nothing 'socialistic.' As before, I had to procure some documents and register with the police: the same police who kept a stern watch on me for no greater crime than my Russian nationality. Before my marriage, I had to report twice daily and had a good idea of their political allegiance. But everybody thought it reassuring: 'law and order were best main-tained this way.' Only the unpolitical Frau Liebknecht shared my bewilderment. She suffered too much from the prevailing 'order' to be contented with its old keepers.

'But what could one expect of Germans?' she commented. Neither of us was exactly Germanophile.

I could not consult Leviné. He was far away. What news of him I did get was scrappy and very disturbing. He was working side by side with the Spartacus League and had very soon attracted the sympathy and affection of the workers, who endowed him with the honourable title of 'our Leviné' – a rare distinction. But he also incurred the hatred and fury of the counter-revolutionaries, who added his name to their black list next to Karl Liebknecht [2] and Rosa Luxemburg.[3] Like them he became a hunted person.

I heard of skirmishes at various places. Leviné was in danger, he might get wounded or even killed. I could not stand aloof, nursing my grievances. Our marriage did not work but we had a child, we could at least be friends. I decided to see him.

To forestall any new attempts at reconciliation I thought it best to tell him that I had a boyfriend.

We met at the editorial office of the newly established *Rote Fahne*.[4] He was so excited that my heart sank, but I did not succumb. I told him quickly of my boyfriend.

'Someone I know?' he asked.

'No.'

He wanted to know who.

'Why?'

Because he wanted to avoid this man in future.

I gave him the name of a casual acquaintance – good enough for a dummy-lover.

Leviné believed me and gave me another taste of his dignity and tact. Not a reproach, not a false word or gesture. Neither did he go in for any penitence. He only told me how he missed me. His triumphs were not complete when he could not talk to me, share with me. Nothing could give his life fulfilment.

We were never closer to each other.

Rosa Luxemburg's head appeared behind a curtain which separated his office. She had been told of my presence and wanted to have a look at me. She scrutinised me unceremoniously for quite a while, gave me a charming smile and withdrew. Leviné was so delighted with the scene that he made a spontaneous move towards me but he remembered and stopped half way.

I played the game until the following day but I was not aware of my cruelty. Leviné seemed as happy as I and he must have known the truth all the time.

The subject was never brought up again but he was strangely

very jealous of the man. Why had I picked on this name? To make up for a feeling which he thought undignified he paid him much more attention than he deserved. I took it as a punishment for my frivolity when I came across an article in which the man referred to Leviné as his 'friend.'

The last phase of our marriage was the happiest of our life. Leviné returned from his Rhineland propaganda journey a changed man.

He belonged to the revolution, but he had not destroyed his old loyalties. He taught me new values and enriched my life too with the joy of self-denial for the sake of a great cause.

His first propaganda tour through the Ruhr and Rhineland was crowned with almost legendary success. These important industrial districts were completely dominated by Christian and extreme-right Social-Democratic leaders who between them carried out fierce propaganda against 'destructive, brutal Bolshevism.'

The workers, essentially patriotic and devoted monarchists, were hardly touched by the revolution. The few scattered Spartacus Groups were helpless against the well-organised Communist baiting. They struggled in vain to gain a foothold among the hostile workers, and asked Berlin for help. Leviné was delegated to try his hand.

His meetings, with the subject, 'What are the aims of the Spartacists?' attracted large masses. But they did not come to get acquainted with Communist ideas. At best they were driven by curiosity, or a certain restlessness characteristic of the time of revolutionary upheavals. Above all, they wanted to settle accounts with 'dangerous spoilsports.' 'Peace and order' were described as the foremost revolutionary virtues. The Spartacists were thus denounced for 'upsetting the quiet course of the revolution and provoking reaction.'

Leviné was regularly received with catcalls and outbursts of abuse but he never failed to calm the storm. He told me jokingly that he often had to play the part of a lion-tamer.

His power lay perhaps in his compassion for the people he came to teach and in his understanding of their frailties. There was no contempt in the patience with which he accepted the hostile interruptions and no condescension in his warm smile. People often spoke of the peculiar, disarming quality of that smile. He made the audience feel that he was one of them and that they could trust him. At the end the workers would surround him by the hundred to express in poignant words their thanks and solidarity. The meetings always ended in large street demonstrations and often in the disarming of counter-revolutionary military units and other revolutionary acts.

Leviné's triumphs reached their climax in Essen. He appeared before an audience of 5,000 nearly all of whom had come to denounce the 'Bolshevik hirelings' and to shout him down. He recalled that it took him a good half-hour to calm them.

He won them over in one single appearance.

The meeting was followed by powerful demonstrations of solidarity with the hitherto hated Spartacists. The *Rote Fahne* of 7th December 1918 reported that, in spite of pouring rain, the entire audience rushed to the editorial office of the largest local newspaper *(Rheinisch Westfälische Zeitung)* in a spontaneous urge to 'settle accounts for its lies and deception.' They tore down the national flag and hoisted the Red Flag. They moved on with revolutionary songs to the railway station, the temporary soldiers' quarters, and persuaded them to support the people's cause. It ended in fraternisation.

I learned more of this extraordinary feat from a participant in the event, in London many years later. He was a member of a socialist students' group who went to disrupt the meeting.

We were imbued with the general belief that the Spartacists were a gang of irresponsible rowdies, Bolshevik mercenaries, or at best their stooges. We wanted socialism of a 'cultured European' blend and we loathed the criminal fools who were 'discrediting' the majestic flow of the revolution.

Leviné's appearance did not fit into the preconceived pattern but we were determined not to be put out by any emotional nonsense. Our group occupied the front seats and was leading the attack. We shouted abuse and pelted him with angry accusations.

He patiently waited for the first storm to subside, listening attentively to our incriminations and often nodding understandingly, like a friend in an intimate conversation. But perhaps it was his smile which conquered us, the warm, sad smile, void of haughtiness or sarcasm despite our ravings. Like all the rest, I soon caught myself hanging on his words. The compelling logic of his arguments and his natural authority did the rest. We forgot all our prejudices and were happy to follow him, to be on his side. But he did not try to 'work us up' or to abuse his influence. It was our reason he appealed to, our common sense, expressing our ultimate aspirations. He made us feel: of course, that is what I thought all the time. How simple!

Leviné said at his trial to the Public Prosecutor:

You will find in your circles a great number of people superior to me in erudition but at a workers' assembly I would triumph. And not because of my personal superiority but only because I would express what the masses themselves felt and desired.

My informant then confirmed in almost identical words Leviné's proud statement.

Leviné became a household name with the workers of the Rhineland. And if they later played an outstanding part in the struggle for socialism, it was not least the merit of Leviné, who was the first to arouse their class-consciousness.

Within a few weeks Leviné succeeded in taking his place amongst the foremost leaders, almost on a par with Karl Liebknecht and Rosa Luxemburg. Radek, who came to Germany as a political adviser, was stunned: the rise was too meteoric and he ascribed it to the skilful manoeuvring of an ambitious careerist. Anxious to obtain additional first-hand information, Leviné tried in vain to see the great man. He was rather curtly refused an interview.

Radek was particularly vexed when Leviné returned from his tour with a mandate to the forthcoming All-German Soviet Congress to which none of the great established leaders were delegated. He thought it inadmissible for a more-or-less stranger to represent the Party on such an important occasion. Better acquainted with the procedure of Party life, Radek's suspicion seems to me incomprehensible.

In accepting the mandate Leviné, of course, acted in complete accord with the Central Committee; even a man of less tact could hardly fail to put the matter to the discretion of the established Party leadership.

Radek later told me how much he regretted his misjudgement: it deprived him of meeting 'one of the greatest revolutionary figures of our time.' The incident is symptomatic of the assessment of Leviné's growth, if not of Radek's flippancy.

Leviné achieved the same popularity with the Berlin workers. His meetings were packed and the Central Committee was overwhelmed with requests for his appearance.

He spoke daily and his chief aim was to acquaint the German workers with the soviet system. After the revolution, the soviets or councils became in Germany a widespread movement; workers, soldiers, peasants spontaneously took to this form of organisation – too spontaneously. Without real knowledge of their structure, they were satisfied with soviets set up by shrewd officials, chiefly members of trade unions and the old socialist parties. The soviets were crowded with people who had nothing to do with the revolution. Universal trustfulness is a common feature of a young revolution, and Germany was no exception.

It was sufficient to declare oneself 'in favour of the principles of the soviet system' to be regarded as a worthy representative of the people. In many places soviets were simply set up by agreement of party officials without any consultation with its members. Purging the soviets of alien elements was a vital task of the revolution. They had to be built anew and from below.

Leviné compared the soviets with a pyramid resting on a multitude of factory cells. In large factories, however, where the workers cannot know each other sufficiently, he explicitly warned against electing councils at general meetings: the mandates could easily fall into the hands of impressive speakers, and authoritative personalities. He advised that initially works or factory councils (*Betriebsräte*) should be elected on the shop floor where the workers are able to 'know their men.' They should be judged by their deeds and not by words and be *recalled* if they failed to defend adequately the workers' interests.

Indeed, the right to recall an unworthy representative without any red tape, by a simple vote, was one of the greatest advantages of the soviet system. The electorate was spared the long years of waiting – four as a rule – to remove an inadequate parliamentary deputy. Under the existing German conditions this was a very important issue.

Disillusioned by the failure of the powerful Social-Democratic Party, which they had helped to build with so much effort and devotion, the revolutionary workers were tormented with suspicion: where was the guarantee that a new organisation would not let them down again?

Leviné was aware of that mood and untiringly emphasised the importance of the unconditional recall at any time of any delegate found wanting:

'This is the essential principle which distinguishes us from the Social Democrats... this must be the basis of our propaganda.'

To my knowledge, none of the other leaders dealt with this problem – in speech or in writing.

Works councils, within the grasp and control of the workers, were designed to restore lost faith and were at the same time an incentive to greater activity.

Leviné worked out his device in minute detail.

Should outsiders in a factory be elected to its councils? Admitted to its rallies? Allowed the right to vote? He naturally advised the workers to seek guidance, in difficult situations, from the foremost leaders – Karl Liebknecht and Rosa Luxemburg – but at the same time, when a council was dominated by Social Democrats, not to be afraid of also allowing men like Ebert to state their case.

To guarantee the assertion of the system and as a means of correctly assessing our own strength, he characteristically advocated re-election of soviets, even at the risk of losing Communist positions to Christians and Social-Democrats.

He dealt with a great variety of problems which are too specific to interest a contemporary reader. They are summarised in his report on 'the All-German Soviet Congress' (Appendix I). But he explicitly warned against actions involving hostilities among the workers themselves. He concluded:

> The factory councils are the backbone for launching our revolutionary counter-attacks.... The struggle ahead can only be waged in compliance with the will of the masses amalgamated in a strong organisation.

It is worth noticing how thoroughly Leviné outgrew his youthful conceptions of the 'heroic leader'. At a time when his own achievments could easily lead him to over-value the individual he alotted him a very modest place in the events; the driving forces were the masses and organisations.

The soviets were not the only ones to suffer from the lack of a strong base in the factory. The Party was paralysed by the same deficiency.

It adopted the structure of the Social-Democratic Party with the members organised on regional principles in so-called street units. The workers were dispersed, they only met at their traditional monthly gatherings (*Fahlabende*). Not much revolutionary effort was demanded of them and it thus fitted in well with the prevailing quiet conditions.

Leviné was the first to fight for transformation of the Party on the basis of building factory cells. He argued that the Party must build its strongholds where the workers are 'welded' into compact units, where they meet daily, know each other and the part each plays in the current struggle.

It was particularly to his credit that he raised at the outset of the revolution the central problem which was to remain with the Party throughout its whole existence.

It is true that the Constitutional Congress accepted the idea. But it is one thing to acknowledge a principle and another to throw off old shibboleths. The problem came up in every revolutionary crisis and was shelved again when things quietened down.

As late as 1924, the 'Middle Group,' politically a most experienced section of the Party, submitted the followingresolution:

> With the industrial proletariat as the leading force in the struggle for power, the Communist Party must possess its foremost basis in the factory, the place where the workers are conglomerated and where the fight has its origins. The fundamental transformation of the Party on the principle of factory cells as the decisive source of its activity is the central task of the Party.

In her time, Ruth Fisher spoke very loudly of the importance of factory cells but her heart was not in it. In her book on German Communism, some years later, she denounced the system as a malicious device of the Russians:

> The very party structure was melted down.... The parties... were atomised into helpless cells, in most cases violently by craftsmen from Moscow.... A new form of organisation, which was to get its name of 'Quisling Groups' or 'fifth column' only later, had been formed in the middle of the twenties. (P. 640).

In its last phase (1928-1933) the Party more or less succeeded in creating a net of factory cells but all was lost in the confusion of its destructive pre-Hitler policy.

Leviné concentrated all his activity on the factories. He hurried from place to place and often organised meetings even during working breaks. Was he ever ill?

To keep alive a happy marriage amidst the sound and fury of an acute revolution demands indeed the skill of a tight-rope walker and at times my 'transformation' had to stand up to other hard tests.

I fell ill with influenza and at a very inconvenient time. I was still living with Lucie Mannheim, who was facing her first première as leading lady on the Berlin stage, and she could not be exposed to the risk of infection. Leviné was preoccupied with no less an emergency: the All-German Soviet Congress was to start in a few days, on the

16th December, 1918. He just found time to take me to hospital by ambulance.

The examining doctor shook her head apprehensively when she learned that I had had three previous attacks in a short time. People were dying like flies from a raging influenza epidemic. I was dazed and not quite conscious.

Leviné could not visit me with the Congress on his hands; occasional telephone messages were our only contact, but he arranged for a private nurse.

She kept on taking my temperature, which seemed a bad sign. I thought of death in blissful resignation. To die now, on the summit of happiness. What a beautiful end!

Leviné could not visit me but in his own indefinable way he made me feel that he was always at my side. A new world was in sight and I was privileged to belong to a direct participant in its creation. Our child would be well looked after in a world of brotherhood and love.

During these months, Leviné often described to me life in a socialist society. There was not a shadow of a doubt in his mind that it was round the corner.

'It is true, we are yet a small minority but we must judge conditions by their tendencies and we are sweeping upwards.'

I was slightly disappointed when I safely returned to life.... Perhaps love and revolution are incompatible after all.

During a short recess, Leviné got hold of a car and came to see me. He had it all well calculated, the car was waiting to take him back in time for the next session.

'I must go' – he kept on saying, but I held him back. It was all a matter of minutes, his visit hardly lasted half an hour, but it had serious consequences. He missed his only opportunity to appear on the forum.

It was particularly precarious as the Spartacists as a group failed to play their proper part at the Congress.

Leviné attributed the failure to the alliance of the Spartacists with the Independent Socialist Party (U.S.P.).[5]

After his experience at the Congress he became a fiery advocate of an independent organisation, the actual creation of the Communist Party.

When, in April 1917, the U.S.P. broke away from the Social Democrats, the Spartacists, after long debates, decided to join the new

Party. Among other advantages it provided a certain shield from the violent persecution of their members and they explicitly reserved for themselves the right of criticism and independent action.

It was not a happy decision and the controversy and doubts never really receded.

Ernst Meyer, one of the leaders of the Spartacus League, told me of a conversation at the Constitutional Congress of the Communist Party with the formidable Leo Jogiches.

Originally in favour of joining the U.S.P., he was later inclined to change his views. Jogiches, who advocated the merger, told him: 'On the contrary, you were quite right.'

The problem was too complex for a straightforward solution. Even when he was writing in 1926-1929 *The History of the Spartacus League*[6] with all the advantages of hindsight, Ernst Meyer still hesitated to pass unequivocal judgement.

One of the conclusions which could be drawn with some certainty was that the Spartacists missed the right moment for consolidating themselves as a Party.

The ferment among the S.P.D. was soaring and many a worker would have undoubtedly joined the Spartacists instead of the U.S.P. had they come *first*.

But the hesitation was understandable. It was to be the first split in the history of the formidable Social-Democratic Party.[7] Even the moderate, essentially pacifist U.S.P. with its considerable influence beyond socialist circles, was for a long time afraid to take the final step. The workers would hardly favour a *second* new party. And the Germans were, as was known, particularly suspicious of small groups.

The Spartacists decided to content themselves with being the 'fermenting yeast' within the U.S.P.

I don't know whether Leviné participated in the debates. At that time, he never discussed Party matters with me and I heard of the debates much later from Ernst Meyer. I only learned of the necessity of a separate organisation from Leviné's passionate speeches: the acute revolutionary situation did not tolerate the ties which a common organisation inevitably imposed.

Fresh from the Congress, Leviné gave a staggering account of the sad timidity and irresolution of the U.S.P. and its absolute treachery in dealings with its Spartacist associates.

The U.S.P. was in no way united in its aspirations. It included on its right the leading economic theorist Hilferding and the pacifist

Haase,[8] while Däumig, on the left, was an ardent champion of the soviet system. He was even in favour of the dictatorship of the proletariat, albeit of a dictatorship of a 'cultured European' blend, based on 'will and spiritual power'[9] rather than on machine-guns.

Däumig chastised the Congress for its 'philistinism and sobriety unprecedented in the history of revolutionary assemblies.'

Richard Müller, ostensibly another strong protagonist of the soviet system, asserted that he was perfectly aware that the soviets were the only concrete gain of the revolution: 'The moment they disappear, nothing will be left. The entire political and economic structure remains as it is.'

Yet he passionately repudiated the very idea that the soviets should ever attempt to seize power. On the contrary, they were only a product of the stormy revolutionary days and must be liquidated as swiftly as possible.

In fact 'the soviets of the workers' and soldiers' deputies represented the entire political power of the country.' In case of counter-revolutionary plots 'the Executive of the Soviets was given the right to also exercise executive powers.'

It depended on the Congress alone what use it would make of its powerful position. Yet the predominant mood of the left section of the U.S.P. was fearful of the right wing, who in its turn had not lived down its allegiance to the old Mother-Party and was striving for reconciliation. And the centre was helplessly swaying in either direction. Some propositions of the Spartacists were rejected for fear of upsetting the Congress; others for provoking the Entente. This, it was said, would never tolerate a Soviet Germany: the Russian soviets had only been saved by their formidable natural ally – winter.

Resolutions which had been unanimously accepted were dropped, pushed aside or thrown into waste-paper baskets, and promises were not honoured. Leviné even accused the U.S.P. partners of tampering with the speakers' lists to avoid political embarrassment.

As a result, the Spartacus Group was prevented from submitting the resolutions on its own[10] and thereby effectively illuminating their intentions and the fundamental difference between the two partners. It would not have changed the course of the Congress. Däumig aptly defined it as 'a Suicide Club,' but it could at least have spared the Spartacists the very humiliating question 'Where was the Spartacus Group?'

Leviné concluded:

The U.S.P. hung round our necks like a millstone.... We must put an end to this unnatural alliance, this marriage of fishes and young lions. We cannot possibly act the part of the whip that drives the independents to the 'left.' How can there be an alliance between a whip and a donkey which digs in its heels and declares: 'You can go on whipping, but I won't budge.' If we continue to ally ourselves with the U.S.P. we shall be the donkeys!

Leviné's report is remarkable for the wide range of its subject matter. He dealt not only with specific Party problems, like reorganisation of the Party on the principle of factory cells, or re-election of the soviets, but also with social and economic problems of the post-revolutionary period: for instance, workers' control and what he called 'factory patriotism.'

The Russian publishers of the report expressed their astonishment that he foresaw difficulties which for a long time were to remain on the agenda in Soviet Russia.

Above all, he tried to arouse the self-confidence and initiative of the masses, and to imbue them with the feeling that they alone were the masters of their destiny. He was teaching them to keep a sharp eye on their leaders: on their deeds not on their words. And he warned that the socialist leaders Ebert[11] and Scheidemann[12] would be no less ready to shoot at fathers and mothers than was Kaiser Wilhelm himself.[13]

Leviné was reporting to a selective audience of the Berlin factory councils. He was received in respectful silence and I was still inclined to regard the workers as an inarticulate mass, a tool in the hands of clever leaders.

I was soon to change my view.

On the agenda of the forthcoming Party Congress stood the Spartacists' attitude to the first post-war parliamentary elections-participation or boycott?

The old cadres of the League strongly advocated participation. It had the advantage of bringing the Spartacists closer to the broader masses and acquainting them with Communist ideas. Nor could a set-back, followed by a period of illegality, even if only temporary, be altogether ruled out. A seat in the Parliament would then be the only means of conducting Communist propaganda openly. It could also be foreseen that the workers at large would not understand the idea of a boycott and would not be persuaded to stay aloof; they would only be forced to vote for other parties.

The Spartacus League was, however, swamped with people who rejected the old Parliament once and for all. They were striving for a Soviet State and thought it inadvisable to waste time and energy on hateful institutions when they should concentrate on fighting the last battle for power. It was a rather hopeless undertaking to persuade inexperienced people to campaign for a body which you aim to abolish. It seemed a contradiction in terms.

It was by no means a clear-cut problem. During the 1905 revolution the Bolsheviks decided to boycott the Duma elections and for similar reasons. The opposition was so strong that it swayed even leaders like Karl Liebknecht. He was quoted as saying:

'I sometimes go to bed decided on boycott and wake up with the conviction that we must participate in the electoral campaign.'[14]

Following both the Party's instructions and his own views, Leviné had advocated participation. He was greeted with a veritable storm of indignation:

'What happened to him? He is not the same man. If Leviné could be dazzled by the parliamentarian rigmarole, whom can we trust?' cried the critics.

Belonging to the same category of fiery novices, I must confess that I also played a part in the obstructions. Everything appears so simple to the ignorant mind.

Leviné suddenly found himself completely isolated, alone against 'the will of the people.' He was carried away, and greatly surprised the Party Congress by voting against participation. It was, however, a momentary lapse: a mistake he very soon rectified.[15]

Leviné was the first to coin the term 'adolescent disorder,' a disease of which the boycott-theory was a typical variety. Barely a month after the Congress, he arrived at the conclusion that the Party was suffering from what Lenin was later to define as an 'infantile disorder' and that it could not fulfil its task unless the deficiency was successfully overcome. '*Jugendkrankheiten*' – adolescent diseases – are also referred to in his thesis, a fragment of which I was able to preserve.

The counter-revolutionary forces very soon realised that they had not much to fear from the socialistic government and came out into the open.

Their first target was the soviets which they assailed with almost the same vehemence, slander and abuse that they generally reserved for Bolshevism itself. In many places, the 'ideological' struggle was supplemented by dissolution of the local soviets, allegedly in compliance with the demands of the almighty Entente.

But they did not stop at that. Under cover of 'border-defences' they built up considerable military forces with special divisions trained and equipped with appropriate weapons for street fighting. These consisted of picked men with a great number of active officers, attracted by higher pay and better rations. The less responsive elements were reassured that they were needed for fighting thieves and marauders.

These counter-revolutionary sallies were increasing in numbers and arrogance. On the 6th December, a military unit staged a plot in Berlin itself. They arrested the Executive of the Soviets and offered Ebert the post of President of the Republic. Ebert was a cautious man and the plot came to nothing. Fourteen people lost their lives and thirty were wounded in the process but the initiators of the affair went unscathed.

The counter-revolutionary forces were not alone in their endeavour. They had their ally in the government itself. Ebert, the leader of the Social-Democratic Party, declared from the start that he 'hated social revolution like sin' and he was fighting tooth and nail against everything which bore its mark. The weakness of the Congress was another spur to his labours.

The so-called People's Naval Division with its headquarters in Berlin at the Royal Stables was a creation of the revolution and therefore a thorn in his flesh. Under Ebert's personal initiative the government decided to get rid of the troublesome elements.

These were ordered out in an appallingly provocative manner with hardly an hour to consider the ultimatum. Seven sailors lost their lives.[16]

The incident took place three days after the closure of the Congress. It was Christmas Eve and the entire bourgeois Press, including the organ of the Social Democrats, attacked the 'criminal Communists,' who did not shrink from causing bloodshed on 'such a day.' Bloodshed was once for all identified with Communism – no matter who caused it and whose blood flowed. A sad example of the manipulation of public opinion.

The U.S.P. half of the government resigned in protest. The balance of power seemed to move further to the right, but this was only on the surface.

The workers did not pull their full weight in the political confrontations but the revolution was by no means over. As Rosa

Luxemburg predicted, it was to come into full swing with the development of the unavoidable economic struggle.

Social conflicts were deepening. Hunger, unemployment, housing and other elementary shortages imperatively demanded a solution. The prevailing mood of the German workers was in no way anti-revolutionary. One could hardly find a significant section of workers which would not favour socialisation of industry and a workers' government.

They were in no mood to surrender their revolutionary positions; on the contrary a large section was even prepared to fight in the coming struggle for further extensions of their rights. They hated the bourgeoisie for dragging them into the war and particularly the war profiteers, the spivs, who had made their fortunes out of the millions of corpses and cripples. But they were made to believe that power, personified by the six Socialist People's Representatives, was in their hands and that it was only a question of using it in the best way. Socialism seemed assured.

There is no doubt that a great number of socialist leaders, including the Independents, harboured the same illusions. Emil Barth, a venerated member of the U.S.P., assured the Congress that 'the question of hired labour will completely disappear in the next few months.'

And Hilferding, the learned socialist theoretician, declared – though not a hair of the heads of the capitalists had yet been harmed – that industry must be regarded and treated as *public property*:

'The factories don't belong to you [individual workers] and even *less* to the capitalists.'

The workers then were prepared to wait but they could not be cheated for too long. Socialisation stood firmly on the agenda and the last word had not yet been spoken.

Only eight days separated the Soviet Congress, held on 16th–21st December, from the Assembly which constitituted the German Communist Party, which was to become the strongest and most influential party on the Continent after the Bolsheviks.

Leviné spent his whole time at conferences and public meetings. I accompanied him as often as I was allowed to, and by now could even be of some help. He sent me to meetings to study the mood of the people and even to find out for him whether the Party, desperately short of leaders, could avail itself of the services of some leftist non-Communist speakers. He knew he could rely on my memory for an accurate report, even if not on my feeble political experience. But he explicitly asked me not to take part in the customary debates which followed major speeches or, for that matter, to make any public appearances.

I was able to bring back records of the indomitable faith of the people in a socialist dawn, but even I could see how unrealistic and downright childish the orators were, who confused their personal emotions with the revolutionary reality.

A memorable occasion was the meeting addressed by a well-known semi-anarchist, Franz Pfemfert, an excellent speaker and a dedicated revolutionary.

He drew a rosy picture of the prospects for the German revolution: it was, he said, difficult to defeat the Russian capitalists, those powerful, brilliant personalities, but the meek, dull German simpletons didn't come up to much as antagonists.

It was quite contrary to the Communist view of the Western capitalists as shrewd, well-organised and cunning enough to corrupt the Social-Democratic parties, and to make them act in their interests. I thought it my duty to correct Pfemfert's views. In revolutionary times, everybody becomes very articulate and is encouraged to speak up. But I obeyed Leviné's orders.

I did not question Leviné's motives but he himself once volunteered an explanation: it would be inappropriate to establish any kind of 'family concern.'

This was not a rational, political approach and could not be the full truth. He must still have suffered from old prejudices. He once pointed Rosa Luxemburg out to me in the street: 'There goes a woman of quite extraordinary brain. She *frightens me.*'

He valued my judgement but preferred to treat me as a precocious child. And he maintained this attitude to the end.

It was late at night when he arrived home for the last time. I had returned earlier and had picked up on my way an announcement of the government which succeeded the Communists, which I found particularly outrageous. I jumped out of bed, half asleep, to show it to Leviné. But he was slow to read the document, joking first about 'sleepy Oslik, so obsessed with politics – just think!'

He was not given the time to adapt himself to my conversion which was none the less serious. My revulsion against society was growing the closer I studied it. I despised my former friends, those people who were so soft spoken, whom I expected to be the engineers of a new, better world 'when the time came.' Now the country was in disarray, exhausted, starving, and they were only trembling for their own snug positions.

We once ran into Jaspers, a prominent figure among the Heidelberg professors.

'Leviné, how fortunate!' he exclaimed, 'I hear so much of the Spartacists, but with Leviné on their side they cannot be just criminals and rowdies, I thought. Now, what are you?'

We went into a nearby café, and Leviné started explaining. Jaspers listened in silence. He seemed very impressed, almost carried away. Not a word of objection escaped his lips. In the end he sighed:

'Oh well, you are a bunch of hopeless idealists!'

He had rejected Communism for its 'atrocities', now for its idealism. All he really wanted was to be left alone.

Professor Emil Lederer, a reputable economist with distinct left-wing inclinations, was, of course, in favour of change.

He was a member of the U.S.P. but was persuaded, he told me privately, to keep this secret, for practical reasons – apparently so as to be more acceptable to Ebert's party. He was appointed to the commission which was to decide which industries were ripe for socialisation. But he was in no hurry, and was quite put out by the impatience of the Communists. A friend of Frau Liebknecht, he sent her a long letter, or rather a treatise, begging her to use her influence to restrain her husband from his 'dangerous policy.' 'We must wait' was the tenor of the message.

'How naïve! He expects me to convert my husband to moderation with amicable table-talk or to change his policy as a concession to his little wife,' remarked witty Frau Liebknecht.

I also knew Hugo Haase, the Chairman of the U.S.P. and one of the six members of the provisional socialist government.

In 1915 I had not the papers, birth certificate, etc. required for a marriage licence. Frau Liebknecht advised me to approach Haase. Her own husband would not like to ask favours of the authorities:

'Haase is on better terms with the people concerned and he is a wonderful man. I will introduce you.'

'It is a dangerous undertaking,' Haase joked. 'You will hold me responsible if anything goes wrong with your marriage. Do you really love the man?'

He got me the licence and remained my fatherly friend and adviser to the end of his life.

If there ever existed a man with a heart of gold, it was Haase. And it was only matched by his purity of mind and modesty.

Regardless of Leviné's ferocious attacks, he recognised me on the balcony of the Congress Hall and waved his greetings. I was quite a distance from his ministerial seat and he did not have to notice me at all.

But it takes more than kindness and humanity to make a revolution. The man who devoted all his life to the socialist cause did not possess the vision and determination for the final leap. His indecision and wavering caused the revolution more harm and *bloodshed* than the calculated acts of its out-and-out adversaries. He was assassinated in the summer of 1919, soon after Leviné's death, in another upsurge of counter-revolutionary activity.

Of all the people on whom I set my hopes to transform the world only G. Lukacz went over to the Communists.

With his somewhat strange Russian wife – as far as I remember she was an artist – he lived an unconventional life outside the so-called academic social circles. I hardly knew him but I always remembered one of his remarks.

Leviné had taken me to a session of an academic discussion club.

One of the professorial ladies said, 'Isn't there a deep inner bond between the factory owner and the worker?'

'Yes, quite decidedly,' Lukacz replied: 'The same as that between the spider and the fly in its web.'

It was Communism in its most expressive terms and perhaps the only sentence which I understood. Haase might have given the same reply but he was too bound up in the old traditions to free the fly. Lukacz had the advantage of having broken with the past long before.

The Congress which laid the foundation of the Communist Party took place from 29th to 31st December, 1918. Like many other ardent Communists, I knew very little of its programme and felt no compulsion to study its procedures. It is surprising how little one wants to know when one hardly knows anything. And at that time the significance of Leviné's amendments were entirely lost on me. His entire policy was distinguished by his struggle for the concrete, seemingly trivial details, by the 'hair-splitting' of which Lenin was often accused. And Lenin said that one of the greatest sins against the revolution was precisely the substitution of the abstract for the concrete. The importance of such details cannot be overestimated and neither can the wisdom such an attitude.

Here are some extracts from Leviné's speeches at the Constitutional Congress of the German Communist Party.

In the name of some comrades with whom we held conference I should like to submit some suggestions for completing and amending the programme. I wish to state in advance that as a whole we accept the programme and are in full agreement with Comrade Luxemburg. Our suggestions aim at providing the agitation with a clearer definition of some items of the programme, with concrete formulations of our aims instead of catch-phrases. We should not say for instance in the second part of item 7 (III b7) 'incisive social legislation' but explain what this incisive social legislation should actually represent. We would also suggest as to item 8 (III b8) that we do not limit ourselves to 'demanding the immediate radical transference of housing, health services, etc. in accordance with the spiritual and proletarian revolution.' We must clarify the meaning of the 'spiritual and proletarian revolution.'

We are accustomed to leave it to the bourgeoisie to deal with the housing problem, which usually consists of constructing with communal help a few additional buildings. We of course as Communists stand for rationing all houses. We also think it essential to state how we, the Communists, intend to transform the educational system. None of this requires much elaboration. For each item only two or three additional lines would be needed.

At the same time, at 1.7, we wish to exploit the experience of the revolution and not restrict the revolutionary tribunal to sentencing a few individuals who are responsible for the war. Nor do we think it advisable to disclose immediately the names of the accused, for the decision must first be left to the revolutionary tribunal, which will also be able to widen its powers and not restrict itself to the four men. It is also designed for trying counter-revolutionaries.

Regarding Comrade Luxemburg's exposition, which demands the building of our organisation from below, it is essential to widen it by having, in addition to the factory councils, councils of unemployed. We must take into account that millions of our fighting comrades will be the unemployed and they must be given the opportunity of building the socialist state.

> To avoid any confusion, we must put in point six instead of 'all organisations and political administrations' 'all political organisations and administrations,' otherwise the word political would apply only to administrations.

> We must also point out that all Red Guards must consist only of revolutionary-conscious workers.

> We have submitted all these proposals to the commission, but we repeat them for the sake of informing all the comrades.

This last proposal was a shrewd way of preventing the commission from eventually dropping the amendments.

Leviné also explained his efforts to avoid abstractions over the agrarian question:

> I would definitely advise the creation of a special Agrarian Commission to supply data as soon as possible and settle problems expertly. One of our proposals should therefore make sure that the Organisation Commission engages specialists or appoints a special commission. This question is of the greatest significance to the local administrations because the workers' and soldiers' Soviets must know what principles to follow in their work.

Remarkable is his early fight against any bureaucratic liberties:

> Comrades, I wish to point out that I do not think it proper for the Chairman to alter the order of speakers without their consent. Should the listed speaker not wish to speak or not be present, then he should forgo his turn or take it later on. But it is inadmissible to alter the order without the consent of the speakers.

The Congress bore all the characteristics which during its entire existence were destined to undermine the Communist Party: a light-hearted attitude towards parliamentary activity and work in the existing trade unions.

The boycott of the forthcoming elections was a foregone conclusion and received an overwhelming majority. The more fatal resolution to abandon the 'treacherous reformist trade unions' was averted by the skin of its teeth by some political tricks: tampering with the procedure, Ernst Meyer told me some years later.

Leviné's fiery speech in favour of the boycott had no small influence on this wrong decision.

His attitude towards the trade union question was rather ambiguous. Having adopted the boycott theory, the second mistake was a logical conclusion. Work with trade unions implied the need for a prolonged struggle to win over the workers for the revolution. This task seemed within reach if not already achieved. Factory councils, more flexible and less dominated by the old bureaucracy, seemed to guarantee better possibilities of penetrating and influencing the masses.

Once you put street-battles for power on your agenda there seems no need for tedious routine work for essentially reformist gains.

However, all the debates and resolutions were overridden by new stormy events.

On the 3rd January 1919, only a few days after its constituent congress, the Central Committee of the newly built Communist Party received an alarming telegram. The workers of Upper Silesia had won a majority in the local Soviet and other top institutions and intended to proclaim a Soviet Republic. They asked for experienced leaders to be sent for their guidance.

Such situations are rother common in young revolutions. Broad masses suddenly awaken to political life. They become aware that things are not quite what they ought to be and that they can be changed. They are carried away by a new experience and ready to storm heavens. And they naively believe that *everybody* has undergone the same transformation – a rare case of human vanity being prepared to forgo the distinction of being ahead of the others.

This fervour – valuable as it is – re-presents a great danger. Lacking the necessary experience, the workers rarely know what they are up against or what obstacles face them. In Upper Silesia the precipitate action could only lead to bloodshed and defeat. It had to be prevented.

To restrain revolutionary energy *without causing disappointment and apathy* is a formidable task, far more difficult than that of evoking ardour in times of upheaval. It demanded someone of great authority and personal tact. The choice fell on Leviné.

I was facing an operation and was only waiting for admittance to an overcrowded post-war hospital. When the time drew near, Leviné tried to centre his activity around Berlin and even planned a last festive evening.

When the day came, he happened to be in town and in the

afternoon I went to his office to fetch him. I found him very upset and supposed that he had to hold, another meeting and we should have to forgo our 'parting evening.'

'It does not matter. I will go with you,' I said, trying to reassure him.

He often spoke on the same subject, and to avoid 'boring' me he would find for me alone new expressions and images.

I was naturally thrilled with his mastery of words and very proud of this secret homage.

'It is much worse. I have to leave Berlin and I don't know for how long. But I refuse to go. I will not leave you now. They will understand,' he stammered in desperation.

We took operations very seriously in those days. And it was a matter not only of depriving me of his presence but of going in fear of his life.

His foolish stammering made me forget my own fears, I was able to listen and understand.

Karl Liebknecht and Rosa Luxemburg were indispensible and no one but he was considered equal to the task.

He had to go but he knew how to bring colour and gladness into the hard duty.

We rushed to the station. He climbed through the window into a crowded train. We hardly had time to say good-bye but we were excited and happy.

III

Our fears and 'sacrifices' proved quite unwarranted. The hospital had second thoughts about an operation and decided to keep me in for observation and intensive physiotherapy instead. But I had no means of communicating the comforting news to Leviné: we were completely cut off.

Leviné had succeeded in averting a hopeless, bloody clash only to be confronted with a similar situation on his return.

In Berlin a storm was raging which went down in history as the 'Spartacus Week' (5th–12th January, 1919), culminating in a severe defeat of the revolutionary workers and the brutal murder of their leaders Karl Liebknecht and Rosa Luxemburg.

The fighting broke out in protest at the attempt to remove the head of the Police Department, Emil Eichhorn. A member of the Independent Socialist Party and a close friend of the late Bebel, he enjoyed great popularity among revolutionary workers of all shades for his personal integrity and genuine devotion to the working class. His position was regarded as a bulwark against counter-revolutionary conspiracy and was a thorn in the flesh of the reactionary forces.

The Communists and the Independents jointly called for a protest demonstration.

A considerable number of Social-Democratic workers were outraged by the decision of their government to remove a trusted, venerated old socialist and joined the movement.

The workers dominated the town. Spontaneously, as was the case in Essen, the workers occupied the building of the central organ of the Social-Democratic Party, the *Vorwaerts*. And with the same purpose: 'to seal its lying mouth' (*'um sein Lügenmaul zu stopfen'*). This time it was the mouth of the Social Democrats. Eichhorn remained at his post under the protection of armed workers who took up quarters in the building.

The position of the government was highly precarious. The workers were in full control and displayed a bold determination not to give in.

The government was saved by the Independents. They lacked the courage for a tough struggle. They could not perceive that their recent associates, the S.P.D. had gone over to the other side for good, and that conflicts could no longer be solved amicably. They advanced the slogan: 'Negotiation!'

The government readily seized upon the offered sheet-anchor. They played the game for as long as they needed to gather reliable military forces to quell the movement. The fate of the struggle with fighters demoralised by the bait of a 'fair, negotiated settlement' was sealed.

But during this short period the Communist Party developed feverish activity. The members were mobilised to a man and were working from dawn to dusk. The *Vorwaerts* appeared with the new name '*Red Vorwaerts*' *(Der Rote Vorwaerts)* under the editorship of Leviné.

The building served simultaneously as fortress, prison-camp and even as a hospital. Leviné was in 'joint' control of all departments. He was in addition, as everybody asserted, an inexhaustible source of energy and courage and a friend and brother to every fighter.

Only by a stroke of luck was he spared the fate of the seven delegates sent to discuss terms of surrender and some hundred of the rank and file massacred by the government troops.

Taking advantage of a lull in the fighting he went to the Central Committee to discuss the 'Negotiation' slogan.

On his way back, the *Vorwaerts* building again came under fire and he had to wait for another lull.

I was very surprised when he suddenly appeared in my hospital. During all that time he was only able to send me occasional telephone messages.

'I am only here for a minute. I must rush off again and try to return to my post.'

He did not succeed. It was the last siege before the building finally fell.

He had 'abandoned his comrades in time of trial' and was stricken with remorse. He was even contemplating giving himself up and had to be cautioned that his life belonged to the revolution.

It seems that such irrational outbreaks, sentimental and even histrionic to the 'strong man', are the hall-mark of the dedicated revolutionary. They enable the cool dogmatist to accept suffering and death. Lenin himself, the most sober materialist of them all, was not free of such feeling and had to be restrained by his friends from giving himself up after the defeat of the notorious 'July Days' in 1917.

Could the workers conquer?

'Spartacus Week' was not a bid for power and was not meant to be.

This fact is best corroborated by the pains the Party had taken to avert such a step in Upper Silesia only three days before. It was an essentially defensive movement against the encroachments of the counter-revolution. The Communists were themselves swept away by its ferocity.

The response of the workers right down to those of the S.P.D. was overwhelming, and the government was utterly helpless. There could be no doubt that in a fight on straight *democratic* lines there were no forces to prevent a 'German October.'

A united proletariat could also defeat an intervening army as was later proved by the famous *Kapp-Putsch*. But such unity did not exist.

The Communist leaders were very well aware of this dilemma. Radek, the expert adviser, advocated retreat. He was very proud of his political vision and told me later with delight that the 'historic letter' in which he formulated his views had been preserved.

The trouble is that once a movement has been unleashed it cannot be recalled any more than a tide can be swept back. The champions of non-violence, the pacifistic U.S.P., would certainly have grasped such an opportunity had it existed. All they were able to do was to paralyse the movement by ambiguous evasion, culminating in the demand for negotiations which again only played into the hands of the enemy.

Negotiations imply mutual concessions. The socialist government which had called in the Army could no longer dictate terms even if it had wished to. And the Army under Hindenburg's control could by its very nature make no concessions to its mortal enemy.

It was not a quarrel over a scrap of territory or a diplomatic clause but a matter of life and death. The Army was called in to restore order: armed workers, rebellious leaders, had no place in a world to suit the taste of the pacifiers. Not a vestige of power should be left in the hands of the enemy. More than that: the Army must eliminate

all potentialities for further revolts. Its first demand was for the surrender of arms and *leaders*. And the classification of 'leader' depends
entirely on the discretion of the victors. Their number may swell into
thousands: every articulate worker who might be able to kindle the
revolutionary spirit is thrown in for good measure. Hence the crammed
prisons and the piles of corpses which the conquerors inevitably leave
in their wake.

It is one of the greatest fallacies to imagine that bloodshed
can be avoided by meek submission. It depends entirely on the general
situation and has nothing to do with the attitude of the workers. The
entire history of civil wars bears out this simple truth. The massacres
were never confined to the battlefield. It was in the aftermath, in the
process of 'mopping up' the remnants of the insurrection that the Army
took its real toll. It was the more ruthless the less it was resisted and the
less it was inhibited by fear of its own losses – not vice versa.

The seven delegates who went to negotiate the surrender of
Vorwaerts were massacred on the spot. The white flag which they
carried was no protection. Hundreds of others were killed and wounded
in the same way.

The bloodshed was naturally attributed to the Spartacists, and
a wild hue and cry after their leaders swept the town. The newly
'liberated' *Vorwaerts* led the chase with a verse:
> 'Hundreds of proletarian corpses all in
> a row – proletarians!
> Karl, Rosa, Radek and company,
> None on show, none on show – proletarians!

The socialist paper was not mourning the hundreds of
proletarians: it was lamenting because the 'company', the most
coveted catch was still missing.

My hospital shared the general excitement. The nurses were
running to and fro like a disturbed flock of sheep, telling gruesome
stories about the bloodthirsty Spartacists. On the 15th January came
the news of the deaths of Karl Liebknecht and Rosa Luxemburg –
'shot trying to escape.'

The special edition went from hand to hand; everybody was
screaming and jumping for joy: everybody except the head sister and
the matron herself.

They were unable, they sadly apologised, to identify Liebknecht with the bloodthirsty brute he was made out to be. His wife had
been operated on in this hospital. They had seen him kneeling in agony

at her bedside, kissing her hands and overwhelming her with tokens of tenderness. The flowers he brought her! In their life they had seen many husbands in the same situation. None was more kind and considerate. And Liebknecht always had a friendly word and smile for the staff. They were very sorry for him and his poor wife.

The human spark seems inextinguishable, asserting itself even in that atmosphere.

To me Berlin now seemed empty, and my own husband was the next target.

It was dangerous for me to remain in the hospital. Somebody might identify me and any attempt at communication would lead directly to Leviné. I insisted on leaving and was discharged 'on my own responsibility.'

On my way home I ran into a demonstration. Workers, crippled war veterans, semi-proletarians, men and women, all those people to whom the two murdered leaders had devoted all their lives, were marching with national flags, jubilantly shouting slogans against the criminal Communists who were at last dead, dead!

The hospital seemed a heavenly refuge from a savage world as I looked in vain for a humane face in that jungle.

Leviné, one of the most hated men after Liebknecht and Rosa Luxemburg, and desperately hunted by the police, could not remain in Berlin, but had to transfer his activities to the provinces. His first assignment was to Brunswick to attend a joint conference of Communists and Independents. Fresh from the battle, he poured out all his bitterness against the treacherous part the Independents had played in the recent events, and won over a not inconsiderable number of the delegates to his side.

Under the assumed name of Berg, he worked for a while in the Ruhr, the seat of his initial triumphs.

The defeat of the Berlin workers and the loss of the two foremost leaders created a profound panic in the young Party. The task of the moment was to salvage the debris. Leviné calmed, encouraged, helped to examine the causes of the defeat and fearlessly laid bare the mistakes that had been committed.

But he was feeling the urge to learn more of the mechanics of the struggle and was yearning to go to Russia and see things for himself. The Constituent Congress of the Third International which was taking place in Moscow in February, 1919, provided a welcome opportunity.

He had the choice of attending the Congress as a delegate of the Party or as the correspondent of Rosta, the Russian News Agency, and he grasped at the latter chance.

Serving unreservedly both the German and the Russian revolution he was strangely anxious to preserve his independence. Already at that stage he seemed to be disturbed by the rigidity of the Party administration, which became particularly apparent in the treatment of the creation of a Third International.

It should be remembered that Rosa Luxemburg and her close friend and collaborator Leo Jogiches opposed the idea of the forming of the new International as premature and tried to avert it.

At the core of their views undoubtedly lay their own quarrels with Lenin and the fear of his domination. Now Jogiches, who was in almost full control of the battered German Communist central committee, tried to impose his views in a somewhat dictatorial manner. It is not uncommon for those who shout loudest about domination to be themselves guilty of the same sin. Hugo Eberlein, the German delegate, for instance, was sent off with binding veto orders.

Leviné could not be treated in the same way, and presented a problem. He did not belong to the old Party veterans and had not participated in the controversy with Lenin. Jogiches suspected him of being closer to Lenin's views and tried to win him over in an amicable conversation.

They met in an obscure café, the refuge of the underground party. Leviné expected a short interview and took me with him – we had so little time to ourselves. I was dumped into a corner where I could hear nothing and only allay my boredom by watching the battling men from afar.

For a battle it was. The brilliant, iron-faced Jogiches was hammering at Leviné for hours, pausing only now and then to assess the effects of his arguments. He was very careful, being particularly anxious not to reveal the real motives underlying his ideas, and therefore not very straightforward.

Leviné was annoyed by these diplomatic tricks and paid him back with almost complete silence and studied politeness which evidently confused and embarrassed his opponent.

The creation of a third International was inevitable. Rosa Luxemburg herself laid one of its foundation stones at the outset of the war, by declaring that the Second International was 'a stinking corpse.' The idea ran parallel to Lenin's: it was not his invention but common to all Left groups of the time.

The fear of Bolshevik domination over embryonic Communist

parties and groups was in no way unfounded. But who could challenge the authority of the engineers of a victorious revolution?

It would be futile to wait for the growth and maturity of the individual parties. For this too they could only profit by the great mentors. The balance of power could be shifted only by a victorious revolution in a key country in the West, not by numbers or strength of its sections. The German Party, the strongest of them all, was at that time a shambles. The establishment of immediate links with a powerful ally could only add to its prestige and serve as a new impetus to revolutionary activity.

Nothing could be gained from postponement and Leviné was in no may inclined to commit himself in advance and have his hands tied. But he felt no compulsion to speak of his views under the circumstances. Unlike Jogiches, he did not expect to convert his partner in a single, even if protracted, conversation. He was more realistic.

Besides, Jogiches was superior in his Party status. Leviné's idealism – which often bordered on naïve sentimentality – never obscured his ability to see people in all their frailties and he was very anxious not to upset their susceptibilities. For the same reason he meticulously observed the accepted conventions. He would address his friends as 'Herr Doktor' and only dropped the title when he himself graduated and became, so to speak, 'their equal.'

This might look trivial but I believe it is worth mentioning because it was part of his smooth relations with people.

Jogiches did not carry the day and might have spared himself the fruitless attempt. Leviné never reached Moscow.

Both he and Eberlein had to travel illegally; they were only provided with a few scraps of paper which, they knew, could not stand up to any scrutiny. The very German Eberlein, blonde, blue-eyed, handsome, highly intelligent, had his own way of dealing with the problem. He demonstrated it to us by pulling a face so harmless and dull as to put off the most experienced investigator.

Leviné's appearance was less fit for an illegal journey. He was duly picked out in Kovno, the border town, and was ordered to leave the train 'for further investigation.' This meant delivery to the German authorities and almost certain death. He had to find a way of escape, to return without an escort. He needed help but had no associates, no friends. His brain worked feverishly. Jews! They were the only people from whom to expect a certain solidarity. He knocked at the first likely door:

'Jews!' he said in Yiddish. 'You would not inform on a Jew.'

Those were magic words, touching on an old sacred tradition. Heaven only knows where he picked them up for they almost exhausted his whole Yiddish vocabulary.

He put himself unreservedly into the hands of complete strangers and they did not disappoint him. They hid him, fed him, they found the right people to bring him to safety.

His manner and personality asserted themselves once more. No questions were asked, money was accepted only to hire professional smugglers. They parted like brothers.

'Safety' was a gross exaggeration. He was a wanted man and had to live under an assumed name and in constant fear of being detected. Following his abortive journey he stayed for a fortnight in Berlin and I got a taste of the life of hunted people. We had to be always on the move, always in search of new accommodation. On one occasion we were startled by a suspicious-looking figure and had to move quickly.

The hotels were crowded and it was late at night when the owner of a shady lodging-house cautiously opened the door and asked: 'Will you drink wine?'

It was the last thing I wanted to do and I nearly said so.

'But of course,' Leviné quickly cut in.

'It was the price of admittance to the sanctuary,' he later explained.

But those were mere 'inconveniences' and only part of the evil.

At the same time, Leviné had to communicate secretly with other comrades who were in the same position, which multiplied the danger, and even to hold small party meetings. Russian revolutionaries had worked under such conditions for years on end though I could not imagine how.

Early in March, 1919 Leviné received instructions to go to Munich. Bavaria was increasingly turning into a hot-bed of revolution. The proclamation of the Hungarian Soviet Republic, the first Soviet Republic in Western Europe, was received with rapturous enthusiasm and as a challenge to follow the lead.

Bavaria was the last spot untouched by the counter-revolution. The workers were largely in possession of arms, and their new revolutionary organisations were still intact. In fact, Bavaria abounded in institutions with pretentious names: the Workers' Council, the Revolutionary Workers' Council – a self-elected body which played an important part in the November revolution, with two anarchists, the poet Mühksam and the author Landauer among its leaders, – and of course, the inevitable Central Council of Workers', Soldiers' and Peasants' Deputies.[1]

Besides the various councils, there existed a legitimate socialist government and a Diet, even if actually only played the role of sleeping partner.

Elected on the 12th January, 1919, with a considerable majority of the middle-class parties over the socialist – 100 seats as against 61 of the S.P.D. and only 3 of the Independents – the Diet was regarded by the working population, including many Social Democrats, as a mockery of the revolution, and the government thought it wisest to evade its convocation.

Power was oscillating between the government and the councils. Thanks to his enormous popularity, the Prime Minister, Kurt Eisner, had so far been able to maintain the balance between the two.[2]

On his way to the Diet on the 21st February, Eisner was assassinated by a reactionary officer Count Arco. The Diet broke up in confusion. Power had unmistakably shifted to the Central Council. The workers were in an uproar and the Communists naively called for a Soviet Republic.

The Central Council refused to answer the call but went another step to the left. It elected a new government comprised of Social Democrats, Independents and a few members of the Peasants' Alliance.

The real power was still in the hands of the Central Council even if it was unwilling to exercise it and the government had no freedom of movement as long as it existed. The situation could, in fact, be compared with the dual power of Kerensky's days in Russia, and a dénouement was inescapable.

Famous for its easy-going, highly inflammable population, with a good sprinkling of artists and cranks, Munich was more susceptible than any other large centre to experiments and revolutionary ideas.

The Communist Party – or rather a conglomeration of eager, enthusiastic people with very vague political ideas – played quite a prominent part in the unstable post-war life of the town.

The leader was Max Levien, of Russo-German extraction, a man of great intelligence and erudition and an excellent speaker.[3] He exercised an enormous appeal on the masses and could, with no great exaggeration, be defined as the revolutionary idol of Munich.

But he owed his popularity rather to his brilliance and wit than to clear-mindedness and revolutionary expediency. One of his little coups made the town roar with laughter.

He had written an article: 'How to make an omelette without breaking the eggs!' The word 'eggs' at that time had a fascinating effect on Munich housewives. The paper was sold out in a flash and the name of the author was for days on everybody's lips.

A few days after his arrival in Munich, Leviné wrote to me:

My friends here are mere children. The experience of the recent events simply by-passed them. Everything is in a state of utter confusion. Most of our party members wear amicably side by side on their lapels, pictures of Karl Liebknecht and Kurt Eisner. When you try to reason they say: 'We won't hear a word against our Eisner, he was a genuine revolutionary.'

...In the same way they treat the anarchists whom they often prefer to their own party members: 'Party allegiance means nothing as long as you are a good revolutionary,' they say.

Not only the rank and file, but the Communist Press itself spoke of Eisner as 'the best and noblest leader of the proletariat struggling for its emancipation' and as 'our comrade.'

The Party Press well reflected the general confusion. After the murder of Eisner, it declared:

The proletariat of Munich and other Bavarian towns *has seized political power*. What is our task today? To defend our political power, the dictatorship of the proletariat.... Today the workers of Munich will be armed....

In the same edition it could be read that power had yet to be seized:

The dictatorship of the proletariat must be proclaimed and established[4]

A few days later it wrote:

The Soviet Congress is meeting at a time when Bavaria is *on the eve or* [!] *in the midst of a social revolution...* at a time when the *proletariat has already* [!] *achieved power*.

It filled its pages with descriptions of the measures needed for securing this imaginary power and other *post-revolutionary* tasks.

Divorced from reality, it was light-heartedly sowing illusions among its own adherents and at the same time provoking the counter-revolution. In an early speech, Leviné summarised the situation:

It seems to me that in Munich far too much importance is placed on high politics and that an excessive preoccupation with the problems of a great future results in neglecting the essential tasks of the moment, vital for establishing that future. True, we defend on principle the Soviet system but we have yet to create the prerequisites to guarantee the establishment of that system. These prerequisites do not exist and while at the Bavarian Soviet Congress, Comrade Levien advocated and defended on principle the Soviet system, he will surely share my opinion that the proclamation of a Bavarian Soviet Republic under the prevailing political conditions of the country would be disastrous and would have disastrous consequences.

...We must speed up the building of revolutionary workers' organisations.... We must create workers' councils out of the factory committees and the vast army of the unemployed.

Leviné was untiringly preaching action in accordance with the existing strength, and circumspection.

The atmosphere was charged with whipped-up emotion. Leaflets appeared from uncertain sources calling for *immediate action*. The danger of another abortive insurrection was acute.

The first copy of the *Rote Fahne* under Leviné's editorship carried on its front page the following declaration:

The moment for a settlement with our adversaries will only arrive when the workers have created the weapons for the seizure of power – councils with a Communist majority behind them.... The Munich section of the German Communist Party most urgently warns the proletariat not to be provoked into precipitate actions before this task is accomplished. All that our enemies want is to trick the proletariat into a premature action.... Our enemies do not want this lull. They wish to make a clean sweep of the 'criminal elements.' *Attempts will be made, therefore, in the near future to strangle the workers' councils and to force the workers' to give battle.* The troops in and around Munich stand by. The provocateurs are at work.[5]

Leviné devoted all his energy to taming the unruly comrades and to building up the forces for the coming struggle.

His was the ungrateful role of what he himself called 'the elder brother': to caution, to teach, to destroy illusions, to reveal the enormous difficulties lying ahead. He had to start almost from scratch, turning first of all to the factories and councils.

Sebastian Haffner wrote:

> To be precise, there was only one Communist, Eugen Leviné, a young man of impulsive and wild energy who, unlike Karl Liebknecht and Rosa Luxemburg, probably possessed the qualities of a German Lenin or Trotsky.[6]

As everywhere else, the Bavarian Councils could hardly be called elected bodies representing the aspirations of the masses. People, however, learn rapidly in revolutionary times and they change their views. To assess the mood of the workers, Leviné immediately launched a campaign for re-election of the Councils. The Party itself was reorganised on the principle of factory cells. Where the cells were not strong enough to carry out their routine tasks, they were supplemented by Communists from other factories.

A down-to-earth attitude with daily reports and exchange of experiences gave a good picture of the prevailing mood and revolutionary potentials and enabled the Party to act with a minimum of mistakes and risks.

These were entirely new methods, a far cry from the former vague and cloudy propaganda stunts and in complete contrast to the approach of a hitherto venerated leader.

It should be regarded as another of Leviné's achievements that he succeeded also in mastering the so-called 'human element' and creating an atmosphere of mutual trust and comradeship.

His quiet, unobtrusive authority also made it possible for Levien to step aside without grudge or hurt, as naturally as he might have given pride of place to an elderly lady.

Still in the infancy of its consolidation, the Party was confronted overnight with a situation as bizarre and complicated as could ever befall a revolutionary leadership.

In an attempt to rid itself of the tutelage of the tiresome Central Council, the government decided to assemble on the 8th April the more reliable Diet.[7]

The majority of the workers regarded the convocation of the hated Parliament as a gross challenge, not to be taken lying down.

Augsburg reacted promptly. On the 3rd April, a meeting of Social-Democratic workers accepted a resolution to send a delegation to Munich, the seat of the Central Council, and to demand the immediate proclamation of a Bavarian Soviet Republic.

The delegation arrived on the 4th April and met no opposition. Niekich, the Chairman of the Central Council, accepted the idea and so did the Social-Democratic Party Executive including the War Minister Schneppenhorst, the Independents and the Anarchists.

The Munich garrison was consulted and declared its sympathy with the workers. Everything was ready for the coup.

The leaders of the three parties devoted the whole of that day, the 4th April, to detailed planning, and the distribution of functions and posts. Feelings ran high. The Communists, who took no part in the deliberations, were generously granted two seats in the government.

Leviné learned of the procedure only late in the evening. When I arrived at our hotel I found a note:

> If you know where to find your husband or Max Levien, get immediately into touch with me. It is extremely urgent.
> Doctor K.

After an extensive search we found Leviné in the hotel where he had returned in the meantime and was preparing for bed. We rushed to the War Ministry.

Leviné was greeted enthusiastically: 'At last!' The absence of the Communist leaders was disquieting but no one doubted that they would accept the event as a generous, gratuitous gift.

Leviné took the floor and said:

> I have just learned of your plans. We Communists harbour profound suspicion of a Soviet Republic initiated by the Social Democrat Minister Schneppenhorst and men like Dürr, who up to now have combated the Soviet system with all their power. At best we can interpret their attitude as the attempt of bankrupt leaders to ingratiate themselves with the masses by a seemingly revolutionary action or, worse, as a deliberate provocation. We know from our experience in North Germany that the Social Democrats often attempted to provoke premature actions which are the easiest to crush...
> ... A Soviet Republic cannot be proclaimed at a conference table, it is founded after a struggle by a victorious proletariat The proletariat of Munich has not yet entered the struggle for power. ... The present moment is extremely unfavourable for the proclamation of a Soviet Republic. The masses in North and Central Germany have been defeated and are only just

beginning to rally their forces again. And Bavaria is not a self-sufficient economic unit, able to maintain itself for a prolonged period.

After the first intoxication the Social Democrats will seize upon the first pretext to withdraw and thus deliberately betray the workers. The Independents will collaborate, then falter, begin to waver, to negotiate with the enemy and turn unwittingly into traitors. And we Communists will have to pay for your undertaking with the blood of our best.

He concluded in passionate defiance:

We don't sit at the same table with Schneppenhorst, the Nuremberg Noske[8], nor with Dürr[9], who demanded the use of gas-bombs against striking workers!

The speech produced the effect of a bombshell. Everybody was screaming wildly, gesticulating, shouting abuse. Schneppenhorst lost his head and forgetting all socialist traditions shouted: 'Punch the *Jew* on the jaw!'

Recalling the scene, the faces of the raving, incensed people, it seems to me that clear-sightedness and even the ability to express his views convincingly is not enough to make a leader. It also requires indomitable courage. How many good causes were frustrated because their protagonists were lacking in that quality?

Leviné's firm stand produced some effect. The proclamation of the Republic which was intended for the next day, Saturday the 5th, was postponed to the 7th April.

Leviné had made his declaration in the name of the Party. He had to act quickly and none of the leaders was present at the War Ministry. He was rather uneasy. What if Levien swallowed the bait as he might, judging by his previous attitude?

Levien was fast asleep when Leviné reached him at two o'clock in the morning; Leviné could heave a sigh of relief; Levien was in complete agreement: proclamation of the Soviet Republic must be averted at all costs.

The postponement offered a short breathing space and left room for some hope.

The rest of the night Leviné spent in writing a long article for the *Rote Fahne* in which he explained the difference between the proposed undertaking and a real Soviet Republic, and the reasons for the Communists' abstention.

What could he say? The Soviet Republic stood in Communist propaganda for the summit of revolutionary achievement. Even if the Bavarian version did not entirely correspond to the Russian pattern it could be still regarded as a step forward. And Bavaria is after all not Russia.

Leviné denounced the Social Democrats for their ruthless and bloody suppression of the revolution in other parts of the country, and the Independent leaders for their ultimate opposition to the soviet system. But his accusations were so far not borne out by the immediate experience of the Munich workers. His arguments had been lost on the more sophisticated and experienced leaders at the War Ministry. How could he hope to convince the people at large?

And there was no power to outweigh the advantage of getting it all so cheaply. With the War Minister at the head, where was the struggle and bloodshed prophesied by the Communists to come from?....

The article ended with refusal to take any responsibility for the event, and the declaration:

> We, however, shall work feverishly for the establish-
> ment of a real Soviet Republic, shall enlighten the proletariat,
> organise it in Factory Councils and Communist cells, shall
> carry the class-struggle into the country, agitate among the
> soldiers and equip ourselves for the moment when we shall be
> privileged to fight for a Soviet Republic and to conquer.

The Party entered on a truly unequal struggle.

All the available speakers were mobilised and went speeding from factory to factory, from meeting to meeting, to elucidate the views of the Party. My hard-earned savings in the Ukraine stood the Party in good stead: they were spent almost to a penny on taxi-fares.

Hope of averting the catastrophe was perceptibly dwindling. The Communists were too weak to carry their point against such an overwhelming majority. Worse still: the general mood could not but effect their own ranks. It takes great political insight and stability for impassioned revolutionaries to stay outside a popular movement, particularly when it seems to be marching along their own lines.

'Won't the movement by-pass us? Aren't we being too cautious? Does not our restraint border on cowardice?,' were the heart-searching questions.

At one of their sessions, the Party activists unanimously decided to present to the two leading parties a list of elaborate conditions for collaboration. Should the conditions be accepted the Communists would have no further grounds for remaining aloof.

When the scheme was later submitted to Leviné for approval, he asked:

'What if the conditions are accepted? Who could guarantee their realisation? Can they be carried out within the present political frame? If we thought it possible, why did we wait for Schneppenhorst to proclaim a Soviet Republic?'

And he concluded axiomatically:

'*One lays down conditions when one wishes them to be accepted. We do not.*'

This was irrefutable and the chapter was closed.

Another incident also nearly swept the inner circle its feet. News arrived that the Munich garrison had declared itself in favour of a Soviet Republic. The declaration was more or less a slip of the tongue following an inflammatory propaganda speech and was soon withdrawn. But in the overheated militant atmosphere the news was received with great jubilation:

'In this case the Communists cannot possibly stay aloof. We must collaborate,' declared Dietrich, one of the most level-headed comrades.[10] He was soon brought down to earth.

Leviné watched the scene in despair.

'A few more weeks,' he often said, 'and even a defeat could be made profitable as an experience for further struggles. But we are caught in a state where lack of adequate forces makes it impossible to meet our revolutionary commitments.'

An unexpected event brought a ray of hope into the gloomy situation. It appeared that the Independents were greatly disturbed by the Communist stand and wanted to hear more of their views. On Sunday morning, the eve of the proclamation of the Soviet Republic, they decided at a committee meeting to invite a Communist leader for discussions. Leviné was delegated for the mission.

He was brief and precise:

A Soviet Republic can be founded only by Soviets, not by individuals and only if a Communist majority stands behind them.

For only Communists can pursue a Communist policy. You say that you fundamentally agree with our policy. Why don't you then join the party which embraces all other Communists instead of remaining in the party of Haase who, during his office as a People's Representative, strangled the Soviets, or of the Anti-Bolshevik Kautsky? I know that you are Communists at heart, but you only recently broke away with great pain from the old Mother Party, having warmed its membership books against your hearts for many years. You are loath to change parties once more, indeed you might regard such a step as frivolous, showing lack of stability and character. I can well understand your feeling. But you must take into account the moral significance of such a conversion, the spur it would be to the rest of the workers, and should no longer hesitate.

I repeat: If you are really Communists, put an end to the party of Haase and Kautsky[11]; if not, all our deliberations are pointless, for we have different aims and ways.

'I understand, I respect your feelings, they are legitimate but you can go one better.

Those placatory words made it easy to bridge the gap and overcome the last reservations. They decided to go over to the Communists as a body then and there. An official declaration, however, would have to be postponed for a time. A few leaders and the Chairman of the Party, Ernst Toller[12], could be only reached in the evening at a plenary meeting. They must not be given the impression that the committee was acting behind their backs, but must be informed of the decision first and invited to follow suit. If they agreed, well and good; if not, the step would be taken despite them. In any case, the announcement would be made that very day. In the meantime, the Committee wanted to study the Communist Programme thoroughly and asked to be sent several copies of the leaflet.

At a subsequent committee session of eagerly waiting Communists, Leviné reported amidst cheers the outcome of his mission and said, 'Let us take that wavering, delicate bride into our strong Communist arms and see to it that the union produces a powerful Communist Party.'

'Have you any money on you?' he asked me when we left, 'I can hardly move and we could drive for an hour in the English Garden. It is spring, spring, and who knows?....'

We took a cab.

He was very excited.

'With the Independents on our side we might yet prevent the proclamation. Much depends on the extent to which the defection will materialise. I fear, though, that there is not much hope. The illusions are too strong and the workers will wish to "have a go." This does not diminish the significance of the event, which will also affect the Social-Democratic workers. Our immediate gains will be the Independents' paper *Die Neue Zeitung* and a number of able functionaries who will help us to fight the impending struggle more effectively.

'However genuinely the Independents are with us "at heart," as long as they remain in their party, they are bound to follow at the decisive moments the instructions of their own leaders. It is therefore almost always a mistake to stay in a party whose views you ceased to share – even with the good intention of driving it to the left.'

We drove for a while in silence. Suddenly he began to recite an old Russian poem:

Tell, oh tell my young widow
That I have taken another wife
I have wooed an early death.

I burst into tears, and his own voice began to tremble. It was his last spring excursion.

The Independents did not keep their word. They let themselves be hoodwinked by Toller who declared himself in full agreement with the fusion and only asked to postpone the official declaration for twenty-four hours. It would be easier to negotiate with the Social-Democrats as Independents than as declared Communists, he pleaded. It seemed sensible enough, they agreed, thus enabling Toller to pursue his own policy in the name of the Party. Toller was too intoxicated with the prospect of playing the Bavarian Lenin to miss the occasion.

To prove himself worthy of his prospective allies, he borrowed a few of their slogans and presented them to the Social Democrats as conditions for his collaboration. They included such impressive demands as: Dictatorship of the class-conscious proletariat; socialisation of industry, banks and large estates; reorganisation of the bureaucratic state and local government machine and administrative control by Workers' and Peasants' Councils; introduction of compulsory labour for the bourgeoisie; establishment of a Red Army, etc. – twelve conditions in all.

Not all the conditions were accepted, but then 'Bavaria is not Russia'.... The Independents were satisfied. It should be remembered that the Communists themselves advocated the presentation of conditions as a basis for their collaboration and without Leviné might have fallen into the same trap.

On Monday, the 7th April, the Soviet Republic was proclaimed. Church bells and huge red posters announced that the 'toiling population had become the master of its own destiny' and acclaimed 'the abolition of the accursed epoch of capitalism.'

A national holiday was proclaimed to mark the great event.

Power officially rested with the Revolutionary Workers' Council, who formed a provisional government of People's Representatives. It consisted chiefly of Independents, Anarchists and two members of the Peasants' Council. Toller, the Chairman of the Independents and the two very popular Anarchists Mühsam and Landauer were the actual rulers.

Hoffmann's government was declared deposed, relations with the two Soviet Republics, Russia and Hungary, established.[13]

The new rulers tried their best to observe the ritual of revolutionary sovereigns. Like Soviet Russia and Hungary, they proclaimed martial law, commanded the bourgeoisie to surrender arms and began drafting decrees for forming a Red Army. But no one took it seriously.

Leviné wrote:

The third day of the Soviet Republic.... In the factories the workers toil and drudge as ever before for the capitalists. In the offices sit the same Royal functionaries. In the streets the old armed guardians of the capitalist world keep order. The scissors of the war profiteers and the dividend hunters still snip away.

The rotary machines of the capitalist Press still rattle on, spewing out poison and gall, lies and calumnies into the people craving for revolutionary enlightenment.... Dictatorship of the proletariat? Another poster gives the answer: It proclaims 'Martial Law' and is signed by the Military Headquarters.

True, martial law was imposed in the early days of the Russian and Hungarian Republics – but they first disarmed the bourgeoisie and armed the workers. And in Bavaria? Not a single bourgeois has been disarmed, not a single worker has yet been armed.... When the workers, thirsty for instruction are flocking to the meetings, they are threatened by the 8 o'clock curfew.

Referring to the proclamation of a *national* holiday, he was teaching the alleged protagonists of the dictatorship of the proletariat that the idea is based on the existence of a divided society, while the word 'national' implies unity between the antagonistic classes:

> Colonel Epp is already recruiting volunteers.[14] Students and other bourgeois youths are flocking to him from all sides. Nuremberg declared war on Munich. The gentlemen in Weimar recognise only Hoffmann's government. Noske is already whetting his butcher's knife, eager to rescue his threatened party friends and the threatened capitalists.
>
> But now will they at last appeal to the proletariat? Will they assemble the workers now, arm them, declare a general strike to keep them on the alert?
>
> Nothing of the kind. Plans are being fabricated, decrees drafted about the creation of a Red Army.... But the decree still remains in draft form. They are in no great hurry....

Nothing had changed except for the feverish activity of the bourgeoisie inside and outside Munich and the mounting apprehension of the workers. They felt that a storm was gathering over their heads and that they were trapped.

The criticism of the Communists was bearing fruit. Besides exposing the helplessness of the new rulers it was teaching the workers to see things in their true perspective. The workers remembered the Communists' warnings and turned to them for protection:

> 'The Communists must collaborate! Only they can save us!'

At many meetings resolutions were accepted to hand over 'full power' to the Communists and to proclaim Max Levien Dictator.

The Communists knew that the workers had as yet no power to confer and that nothing could be gained by joining the government, but they knew that some time or other they would be forced to appear on the scene and they set out to create organisations of their own to be equal to the new tasks. They turned to the factories, calling upon the workers to elect a new body reflecting their real aspirations. 'For only such a body is entitled to decide *when* a Soviet Republic should be proclaimed and when the struggle should begin.'

The manifesto published in the *Rote Fahne* explains in great detail what was demanded of the new Committee.

> Not even the Workers' Committees are authorised to make the decisions, for they too were elected for quite different tasks.... You elected people versed in laws of an economic and administrative nature; now you will have to elect people imbued with revolutionary spirit... capable of making quick

decisions and at the same time of judiciously assessing the balance of power and of choosing soberly and circumspectly the moment of action.

The document contains further details (in factories of an overall of 1,000 workers one representative should be elected; in others, one to every 1,000), and an appeal to elect Communists. It explains:

It is not possible to do away with political parties through the decisions of a few confused and zealous leaders. Now, as ever, the Communist Party will embrace all who strive to fight for the same objective and with the same means. Now, as ever... we shall draw a distinct demarcation line between ourselves and those social traitors who have hitherto combated the soviet system and the perpetually vacillating Independents who water the system down.

We exhort you to watch with the greatest suspicion every move of the founders of this sham Soviet Republic!

We exhort you to take all the necessary steps for the struggle and for the realisation of a real Communist Soviet Republic!

There can be little doubt that the form in which the Munich events proceeded was to the greatest extent determined by Leviné.

The firm stand against the proclamation of the Soviet Republic was entirely his work. And it was entirely his truly visionary assessment of the situation which enabled the Party to transform a farcical undertaking into the greatest event of the German revolution.

Why didn't Leviné simply step aside and leave the Tollers to their own destiny? Why didn't he wash his hands of an enterprise which, he was convinced, was foredoomed to failure?

The Independent author of a pamphlet *The Munich Tragedy*,[15] ascribes Leviné's attitude to mere confusion:

At the decisive moment Leviné allowed his clear, sober realisation that the time for a Soviet Republic had not yet arrived... to be obscured by the hope that it might yet be brought to successful solution.

The German historian Professor A. Rosenberg ascribes it to the sheer romanticism of an impassioned revolutionary:

Leviné thought it the duty of the Communist Party to throw itself into the breach and to save the honour of the soviet idea.[16]

Leviné's policy puzzled even many Communist leaders, and above all the then head of the Party, Paul Levy, who thus failed to exploit the rich experience of the Munich events for the benefit of the revolution.

It was, however, exactly Leviné's 'clear, sober' mind which governed his policy. He reasoned:

Our enemies have well perceived our weak point, which is our lack of organisational power. They know that time is on our side and that the workers grow increasingly susceptible to our ideas. They cannot idly watch us mustering our forces and wait for us to decide that the moment for action has arrived. They are therefore trying to provoke premature action so as to nip it in the bud. They have succeeded in doing so with the help of the Social Democrats in a number of towns. In Munich we refused to fall into the trap. But the die is nevertheless cast. Whatever, the attempts of the present Soviet Republic to dodge the real issues and limit itself to problems like 'revolutionary reorganisation of universities' and other questions of no great immediate danger to the bourgeoisie – a bitter struggle lies ahead. The workers are in a turmoil. The revolutionary phraseology could not but create illusions that they actually possess some power and they will not meekly accept military intervention.

They have not yet come face to face with the counter-revolution but they feel threatened and come to us for help. We cannot avert the catastrophe, but *a revolutionary leadership* is responsible for the state in which the workers emerge from it: as a downtrodden, disappointed herd or as high-spirited revolutionaries ready to resume the struggle. We will tell them the truth: an honourable *death* and *experience for the future* is all we can salvage from the present situation. But this is a great contribution to our final task and is in our power to achieve. For this purpose we must try to transform the bogus Soviet Republic into a genuine one and thus give the workers an object lesson about its real nature and of what they can gain from it. *We shall have to pay the bloody price either way for there can be no peaceful solution.* But we must not die in vain.

This was how Leviné presented the situation to the workers and this was the condition for the Communists' collaboration. He was not beating about the bush:

I fear we are lost either way. Many of us will have to initiate the era of freedom with our lives. But I know from the Russian experience in the towns – where a genuine Soviet Republic was overthrown by a stronger enemy, it was so deeply rooted in the minds of the workers that it almost automatically sprang up again, when they recovered their fighting powers. It was different when the struggle was forced on them for illusory positions as in our case, and where they had to ask the ominous question: 'What have we been fighting for?'

We must not make it easy for the counter-revolution to shed our blood. If they find us ready to defend ourself they will learn that playing with Soviet Republics could be a double-edged sword on which they might cut their own fingers.

But were the Communists as a Party obliged to take over instead of letting the Tollers extricate themselves from a situation created by their own folly? It is only natural that this highly controversial question should also arise in Communist circles.

Leviné anticipated this mood:

If we tried to approach the problem from our narrow party interest, stay aloof to spare our forces and keep intact our organisation, it would in no way help us. The counter-revolution knows where to look for its deadliest enemies. Its vengeance will fall heaviest on us. We shall be their first targets.

Not only the workers but the government itself asked the Communists for help. After three days it was at the end of its tether and was quite ready to abdicate.

On the 9th April, the Revolutionary Workers' Councils assembled to discuss the situation. Leviné again explained why it was useless to join the government:

We are convinced of the inevitability of military intervention and we shall be at your side when the fight breaks out. But we can only take responsibility for a Communist policy and we will only take over if you are ready to carry out our programme.

The meeting then resolved to demand the resignation of the provisional government and to transfer the whole executive power to the Communists. Toller who was present at the meeting, declared his full solidarity with Leviné and guaranteed the abdication of his government: a condition made by the Communists to avoid strife among the proletariat. A committee of twenty members was formed to work out a plan of action. Toller left the meeting to inform his government of the resolution.

He soon returned and stated that he was unable to reach his colleagues but he asked for the floor to make a 'personal declaration.'

He made a violent attack on the 'ruthless Communists.' Their policy would provoke the peasants to hold back supplies and he could not bear to think of the resulting hunger, with children and invalids deprived of milk.

'I see before me an assembly of madmen ready for selfdestruction,' he cried histrionically.

He solemnly promised to carry out personally all the measures demanded by the Communists. But he 'loved the proletariat' and would act carefully and peacefully whereas 'the Communists only loved their dogma' and were set on fighting and destruction.

Toller was an excellent speaker and his promise to avoid the struggle was an irresistible bait. The meeting wavered and then openly cheered him.

Strangely, it was I who first became conscious of the changed mood. I might have been prompted by the hope that the Communists – my husband – could then somehow 'get out of it.' Or perhaps my betters were too exhausted to understand the hidden implication of those cheers.

'You see,' I said excitedly to Leviné, 'they still trust Toller and not you.'

But overawed with respect for the sanctity of 'the will of the people,' so often spoken of lately, I concluded that Communist leaders were obliged to comply with it unconditionally:

'You must ask them to think again carefully and to make a *final* decision.'

This was a great mistake. Without a determined proletariat behind them, the Communists could not play their part and its representative body, the councils, were evidently divided. It was wrong to offer any reconsiderations. Leviné said afterwards, 'You wrongly influenced us.'

But in the general turmoil, everybody was so impressed by my quick assessment of the mood that my advice was accepted lock, stock and barrel: the meeting was allowed a second vote.

The Communists were the last hope. Only a short while ago Toller himself had asked them to take over. They could not be rejected and the meeting 'finally' ratified its former resolution.

The meeting closed at three o'clock in the morning. At six the sirens were to announce the general strike, the first measure of the Committee of Twenty. But the sirens were silent and nothing happened.

The workers accepted the Soviet Republic like 'a gifthorse' and were ready to give it back when it proved useless to them. When, striving to postpone the institution of the Soviet Republic, Leviné asked the workers: 'Where are your shining eyes? Where is your enthusiasm for the great event? Your will to fight for it?' he proved that a leader must and can be capable of sensing the mood of the masses and of taking cognizance even of such imponderables as 'enthusiasm' and 'will to fight.'

Now they listened to him and agreed that he was right in his prognosis. But it is not enough to follow a leader who demands such great sacrifices. *Not when there are other leaders*, warm-hearted chaps like Toller, who assure the masses that they know of better and easier ways of solving the problem.

'Leaders can only formulate what the masses instinctively feel themselves,' said Leviné. But that 'feeling' arises from personal experience. The Munich workers had no such experience and therefore lagged behind.

The ensuing confusion was aggravated by a tragi-comic incident: almost the entire leading body disappeared into thin air. Messengers were running in vain from place to place. Our telephone never stopped ringing. The leaders could not be found.

On leaving the meeting, they had assembled to work out a plan of action, to issue proclamations and so on. But the inhuman strain of the preceding days asserted itself. Since the 4th April, they had hardly had an hour's sleep.

No sooner had they sat comfortably down than they passed out. A leaden sleep held them for hours in its grip and they were the last to learn of the previous night's fiasco.

The failure again explodes the myth of the Communists' dictatorship over the masses. To whom could they turn when the workers refused to follow?

The workers were still divided. The Committee of Twenty therefore requested the Revolutionary Workers' Council to relieve it of its mandate, and offered instead to stand by the Toller government in an advisory capacity. Their proposals were eagerly accepted but were never carried out. The workers did not stir; the situation was aimlessly dragging on.[17]

The Communists were then inclined to believe that the Soviet Republic would collapse of its own weakness and that an unconditional capitulation of its government might yet spare Munich the horrors of military intervention.

The whole history of the Soviet Republic, which the Communists decried in advance as an act of provocation, was too compromising for Hoffman's Government to indulge in a serious struggle against rivals who rather resembled a group of children playing Red Indians.

However, the Communists were still reckoning with tougher counter-revolutionary measures, a period of illegality, and were about to work out corresponding plans.

On Saturday, 12th April, Leviné sent me home early. He promised to follow me shortly and predicted quieter times.

'It will all be resolved amicably. In a few days the venture will be liquidated.'

I waited in vain until the early hours of the morning. During the day he sent me a message not to leave the house until further notice. But I was not unduly disturbed. I could see through the windows people promenading and children playing; it all seemed peaceful and reassuring.

Towards the evening systematic shooting could be heard.

So Hoffmann did not want a peaceful solution! The outcome of the struggle seemed all too obvious, and I trembled. No news from Leviné. Should I ever see him again?

He suddenly appeared next day, the 14th April, and in broad daylight.

'I am taking you out for lunch,' he said coolly, apparently to bring some sobriety into my stormy reception.

We were not alone; he was brought by a friend in his car, and no one was ever allowed a glimpse into his intimate life.

On our way to town he told me, 'Soon after I sent you home we received disquieting reports of unusual activity in the Republican Defence Force. This put us on our guard. With the Munich garrison, who only a few days ago sympathised with the Soviet Republic, it issued a joint proclamation next morning declaring the Soviet deposed, arrested several members of the provisional government, including the Anarchist Mühsam, and proclaimed martial law.

'Under the leadership of the Social Democrat Aschenbrenner[18], the commandant of the railway station, they occupied the building to secure communication with Hoffmann's government and his already mobilised army, as well as a number of other positions of military importance. The Social Democratic Executive naturally sided with the Putschists. It issued a manifesto calling for "energetic support for the legitimate government." To appease the workers they promised "to carry out the sound principles of the soviet system." They did not fail, however, to warn against the "criminal elements" and to whip up hatred against the Soviet Republic.

'When the news of the Putsch spread, the workers were roused to a pitch. The indignation against Hoffmann's Government, whose own members provoked the Soviet Republic which they set out to suppress by force, was universal. The Social-Democratic Executive did not dare to appear at meetings for fear of their own rank and file. The appeal of the Revolutionary Central Council for protest demonstrations only evoked scorn and contempt. When the Putschists started attacking the Communist localities[19] the workers rushed to their aid. The unity about which there had lately been so much wrangling was born in one single moment out of the will: to conquer or to die! Together they repulsed the attack and went into the offensive.

'By ten o'clock they captured the railway station and soon occupied a number of other important buildings. The workers had not arms. Toller was forced to confess that he did not even know what quantity of arms he possessed. It turned out that he had at his disposal 600 guns, mostly defective, and little or no ammunition. Within a few hours, the workers were armed. How could it have happened? When the proletariat is driven to extremes and really loses patience it breaks all fetters and removes all obstacles.

'We appealed to the workers only a few days ago: "Get rid of the Revolutionary Central Council and of Toller. There is no time for fine talk.

'Yesterday action was taken over the heads of all of them. And there was hardly any shooting. At such moments the enemy feels that the game is up and scarcely puts up resistance. There was a total of seven casualties. Aschenbrenner, who ordered the shooting of the three of our men who went to him for negotiations, escaped on an engine.

'The Workers' and Soldiers' Councils then formally deposed the Toller government and transferred full power to a Committee of Action of Fifteen, which in its turn singled out an Executive and Control Council. Both are directly responsible to the Executive of the Workers' and Soldiers' Councils. In this way the government established direct links with the workers and can constantly test their mood and express their will.

'The enthusiasm is enormous. We declared a general strike and the arming of the proletariat is in full swing. We need the strike to speed up our work and also to demonstrate our strength.'

Here Leviné stopped.

'And your husband is the head of both institutions,' remarked our friend, 'and you are something like a queen.'

Leviné simply winced and whispered to me: 'You will never, never repeat such jokes, will you?'

He wanted to be 'quite sure.' Yet he was not modest in the accepted sense: he was too conscious of his inner powers. I sometimes teased him for his obsession with keeping copies of his letters and preserving every scrap of written paper. 'You seem to anticipate immortality.'

He used to laugh good-naturedly but refrained from discussing this strange habit.

He might have felt that his life would leave some marks but he spurned official status in the same way as he rejected wealth and privileges in general. And it seemed that only he could be free of any desire for acquisition and acclaim who had actually enjoyed them in the past.

'And what is Toller doing?' I asked.

'He has put himself at our disposal. He wants to "prove his love for the proletariat with his blood". He has joined the armed forces and already wears a uniform.... I am afraid he will cause us no end of trouble but it was the best gesture he could think of. You cannot shake off a man who "wants to die for the proletariat"'.

Our friend departed and we were left alone in the almost empty restaurant. There were no more politics. Even at that moment Leviné was able to change into the romantic, chivalrous husband. A woman offered flowers and I was rather surprised when he sent her away:

'No, thank you.' He had never done this before.

'Will there be no more flowers in a real "proletarian" life?' I tought.

Later I found him knocking in vain on several flower-shop doors.

'Oh,' he laughed. 'I was trying to break my own orders. I had quite forgotten that we decreed today to close the shops.'

'Why didn't you buy them in the restaurant?'

'But you would not know that today I *wanted* to give you flowers if I bought them by accident. And now everything has been spoilt,' he said sadly.

He was wrong: I really never forgot those unbought flowers.

He had a short break while his office was being organised, and we could walk for a while. He immediately returned to politics. The town was brimming with it.

We stopped by a poster announcing: 'The military Commander of the Town is henceforth the undersigned.... Anyone who fails to hand over his arms within twenty-four hours will be shot. Egelhofer.'

I was startled by the violent language.

'But', said Leviné, 'they don't need arms, unless they want to turn them on us. The first shots in the German revolution were fired by officers. In Russia terror was first introduced by the bourgeoisie. You know that, and yet you are shocked when we try to prevent the counter-revolutionaries plunging us into a blood bath. It is time to learn not to be frightened when the proletariat begins to give orders. If it would only learn to command soon!'

We were approaching the Ministry of War. The building was positively besieged and swarms of people kept thronging towards it. These were the people who had come to surrender their arms. Their faces were impenetrable, solemn. Some were contemptuously smiling, probably those who had succeeded in hiding their main stocks in the rooms of their caretakers or other 'loyal' proletarians exempted from arms-searches and unaware that the arms would be used against their own friends.

They were all pressing forward to get rid quickly of the dangerous objects concealed under their coats.

'This is the vote of confidence of the bourgeoisie in the new government,' remarked Leviné. 'When the bogus Soviet Republic demanded the surrender of arms, they did not think of obeying.'

The streets were filled with workers, armed and unarmed, who marched by in detachments or stood reading the proclamations. Lorries loaded with armed workers raced through the town, often greeted with jubilant cheers.

The bourgeoisie had disappeared completely; the trams were not running. All cars had been confiscated and were being used exclusively for official purposes. Thus every car that whirled past became a symbol, reminding people of the great changes.

Aeroplanes appeared over the town and thousands of leaflets fluttered through the air in which the Hoffmann government pictured the horrors of Bolshevik rule and praised the democratic government who would bring peace, order and bread.

In the evening all leaders assembled in a huge hall of the Wittelsbach Palace, the seat of the new government. Hard work with almost permanent committee sessions lay ahead. Suddenly somebody started singing the Internationale. The others followed and the Royal Palace resounded with the ecstatic voices of a bizarre crowd choking with emotion, much closer in appearance to a dedicated church congregation than to tough Communists.

I cried and some of the 'ruthless blood-thirsty criminals' were struggling to suppress their own tears.

The Wittelsbach Palace was flooded with people from morning to night. Inventors appeared with world-shattering schemes which, put into effect, would guarantee wealth, peace and other dazzling prospects; authors of new educational reforms; protagonists of marriage reform, which was regarded as the 'first and foremost task of a Soviet Republic'; artists who offered 'the people' their art and were very offended when asked to help to design effective propaganda posters; actors, ready to act for 'the people' in new, self-designed theatres. They were all determined to submit their ideas direct to the Executive Council, above all to the hitherto most popular comrade, Max Levien.

Radical writers turned up with grandiose schemes for mass propaganda. All they demanded of the Government was to supply them with the requisite paraphernalia, such as aeroplanes, cars and a staff of reliable, talented comrades; and they were offended and unwilling to perform less ambitious tasks or to use for the time being their own initiative in finding the necessary equipment.

Astrologers also besieged the Government offices. They proposed to ask Providence about the destiny of the founders of the Soviet Republic and were seeking information about dates of birth and other weighty aspects from their relatives and friends. The stars were so far benevolent, the Soviet Republic was to win through.[20]

Amidst this chaos an embryonic Communist Party was destined to build a machinery which for two unparalleled weeks dominated the entire life of the country.

A leadership so far untested in action, with Leviné, an alien and a stranger to Munich workers at its head, succeeded in uniting the workers in defiance of the old established parties, and in securing their enthusiastic collaboration.

The scarce Communist cadres were replenished by many a man chosen from the mass of the invading dreamers and cranks, and set forth to carry out the monumental task.

On the third day of Communist rule Leviné reported to the assembly of the Workers' Councils:

'I have come straight from a session of your Committee of Action. Together with representatives of the Banking Council they are discussing measures for breaking the resistance of the capitalist exploiters who, just as in the early days of the Russian Soviet Republic, are subtly plotting to slow down the triumphal chariot of the revolution. We are resolved to confiscate the banks and to install our own delegates in them. We shall order the banks to open immediately to secure the payment of wages and unemployment relief. For the same reason we shall compel the bourgeois municipalities to carry out their duties under the supervision of the proletarian government.

'It is possible that the capitalists have already hidden away their valuables. To find out, all safes will be opened in the presence of their holders who will be asked to appear with the keys. The safes of those who fail to turn up without satisfactory reasons for absence will be opened under the surveillance of the Banking Council and the contents confiscated for the benefit of the poor. The safe-holders will, moreover, be forbidden to withdraw a single pfennig without official permission.

'I have mentioned only the decisions taken just before I was delegated to come to you, but there are infinitely more matters to settle. I appealed to you yesterday to assign comrades for help.

'We have not much time to spare for meetings. Of course, we want to report to you. We want to have your criticism. The moment we lose your confidence you must put others in our places.

'Our main task has been to arm the proletariat. In one night you have done more than was done in seven days by the former Central Council: You have armed yourselves. This is the essential nature of the proletarian government: it can do nothing of itself, it can only appeal to you, submit to you proposals. You yourselves must act.

'When the Military Commander issued his proclamation, it was a joy to watch the bourgeoisie handing over their arms. The proletariat will never forget that moment, and should it be defeated this time, it will rise again to relive this experience. What does the surrender of arms mean? They might have included a few souvenirs but most of them were kept to bring you death and destruction. And yet, people still reproach Comrade Egelhofer for threatening to shoot for disobeying his orders. Revolution cannot be made with soft, compassionate hearts. It demands a stern, relentless will.

'Calling for a general strike, we exempted the employees connected with the payment of wages. But influenced by the bourgeosie a
good many black-coated workers refused to turn up. We shall, therefore, immediately install our commissaries in all banks and municipal
offices and compel those gentlemen to collaborate. We can dispense
with the higher ranks, and when we raise the miserable salaries of the
subordinate officials I wonder whether many an old employee who
formerly staked his hopes on the Wittelsbachs will not welcome the
proletariat as his liberator.

'I am able to give you good news: the Peasants' Council
approached us of its own accord and declared its willingness to work
with us hand in hand and moreover to influence the peasants to abstain
from withholding supplies. An aeroplane is already on its way with
leaflets designed to explain the situation to the peasants and to appeal
for supplies.

'The small peasant fears the confiscation of all his possessions.
It will be your task to reassure your friends and relatives in the country-
side. We propose to expropriate only the big landowners and then only
from the land which they cannot cultivate themselves. The smallholders
and farm labourers, however, stand only to gain from the proletarian
government. When the peasants are properly acquainted with our aims,
there will be no need for us to have recourse to machine-guns when
the rich farmers make difficulties. We shall appeal to the poor and the
farm hands.

'A further task was to constitute a Propaganda Committee.
Besides writing leaflets and holding meetings it will enlist and send out
propagandists to the villages and barracks. The Committee comprises
the Comrades Levien, Morten and Werner. 'In granting the soldiers
five marks extra pay, we did not intend to bribe them. But we appreciate
the present precarious situation and we try to relieve their anxiety about
their families and free their minds for fighting for the proletarian cause.
As a result of our propaganda, you will be pleased to hear, the Barracks
Council has unanimously declared itself in favour of the proletarian
rule.

'We have to fight not only the enemy within our boundaries,
but also the enemy without. It recently declared that Hoffmann would
not besiege Munich but only starve it out. It is, however, possible that
we shall break through the blockade. We have formed a Military Commission which includes Comrades Egelhofer, Wiedmann, Reichhart
and Reichelt. This Commission has already taken measures and even

outside Munich, for instance, in Rosenheim, where counter-revolutionary plots were discovered.

'A Transport Commission was set up with Comrades Schreiber and Bauer to control the post, telegraph, telephone and radio station. We have already had the pleasure of sending a radio message to Lenin, in which we informed him that the bogus Soviet Republic collapsed under the asault of Hoffmann's government and a real proletarian rule had been established in its place.

'The telephone personnel sided with the bourgeoisie and decamped. We have appointed comrades to mobilise new personnel and to select people to monitor telephone conversations. We have also confiscated all private cars for the use of our military forces. However, we have exempted taxis, because they mostly belong to proletarians and some of the vehicles have not even completely passed into their ownership. But we have reserved the right to confiscate them in case of emergency.

'The Transport Commission will also check all vehicles to prevent the bourgeoisie from escaping with their valuables and arms. It is closely collaborating with the Military Commission which, equipped with heavy artillery, controls all railway lines leading to Munich.

'Our Economic Commission, which has already started dealing with the banks, is in the process of taking steps for their socialisation. The Commission is also entrusted to guarantee smooth delivery to Munich of food, raw materials and coal. A number of the old staff is collaborating with us on this field. In the next few days, several of the luxury hotels will be confiscated for homeless proletarians and some members of the government who live too far from their offices. The Regina Palace Hotel has already been requisitioned. [Stormy applause!]

'Also to be requisitioned are stores of provisions from the hotels and homes of the bourgeoisie. At the house of a certain baroness, we found a bath-tub filled with eggs. The requisitioning will be carried out by an Anti-Profiteering Committee. Here we might follow the example of Noske. Just as he had workers' quarters cordoned off and had them searched house by house, cupboard by cupboard for arms, we shall cordon off bourgeois quarters and have them searched for bacon, eggs, and butter. Comrades Strobel and Mai are on the Economic Commission, and Comrade Axelrod[21] is attached to it in an advisory capacity.

'In addition we have formed a Committee to combat countre-revolutionary activities. The Committee has already made a number of arrests, and seized hostages. We still need people to assist this Committee.

'The Government will have to carry out all these measures as well as dealing with information and complaints. Unlike bourgeois governments, our Government is available to everybody. But you must bear in mind that each of us has only two eyes and two ears and the day only twenty-four hours. All those who have important matters to discuss are welcome but not people who come to satisfy their curiosity.

'The Executive Council with Comrades Duske[22], Männer, Levien and Dietrich is designed to supervise the activity of the individual committees and ensure the co-ordination of their various measures. In case of emergency, or should the Committees be out of session, the Executive Council is entitled to make decisions on its own authority. In addition, it has to determine various matters of principle which require supplementary sessions. So you see that it is not from lack of goodwill that we do not appear before you frequently. I suggest that we report to you on our activities daily for one hour.

'Up to now the strike has been directed by the Government. But it would be more appropriate for you to build your own strike committee. It is not our task to direct the strike, for the strike is intended to support us. And we cannot call it off right away. Until we have the situation well in hand the strike must go on.

'We wish you to parade the streets with your guns as often as possible. The bogus Soviet Republic prescribed a holiday, the proletarian Republic became a holiday. It would be a good thing for you to submerge the town in a sea of red. Use all your red cloths and curtains to demonstrate that the proletariat is celebrating a holiday. And sing in the streets. We shall distribute sheets with revolutionary songs.

'The ground we have covered so far represents only a fraction of the first rung of the ladder leading to final victory. You alone can guarantee the ascent to its summit. We request you to name the comrades able to take over various functions. The essential work must be performed by the proletariat itself.

'The government must only hold the threads and control them; but they must be woven and brought into its hands by the proletariat. I do not appeal to you for collaboration, I appeal to you to do the job, just as you yourselves have won the battle.

'The danger has not passed. The White Guard might assail us. Hunger might knock on the gates of Munich. But Ebert, Noske, and Scheidemann can only hold out for a matter of weeks. Saxony is in a ferment; in Brunswick a Soviet Republic has been proclaimed. Abroad the news of the establishment of the first proletarian Soviet Republic has been greeted with jubilation. Hungary is a Soviet Republic. Italy looks with hope and joy to Bavaria. In France, England and America the capitalists are at the end of their tether, for the spirit of Bolshevism has seized the proletariat. The Russian Soviet Republic has been recognised by the Entente.

'We are holding an advance post. The Russian proletariat also held a front line position. They persevered and proved right. We keep a watchful eye on the East, South and West and we can say on this the third day of the revolution, that it has not been in vain.

'We do not know whether our first onslaught will suffice, whether we shall be able to hold out to the end. We shall try. And we know our struggle will not be in vain.'

In his report Leviné spoke of hostages. Later on, at his trial, he did not repudiate the accusation of taking hostages. He only hit back by reminding the Court that it was first practised, with the connivance of the authorities, by the German Army during the war.

Perhaps he knew of an isolated case and did not wish to disclaim responsibility, just as he refused to condemn the highly regrettable murder of the ten hostages, though his lawyers pointed out that this was the only basis on which the Prosecution could demand the death penalty. He thought it immoral to attack the defeated proletariat. (The accusation was afterwards dropped by the Prosecution itself.)

The hostages, members of the so-called 'Thule Association'[23] an early fascist Group who were shot *after* Leviné was removed from power, were arrested for manipulating faked government seals for overt counter-revolutionary purposes and could, in fact, hardly be described as 'hostages'.

Leviné admitted that 'revolutions are not made with tender, compassionate hearts' and the Soviet Republic, in fact, formed a special body for combating counter-revolutionary activities. He was, however, worried lest anyone should become a victim of spite or revengeful instincts. Even before he made his report he took me aside and said:

'Listen carefully. We have created a Special Commission for dealing with counter-revolutionary activities. It is indispensable for a young revolution', he added to reassure me. 'People will be brought in for interrogation, of course, frightened people. I would like you to join this Commission. If you agree, I shall propose to co-opt you. You will have nothing to do with the sentences. I only want you to watch and listen and report to me directly if you are not satisfied with the procedure. It would set my mind at rest and above all it would be a service to the revolution. We must not mar it by unnecessary suffering and miscarriage of justice, we are not fighting individuals. I know you have a soft spot for your enemies'.

As there were many documents and letters to examine, another woman was co-opted, a doctor's wife. She was very beautiful and, I think, reassured at least all the male prisoners. The head of our department was Strobl, a very young man, a dedicated and intelligent Communist but very embarrassed by his role and too apologetic even for my liking. I never heard a mention of hostages, though some may have been taken in the course of military operations.

Leviné did not expect to win even if he said at his trial that he had harboured some illusions. Perhaps he tried to hope. With the great task on his hands, he needed the strength of confidence and could not afford to be too analytical. Once I caught him listening with a somewhat sad and ironical smile to some proposals, realisable only in a future stabilised state.

'Don't you believe at all in the survival of the Soviet Republic?' I asked.

I received no reply. But his answer was manifest in his whole policy: there was no striving for consolidating reforms.

The art of a leader, as indeed of a teacher in general, consists in setting himself and others realistic, practicable tasks. The present task was only to salvage as much as possible from the debris of an unavoidable defeat: an honourable death and an object lesson in the essence of a Soviet Republic was all Leviné promised.

This promise he kept and sealed with his own life.

This aim also required the awakening of a corresponding spirit in the workers themselves and Leviné never ceased to try to raise their self-confidence and dignity. All his speeches abounded in encouragement: 'You have fought, you have accomplished everything by yourselves, you are the engineers, we are only your temporory advisers. Control us and chase us away if you find us wanting and replace us by worthier men!'

Proud of their victory the elated workers performed true miracles and for a short while followed the Communists unreservedly. Their teaching was proved in action and left no room for evasion. But this spirit could not last.

But this powerful demonstration at the end of the general strike was the last of the Communist victories. Leviné proudly recalled the event at his trial:

The Public Prosecutor will know how ... the workers, with hundreds of post office employees, men and women, in their pale blue uniforms in the vanguard, marched to the Wittels-bach Palace to demonstrate their solidarity with the men who are portrayed in this Court as terrorists and enslavers of the Munich proletariat.

The White Army was closing in on Munich, and the approach-ing calamity could not but arouse fear and perplexity. All those among the workers who were weak and half-hearted began to look for some means of escape. They naturally turned to leaders who were equally incapable of looking the danger in the face: Toller, supported by his close associates Männer and Klingelhofer, again raised his head.[24]

Two camps were now confronting each other: one with Leviné appealing to the noblest feelings of the workers, their striving for freedom and courage and one with Toller playing on their indolence and despondency accumulated in age-long enslavement.

The last meeting of the factory councils was dominated by impotent fury at the grave situation and a desire to escape with a mini-mum of harm to themselves. Männer was the first to speak:

'The demand of the Committee of Action to hand over the keys of safes to the political Commissar is nothing but political theft. He might have understood, he went on, if they had ordered the confis-cation of money. But jewels and other valuables are useless: the workers cannot eat them. Of course, he was in favour of the Soviet Republic but he must, nevertheless, so act that he might be able to look Hoff-mann's Government straight in the eye'.

To look Hoffmann's Government straight in the eye had, of course, its advantages. It was, unfortunately, incompatible with ful-filling the tasks of a revolutionary government.

Klingelhofer spoke in much the same spirit:

The Communist leaders are whimsical theorists. Their unrea-listic policy with its provocative demands is bound to have dangerous repercussions.

But these were only harmless preliminaries to Toller's decla-ration:

I consider the present Government a disaster for the Bavarian toiling masses and I regard its leading figures as a menace to the Soviet idea. Incapable of any constructive work, they indulge in senseless destruction. To support them would, in my view, compromise the revolution and the Soviet Republic. The

terrible thing is that the workers are kept in complete ignorance of the true course of events.

He added, though, that the Party as such was not to blame
but only some individuals who happen to belong to it:

There are dishonourable elements in every party. When Leviné
said that he had always been delegated by the Party wherever
it thought it necessary, he ought to have been dragged down
from the tribune.

Reports of the Provision Sections, food, coal and others, followed. They were highly tendentious and clearly aimed at arousing
further despondency and panic.

Personal aspersions followed. Rumours were circulated that
the Communist leaders had secured for themselves fifty faked passports
together with a large sum of money and an aeroplane, ready to flee the
country.

The speeches, even of Toller and his friends, bristled with
suggestive terms: 'Alien elements', 'Prussians,' 'Russians' – even the
inevitable epithet 'Jews' could be heard.

The meeting included a considerable number of truly 'alien
elements,' who penetrated the hall without mandates. Some spies and
counter-revolutionary hirelings who tried to provoke skirmishes had to
be forcibly ejected. The police and the bourgeois Press, who still formally had their representatives on the Workers' Councils but hitherto
had preferred to keep aloof, now appeared in force.

There was no room for Communists in that assembly and no
revolutionary policy could be expected from openly anti-Communist
rebels. The government, therefore, offered its resignation.

But the assembly flatly refused to let them go. It was safer to
let the Communists face the White Army than to accept responsibility
themselves.

A bizarre farce ensued: the abused and maligned Communists,
'the misfortune of the Bavarian people' were angrily commanded not
to go but – to remain at their posts!

'You must stay at your posts and open negotiations.'

'But we refuse to negotiate. We are convinced that it would
only serve our enemies. We propose, on the contrary, to spare no
efforts to organise the defence of Munich. We have different aims and
are ready to make room for people to suit your wishes.'

It was in vain.

Leviné resorted to the crudest analogy:

'Surely you would not elect the Wittelsbachers to lead you into a revolution. In the same way you cannot look to us for a policy of meek surrender.'

But it was futile to expect a rational response from panic-stricken people:

'You must stay at your posts!'

Leviné then threatened to introduce some stern emergency measures and first of all to arrest a great number of saboteurs and other known counter-revolutionaries.

The threat proved most effective: quite a number of those present might have fallen into that category. The assembly took fright and decided on a vote of no confidence.

This was not what Toller's clique desired. It took them, furthermore, by surprise. They had repeated too often and for too long the tale of the Communists' lust for power and had not expected them to voluntarily cede it.

The last means to avoid responsibility, then, was to scatter it. Here they unwittingly adopted the practice of the shrewd Russian muzhiks who, as a rule, secured for themselves the signatures of the whole community before going into action.

The new government consisted entirely of the members of Factory Councils; none of the trio who actually determined the policy belonged to it.

The first move of the new Committee of Action was an offer to negotiate.

Even before the Communists were removed from power Toller secretly tried his hand in effecting a negotiated settlement. Hoffmann demanded as a basis for any negotiations the immediate surrender of all Soviet leaders. At that time this was obviously beyond Toller's comperence. And perhaps he had not yet reached the degree of panic and hatred which might have made him agree to accept the condition.

But Hoffmann's Government had no more say in the matter and the heads of the White Army had their own ideas about quelling a revolution: the offer of negotiations was contemptuously ignored.

This did not awake Toller to the stern realities. He only intensified his struggle against the Communists. He no longer promised to carry out their programme as he had on the memorable night of the 10th April. He did not even dissociate himself from a campaign of the crudest calumny against his recent allies, such as: 'Leviné and Max Levien have absconded with the funds of the crippled war-veterans.' He anticipated, in fact, the verdict of the counter-revolutionary Court which charged Leviné with 'dishonourable motives.' 'If the proletariat tolerates leaders like Leviné, it does not deserve a Soviet Republic,' Toller said.[25]

The author of *The Munich Tragedy* gives vivid evidence of the harm caused at that crucial moment by his own Party associates. He even unwittingly confirms the truth of Leviné's claim that a weak, defenceless, proletariat would incur more ruthless treatment than a strong, defiant one.

> Toller's statements, which were of course, immediately communicated to the Hoffmann Government by countless spies *positively provoked it to take vigorous action.*[26]

The town did not fail to notice the changes. Gay, elegant people reappeared in the streets, cars and taxis were about again, shops were crowded, everybody spoke of the Communist reign of terror which would soon be brought to an end. The road for the conquerors lay open.

Leviné was in fact bluffing when he threatened to take stern measures. It was precisely because his government had no longer the power to perform its revolutionary duties that it was determined to resign.

In the last few days Toller had succeeded in forcing through a number of the measures of his group, like lifting the ban on the bourgeois Press, denationalisation of motor-cars and the release of counter-revolutionary prisoners. The endless quarrels with their reluctant allies, with their subtle sabotage, threatened to demoralise the Communist leaders themselves.

One morning Dietrich's wife came to say that her husband had suffered 'a complete breakdown' and would not be able to attend the sessions. He was hoping to come tomorrow.

Levien appeared, his face contorted. He complained of pain in one of his ears and diagnosed inflammation. He was not sure whether he would be any good at work in this state. Hadn't he better stay away for a day or so? He left the room moaning.

'They are leaving the sinking ship' flashed through my mind.

Leviné guessed my thoughts and cautiously stroked my hand. Was he comforting me or himself? He could not bear the slightest doubt in his comrades but his helpless smile was indescribably sad.

The workers were still observing their daily pilgrimage to the Wittelsbach Palace where Fröhlich used to address the huge crowds from the balcony.

That day he was almost in tears. 'I don't know what to say, I am so tired.'

The Soviet Republic was perceptibly crumbling but the Communists had yet to perform a last duty.

Supported by the Red Army who refused to disperse – characteristically even Toller did not dare to make such a demand – and by a considerable number of Factory Councils, they concentrated on the defence of Munich.

It became dangerous to hold public meetings or even to meet openly. In the tense atmosphere of a besieged city, Toller's declarations actually made the Communist leaders – 'the bane of Bavaria' – outlaws. Anything could be expected, even before the invasion. As the danger reached its climax, I thought of the many protestations of the intellectuals of their desire to serve the people, of their remorse for former indifference and their sympathies with the Communists.

I challenged one of them to prove his sincerity in action and to help me to find a hiding place for Leviné. Professor Salz, who had known Leviné from his university days, indeed volunteered to put us both up with his friends – separately, which, as experience had taught, was safer.

This disappearance played a great part at Leviné's trial. His death sentence rested on a charge of 'dishonourable convictions' which was based, in its turn, essentially on his 'cowardly' absence from the battlefield.[27]

A natural emotional reaction against 'running away' undoubtedly also existed among the Communist rank and file, and any demagogue could play on this feeling. Toller who, despite his military duties, disappeared on the mere 'assumption that there would be no fighting' did not fail to speak at his trial of his 'crushing experience on learning of the disappearance of the Communist leaders.'

It will therefore not be amiss to dwell on this sensitive subject.

Many of us indeed feared that Leviné would refuse to go into hiding. An incident at the meeting of 27th April was instrumental in breaking his resistance.

A shot was suddenly fired. Somebody shouted 'The White Guards!' and everybody rushed to the exits. I was sitting a few rows behind Leviné and he made a spontaneous move in my direction. Anxious not to lose him in the stampede, I seized his hand. He thought I was trying to induce him to flee, tore himself away and rushed towards the other end of the hall.

It turned out that the shot had been fired in a private quarrel, but Leviné took his momentary impulse to protect me very seriously. He had thought of me first while he was on duty and might have been needed to prevent panic or set an example!

The incident was later discussed with his close friends and he was severely taken to task for his lapse into false ideas of personal heroism. It was his duty to escape, his friends argued, and not to facilitate the work of the enemy in depriving the workers of their leaders.

Even from the point of view of a fair distribution of danger, the leader, who is far more exposed, has a right to greater protection.

Cold reasoning could not, however, suppress Leviné's desire to share the fate of his comrades.

He said: 'To my *personal consolation* I shall bear in mind that Karl Liebknecht and Rosa Luxemburg met their deaths without fighting hand in hand with the workers.'

He was also obeying a strict order of the Party Executive: 'The military section will take up their positions. You have no further functions to perform and must for the time being disappear.'

Leviné said nothing about his struggle to remain in hiding while the workers were being butchered. But his host and fellow defendant told of his torment and so did a short note which he sent to me. To him this was undoubtedly his hardest task.

He was ready for the end and regarded the last six months as a gift. His famous: 'We Communists are only dead men on leave' was not just a phrase but a deeply felt awareness.

On the 28th of April, Leviné returned late at night from a hard day's work. He was not tired, at least he showed no sign of it. But I found him fast asleep when I had left the room for a moment. He planned to get up early. At 12 o'clock we were to meet Mr Salz and he wanted first to buy me a present, a ring, or some other ornament – a *lasting* keepsake. He could not make it, however. For the first time in the course of those six months he lapsed into one of his old moods. I left the house first so as to be in time for the appointment, hoping that he would soon follow me. But I waited in vain. We were then actually separated and spent the whole day frantically looking for each other. Only towards the evening did one of his messengers run into me in the street and take me to the building of the Luitpold College – the last meeting place of the Communists.

Leviné was for a while quite mute with excitement and remorse.

I (above) Leviné's mother as a young lady and later at St. Petersburg
   (below) Leviné with his sister Sonya in 1890

II Leviné at 20, when he was trying to conform

III   Leviné's first imprisonment at St. Petersburg, 1907

IV   (above) The Authoress in 1915
(below left) a Czarist passport photograph
(below right) The Authoress in 1923

V   Rosa and Eugen Leviné with their son at Bad Rappenau in 1916

VI The leader of the Munich Soviet Republic just after his arrest,
May 13, 1919

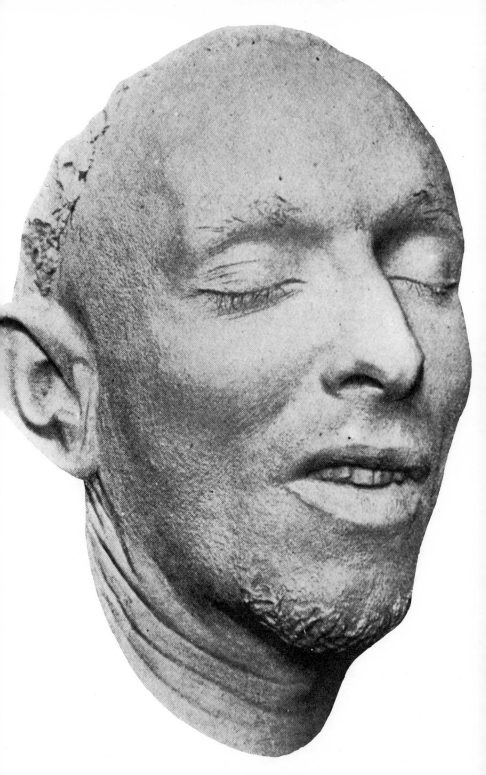

VII Leviné's death-mask

VIII   Leviné's grave at the Israelitische Friedhof in Munich

'All I can say in my defence is that on my arrival here I dropped onto a table and slept for two solid hours.'

It was also the first time he had ever apologised for letting me down.

He was already back at his work and only spent brief moments in the room where I was waiting for him. He wanted me to read the final proclamations. I was to serve as a testing ground.

Once he appeared with a plate of food, a pancake, the most luxurious meal he was ever served during his time of office. He came to share it with me. Holding no official post, I myself was not entitled to food. I somehow convinced him that I was not hungry and he left. The young secretary complimented me on being a good liar and later on insisted on sharing her meal with me. Leviné saw us eating and concluded that I had permitted myself to break the regulations. He was very upset. 'How could you do it?'

This was the first time that Leviné had upbraided me in the presence of another person. No personal discord could ever have provoked him to such an offence.

The girl laughed, 'I have the same right as you to offer your wife food, and she happened to prefer mine.'

But when Leviné left the room she said, 'That was a lesson in truly Communist behaviour. And they are accused of recklessly squandering public property. I shall remember this example all my life.'

Later in the evening, Leviné read out to me the last Party manifesto and I remember some of the sentences:

The White Guards have not yet conquered and are already heaping atrocity upon atrocity. They torture and execute our prisoners. They kill our wounded. Don't make the hangman's work easy. Sell your lives dearly. This is the only way of wresting concessions from the enemy and checking the White terror!

I asked for the last time, 'Is this right? Couldn't you be mistaken? Is it necessary to fight?'

Not only did I, like any normal person, instinctively abhor bloodshed, I was in a way fighting for the life of my husband which I believed might be less endangered if he called off the battle.

I ought to have known better after my recent experience.

An ostensibly peaceful movement for socialisation initiated in the previous March by the Berlin Workers' Council 'calmly and circumspectly in contrast to the Communist ways,' was seized upon by the government on the pretext of ridding itself of the undesirable Republican-Security Troops and turned into one of the most sanguinary episodes to date of the German revolution. It was estimated that it claimed some 1,200 casualties. The bloodshed was duly ascribed to the criminal Communists, and their foremost leader, Leo Jogiches, was brutally murdered for good measure.

The experience shook me deeply, yet I was still trying. It is difficult to absorb lessons which run contrary to what one regards as one's own interests.

Leviné saw my fears and spared no effort to make me understand his policy:

We are facing an incensed soldiery sent to make 'a thorough sweep of criminal elements endangering the very life of the country.' It is a fallacy to believe that meek surrender is a better way to avoid or reduce bloodshed. On the contrary: only when they find a bold, determined army and realise that the battle might claim casualties in their own ranks will they be inclined to make concessions. No warlord ever considered laying down arms *in advance* as a means of achieving better peace terms and this is preached to the proletariat which is engaged in a struggle a thousand times more ruthless.

The workers, the best of them, will fight whatever our instructions. A revolutionary is no less ready to give his life in upholding the *honour of his cause* than the patriot who fights to the last ditch preferring death to surrender. The workers would only despise a leader who fell below their own standards of revolutionary honour and preached, *in advance*, the laying down of arms. It might seem irrational but then no great achievements were ever accomplished without this spirit.

The White Army will, in any case, find a pretext for a bloodbath. They need this, and the extent of the slaughter will be determined by political calculations alone, by nothing else. Is workers' blood so cheap as to let it flow unopposed for the satisfaction of newly converted pacifists?

I know it is difficult to accept this hard truth. Toller's protestations of his abhorrence of bloodshed are much more appealing. Yet during the war our roles were reversed: The party of the soft-hearted Independents was not afraid of bloodshed and supported the capitalist government in the alleged 'defensive war,' and we were in the front lines of the fight against such carnage. It all depends on your aims and on where you stand. Could there be a more clear-cut defensive war than the one which is forced upon us? No one would be happier than the bloodthirsty Communists if the Independents could persuade the White Army to abstain from fighting. We don't want the fight, nor do we need it.

Are you convinced? Hard days lie ahead. We must at least be able to feel that they could not be averted.

It was the last private lesson Leviné afforded me.

Leviné's decision to give battle was never understood even by Communist leaders. All or most of them had studied their Marx and were acquainted with his views of defenceless retreat, but accepting a theory and having the courage to carry it out in practice are two different things.

The then highly authoritative German leader, Paul Levy, took from the start a by no means unequivocal view:

To head a movement which has been set in motion against our explicit warnings and is leading to disaster – this we are not obliged to do.

He was much more inclined to advocate unconditional surrender, though admitting that this solution could not be achieved because 'a great number of workers would fight in any case.'[28]

The Party limited itself to lavishing praise on Leviné's personality and tacitly avoided, to the great harm of the German revolutionary movement, dwelling on the controversial issue. This was left to other sources.

The author of *The Munich Tragedy*, published by the Independents in attempted apology for their own sorry part in it, staunchly upholds the prestige of his Party friends Toller and Klingelhofer, who laudably tried 'at all costs to prevent bloodshed.'

'Negotiations with Bamberg,' he concluded, 'would certainly have led to some kind of agreement and would have been politically more expedient and more prudent than any other course of action that could be envisaged.'

Unfortunately, the expediency and prudence of the generals are at variance with those of the revolution as the same author had to admit: 'This policy was, of course, paralysed [!] by the declaration of the generals that they refused to negotiate. In an interview given to the *Berliner Tageblatt* General Haas emphatically stated that they refused to enter into negotiations. Noske, the Reichswehr Minister, was of the same spirit. In an interview with the same paper he said that the Munich madmen must be swept away, "even at the cost of bloodshed".'

What then? The author prefers not to answer. He was from the start not very confident about the value of negotiations. All he could promise was 'some kind of agreement' which is an exceedingly vague notion.

More criticism followed:

'An actual military struggle became unavoidable only after Leviné decided that it must be so, a decision based on unwillingness rather than inability to surrender a hopeless position. Defeat, not struggle, was unavoidable,' says Alan Mitchell, the author of *Revolution in Bavaria 1918–1919*, and he boldly condemns Leviné's decision as 'foolish and unjustifiably criminal' (p. 329).

This belated critic aptly summarises all that has been said over many years.

Who decided 'that it must be so' during the first encounter? Why was the struggle not avoidable under Toller's reign?

Why had Toller felt obliged to issue 800 rifles after all, as the critic testifies himself? (p. 321).

Why did the workers take up arms in defence of a hopeless position, Leviné having *repeatedly* warned that the position was hopeless?

Why had the Workers' and Soldiers' Council, entirely dominated by the Independents, referred the power to the Communists?

The critics prefer not to go into details and difficult analysis. Least of all have they taken the trouble to explain in *concrete terms how* the surrender should have been carried out in practice?

Evacuate the town? Arrest and deliver the leaders? How many? Hand over all arms? Who would do the job?

Would not the generals rightly consider themselves better fitted to carry out their intended 'clean sweep' of all relics of the revolution?

The critics would not know the answers and nor did Toller. For Hoffman preferred to liquidate the 'hopeless situation' in his own way.

It had been forgotten that Munich was regarded as a trouble spot and was for some time due for 'pacification.'

Leviné denounced the proclamation of the Soviet Republic as a pretext for bringing in the army, as a *provocation* and such sincere political observers as Philip Price, Sir George Young and *The Times*, obviously shared his opinion.

Sebastian Haffner summarises the situation in the following words:

Never before was a revolutionary party forced into action in an inflammable situation against its will and with such cynicism.

Never were the militant workers so severely punished for it.

Never was a game so clearly envisaged by a superior, not only 'equal' opponent.

Never had a revolutionary party resisted with such determination taking part in an ostensibly revolutionary action.

Never had a revolutionary party to master such a bizarre, daily changing situation.

Ebert urged for a speedy intervention, cautioning that 'people might get used to it.'

Yet the Communist danger no longer existed. The new government did its utmost to demonstrate its servility. Under the prevailing conditions there was no need for military intervention.

It is true that the Red Army still existed. But it was determined to fight because it was not given to them simply to surrender arms. Unlike the regular soldier the Redarmist is punishable for merely carrying arms. By no stretch of the imagination, however, could the Red Army at that stage be feared as an attacking power. It was then up to Hoffmann's Government to conclude the Republic peacefully.

Shedding blood appears, however, to be the prerogative of the strong and mighty. Characteristically none of Leviné's valiant critics had ever questioned the right of Hoffmann to restore his sovereignty by bloodshed, though his first assault was directed against a *non-Communist*, harmless, 'human' Soviet Republic and at a moment when it was already tottering and when even the sceptical Leviné believed that 'everything would resolve amicably.' It was in fact this armed intervention that brought things to a head and laid the foundations of the Communist Soviet Republic.

Neither was there an undue outcry against the massacre of the hundreds – thousands? – of those who did not answer Leviné's call for resistance.

In this connection it is worth noting that equal indulgence was shown towards the workers who took up arms against Hoffmann in an equally 'senseless' battle. Leviné never promised ultimate victory, he never failed to outline the strictly limited objectives of the struggle.

That time the workers had conquered and – as victory goes – they disposed a great number of people in their favour. The Communists who ostensibly inspired the fight were acclaimed heroes overnight. It was for a while generously overlooked that a more serious military encounter against an exclusively Communist rule was imminent.

Leviné's reasoning might be dismissed as the conjecture of one of those cranky dogmatists, indifferent to human suffering and life.

Here is the testimony of a non-Communist, a well-known writer, Laurens van der Post, strongly corroborating Leviné's views. He witnessed the moral results of a defenceless surrender in a Japanese prisoner-of-war camp for Allied Captives, and said in a radio talk in 1966:

> This is the thing which is very difficult for people to realise – that the human being is deeply humiliated by capitulation – particularly by the kind of capitulation that had been inflicted on our people in Java. They had no guns, most of them, and those who had guns had not been allowed to fight. They had to surrender without making a fight for it. If you have fought to the last bit and surrender is forced upon you, there is a kind of redemption in it. But if you have surrendered without a fight, as these chaps did, they felt bitter about it, they felt humiliated. They felt that the general defeat had become a personal defeat. Everybody felt the defeat, nobody trusted one another. The whole order of life seemed to have broken down.

In an attempt to raise the morale of his fellow-prisoners Van der Post 'foolishly' told them:

'There is a way of losing which becomes a form of winning and this is how we are going to lead our lives in the camp.'

Van der Post learned this lesson 'from within'. It is the gift of Leviné to correctly assess a condition without immediate practical experience.

Sebastian Haffner says in the *Betrayed Revolution*, 'A fortress which surrenders without fighting to the last ditch carries the curse of dishonour.'

A further testimony may be derived from German history.

In October 1923, the Communist party leader Brandler called off a battle 'to save the workers from a useless massacre' – with catastrophic results. The outraged workers lost their heads and made a sweeping dash in an ultra left direction from which the German Communist movement never recovered. Characteristically, the workers turned their back on their 'saviour' Brandler, and cherished the memory of Leviné who called for 'senseless resistance.' And the abortive battle of the so-called 'Hamburg Barricades' *unwittingly* unleashed at the same time by Thälmann, stood him in good stead and largely contributed to the heroic image the Party created of him.

Leviné took me to the assembly hall to say good-bye to our friends. None of them failed to take his stand, none 'deserted the sinking ship.' They were now in their true element, no longer exhausted by the fruitless quarrels with alleged allies. And they knew how to meet danger. Each of them had pledged his life and was prepared to face the end destined for him.

As on the first evening of their rule they again resembled a church congregation, serene in their triumphant belief in the impending ultimate victory. The present defeat, which could not be denied, was regarded as a momentary episode which would soon be swept away.

We both left the hall. It was the last time I saw Leviné at liberty.

IV

I was walking through deserted streets to my place of hiding. It was late at night. Sirens were screaming, distant shots rang out, here and there patrols could be seen – were they friends or foes? The town was divided into two camps and I was again an outcast.

A short while ago we were the oppressors. Was it better? I recalled what Leviné had taught me in the last six months:

'Up to now a small minority has ruled over an overwhelming majority and we propose to suppress a small section of people, and that only *temporarily*; only during the acute danger of a violent restoration of the old order.'

This period could not possibly last, he explained; his faith in the imminent world revolution was invincible. And afterwards:

The privileges of the "suppressors", the workers, will be wide open to everybody, including the bourgeoisie. All they need is to accept our mode of life, which is to work 'according to their ability.' Never before in history, for obvious reasons, could the privileged classes offer the masses such complete equality.

Leviné did not shut his eyes to the cruelty inherent in the struggle: 'Revolutions cannot be made with soft, compassionate hearts, it demands a stern, relentless will.'

Lenin expressed it in his unequivocal admission that 'Dictatorship is a harsh word, a painful word, a bloody word.'

'Isn't there another solution?'

'Yes, to wait until man has become so perfect that "the wolf would lie down with the lamb." That would certainly be the ideal form of human relationship. The Christian Church has been preaching it for 2,000 years and the wolf has not stopped devouring the lamb.

'We Communists have lost our patience and are trying to

begin at the other end – to remove the teeth of the wolf – don't be alarmed: we only want to remove the power to molest others.

'This is what was always considered as the first step to socialism: to deprive the capitalists of the power to exploit the people for their own selfish ends.'

'Wasn't it always held that socialism will arise out of a world of plenty?'

'That view will have to be amended. Experience has taught that it was poor, ruined Russia and not America or England who first made the revolution. And in Germany? Never before during the period of plenty did the masses cry out so tempestuously for socialism.

'The misery and destruction caused by the war demand drastic measures. The Government promises socialism in words.

'Socialisation on the way!' scream its official papers, for it does not dare to oppose it openly. All its campaigns against the revolutionary workers were conducted under that very cover. But it fights every attempt to put it into practice. And the Independents provide the quasi-theoretical excuses: "Socialism must arise out of plenty." And they leave the factories in the hands of the capitalists.

'The shattered industries must be rebuilt – on what basis?

'They intend to re-erect the capitalist fortress first and to storm it afterwards. We believe that history offers us a chance to rebuild the country on socialist principles, without the capitalists, now. We must seize it, or we forfeit the right to call ourselves socialists.

'It will be a hard struggle. The bourgeoisie will not relinquish its privileges peacefully. Injustice, blunders, even acts of cruelty can unfortunately not be prevented. One must decide on which side one is and what one is striving for. Any changes that humanity has attempted on a large-scale have involved great sacrifices. The present European parliamentary states which are held up as an example are all the result of violent revolutions.

'But parliamentary democracy has never been practised in its true sense: *government by the people*. We regard the Soviet system as the most effective means of making democracy a living reality. The man in the street is called upon to play his part in the destiny of the country not, as is the rule in a parliamentary state, once in a fixed number of years, but hot on the heels of any crucial event. He is thus encouraged to reflect, discuss, watch, form an independent opinion. He is trained to participate in political affairs. He is empowered above all to recall at any time an incompetent or unworthy representative.

'Far from stifling democracy – another accusation hurled at us – we endeavour to remove by these means all dictations from above and create the conditions leading to the abolition of the state itself.'

Leviné persistently stressed this aspect of the Soviet system:

'You are the engineers, we are only your temporary advisers. Control us and chase us away if you find us wanting and replace us by worthier men.

'...The government must only hold the threads and control them but the threads must be woven and brought into its hands by the proletariat. I do not appeal to you to collaborate, I appeal to you to do the job, just as you yourself have won the battle.'

It was not mere propaganda stuff. This was the society the socialists were always striving for. Lenin wrote:

Very often delegations of workers and peasants come and ask what to do. I say to them: You are the government, do as you please, take all you want. We will support you. But take care of production. Take up useful work. You will make mistakes, but you will learn.[1]

Leviné helped me to get rid of my aversion to 'Marxism' which was skilfully inculcated into people of my class and environment. We confused it with personal cynicism and ruthlessness. The device 'dictatorship of the proletariat' seemed a good case to prove it.

Cloudy conceptions and highfalutin words are much more attractive than the cold 'materialistic' teaching that our very thought and feeling is determined by the material conditions of our life, yet it has nothing to do with lack of personal idealism. Indeed it would be inexplicable why so many of the hard materialists devote their lives to creating a better world, while the adherents of the idealistic philosophy find it possible to share in the privileges of a society based on injustice and corruption.

A revolutionary party could not be created without attracting the best elements of our society – the idealists. Without satisfying their moral aspirations, it would fall to pieces.

The later apologists of Stalin's atrocities alleged that everything is permissible as long as it serves the revolution: 'Ends justify means.'

A revolutionary party must beware of means which are not in harmony with the ends, or it might find that the achieved ends are not at all the ends they were aiming at.

Working-class consciousness cannot be genuinely political unless the workers are trained to respond to *all* cases of abuse, tyranny, oppression, violence, no matter what class is affected.

We have nothing with which to fight capitalist society, equipped with all the power of a modern state, except the power of our ideas.

It is another of those misconceptions to believe that we can have an unbiased view in matters of class-struggle. Our judgement is built from the start on the premise of the sanctified present social order; it has been instilled into us for generations. The so-called objectivity is therefore in the last analysis a stand against revolutionary changes – against the working class. To be really 'objective' we must first decide on which side we stand: with the oppressed or with the tenacious champions of the privileged minority.

I made my choice and was ready to accept what was destined for me as Leviné's companion. I shall try not to fail him to the end of my life.

My host was a Turk, a man of some distinction whose friendship with Salz dated from the German-Turkish war alliance. He occupied as a sub-tenant a luxurious flat, complete with a devoted servant-girl. As an inmate of such a flat I was beyond suspicion even if I never left the house. This was explained by my delicate condition which was not far from the truth.

The good-natured girl, therefore, lovingly looked after me. To cheer me up she also supplied me with current news.

'They have just carried away a Communist leader! Levien was arrested and terribly beaten up! Leviné was discovered disguised in a cellar!' she would gleefully announce, running in and out of my room.

With bated breath I would ask for some description of the captives. No, Leviné and Levien were not among them.

She brought guns, a great many, a whole arsenal:

'We were clever' she said: 'We stored our arms with the caretaker. He was exempted from searches and we could rely on him. They could then search us to their hearts' content.'

On the whole the day passed quietly. It was May Day. Presumably as a concession to its sponsors, a predominantly Social-Democratic government, the Army decided not to provoke the workers, by an ostentatious disregard of a cherished traditional celebration and to enter the town on the second, the next day. But something forced the Army's hand.

It was discovered early in the morning that ten hostages held by the Communists in the cellar of the Luitpold College had been shot dead.

It was never established who ordered the shooting.

None of the Communist leaders were at that time in the building. Leviné for one left it long in advance of the deplorable act and was officially cleared of having any part in it.

The shooting was presumably an act of desperate people aroused by the atrocities of the White Guards, who, felt that all bridges were burnt behind them.

The indiscriminate shooting of everyone connected with, or even suspected of connection with, the Communists clearly justified this feeling if not the unfortunate conclusion.

The assassins paid dearly for their folly: Six of those responsible for the shooting were sentenced to death; ten to fifteen years' hard labour; three of the accused received their sentences for no other reason than 'encouraging the murder by their readiness to eventually carry out the order themselves.'[3]

The victims were members of the notorious Tula-Society, an early Nazi group, whose membership included Rudolf Hess, and were arrested for acute counter-revolutionary activity. They could not in any way be classified as hostages'.

In its official proclamation the new military Governor supplemented the unfortunate news with the statement that 'the corpses had been mutilated beyond recognition.'

This unleashed tales of cut off fingers, put out eyes: the entire vocabulary of wartime atrocity came back to life.

The fury within and outside the town reached its pitch. The act called for immediate revenge. The Army advanced and by the early evening of the 1st May, the battle was in full swing.

The news was brought to me by Salz himself. I had learned to be careful about 'Communist atrocities' but this was an officially confirmed act. Salz was shaking with indignation and – fear. It was one thing to shelter a fugitive revolutionary, another a man guilty of a sadistic massacre.

'I ought to have known better,' Salz muttered, pacing the room. 'And I put a close friend in danger. I must do something... something,' he kept on repeating.

'Something' was nothing short of delivering Leviné directly into the hands of the executioners. There was no room for him in the whole large city. Salz was well aware of it, and this only deepened his conflict.

The temptation to rid himself and his *friend* of an overt danger was almost irresistible. I was watching him in horror. If I could only reassure him of Leviné's innocence! But he was there, I had left him in the Luitpold gymnasium, the scene of the murder. What did I know of the implications of a revolutionary struggle? What forced Leviné to commit an act which to all intents and purposes could only 'mar the revolution' – which he was so anxious to avoid?

I reminded Salz that he sheltered a *revolutionary* – how did we know what that meant? – and implored him not to condemn him out of hand.

He was still pacing the room in desperation but his natural integrity prevailed. He touched my shoulder:

'He will be safe with us, whatever the price.'

It was a high price, demanding great moral courage. It is true, the court was very lenient and found 'no convincing basis for a crime of aiding and a betting high treason, nor sufficient evidence of encouraging it.'

It released Salz and Leviné's host, Botho Schmidt, immediately after Leviné's trial. But three weeks in prison in the heated atmosphere of a besieged city was no small ordeal. Salz was, in addition, dismissed from his professorial post and compelled to leave Bavaria.

The Army took the town almost unapposed. The Workers' Councils, as the official Soviet Government, tried their best to demonstrate their goodwill and submissiveness. To prove it they called for a peaceful 1st May demonstration 'with wives and children.'

Toller also took the line of appeasement. He testified at his trial that he was knew very well of the atrocities committed by the Whites but deliberately concealed it from the Workers' Councils.

The Executive of the Social-Democratic Party vouched that 'the troops of Hoffmann's Socialist Government are not enemies of the workers, not White Guards. They come to safeguard public order and security.'

It appealed to the workers not to resist but to 'help the soldiers to carry out their arduous task... to obey the orders of surrendering arms.'

Only a handful of workers rallied to resist the onslaught. As Leviné predicted: 'There will always be a number of foolhardy heroes ready to fight for their lives and defend the honour of the revolution.'

According to official figures, no more than 93 Red Armists and 38 soldiers fell in battle.

Nevertheless, the military operation lasted several days. To achieve security and order of their type it was essential to thoroughly 'smoke out the Spartacists' nests.' According to official estimates this operation cost 370 lives. Other sources more qualified and objective put the number of victims into the 600–700 bracket. Lastly, Professor Gumbel, after a thorough investigation, quoted in his book *Four Years Murder* the ominous number of 2,000!

People were dragged out of bed, shot, knifed, beaten to a pulp.

The savagery of the troops did not frighten off the Executive of the Social-Democratic Party. It still gave assurance that 'The Hoffmann Government is not opposed to the Soviet principle' and that 'comrade Hoffmann... is a thoroughgoing champion of the socialist movement. His collaborators are Social-Democrats like yourself.'

And they also endorsed the proclamation of martial law, which was staring from the walls in sinister large black letters. It was signed jointly by Lieutenant General and Commander in Chief von Oven and Dr Ewinger on behalf of Hoffmann's Government.

A 'regrettable incident' put an end to the indiscriminate butchery. The victors committed a great blunder. Instead of Communists or 'red suspects,' they murdered twenty-one Catholic journeymen who innocently gathered at a regular meeting and were denounced by some zealous burgher.

The unfortunate lads were beaten, kicked, pierced with bayonets, stamped upon. Broken sticks and bent sabres were exhibited at the subsequent trial.

The incident had a very sobering effect. Death was penetrating into their own midst, the victims could not by any stretch of imagination be identified with Reds. People who had rejoiced in the blood bath and overwhelmed the soldiers with gifts and cheers became apprehensive. The troops issued a proclamation, forbidding 'taking the law into your own hands.' Lynching and indiscrimate shooting was thus discouraged.

But this was only one and perhaps a less essential part of 'mopping up the revolution.' The working class, divided and still under the influence of the socialist parties, presented no great danger. It became a serious menace only under the guidance of the Communists and chiefly of Leviné. He must be rendered innocuous, silenced forever.

Everything was concentrated then on his capture. A reward of 10,000 marks attracted a horde of professional and amateur spies. The authorities were assailed by eager informers. They were growing very impatient. The hunt was progressively intensified.

Salz visited me regularly and kept me informed of the general mood and events.

He was satisfied that Leviné had had no part in the shooting of the hostages and showed great sympathy with both of us. On his last visit, he reassured me that everything was being done for Leviné's safety. His host would keep him for as long as was necessary. He had grown very attached to Leviné and admired him to a point of worship. The flat had been searched twice and Salz was told that Leviné was saved by his own truly supreme composure.

'He has cast a magic spell on his host. No wonder you love him so much,' Salz smiled.

I dared then to make a heartfelt request. The tenth of May was Leviné's birthday and I wanted to send him flowers. Could Salz do it for me?

It was not an easy assignment and Salz sighed:

'Oh well, we are all crazy.'

It was the last I ever saw of him but he fulfilled my request. Two days later a new intermediary appeared and brought me a letter, the first direct link with Leviné himself:

> 12th May.
>
> Dear Oslenochek!
>
> At last I can send you a few words, my love, my dear. You were all the time beside me and my heart rejoiced when I thought of the last period of our life.
>
> During all those desperate hours, hours of terror, I was full of those memories. I recalled our talks, your words, your kisses and caresses. Don't be sad Oslishechko. I am cheerful and full of energy. In spite of all the distress, I am looking to the future with confidence. As to us, I firmly hope that we shall be together very soon. And together with the child before my departure.
>
> I am writing in a great hurry, my own one. The deliverer of the letter has to leave. I kiss you, kiss your eyes,

lips, shoulders, kiss you, fondle you and feel the joy of your presence. Don't despair Oslishechko. Your flowers gave me great pleasure. I knew they would come, relished them in advance and enjoyed them when they really arrived. They were brought to me by the deliverer of this letter. I am fond of him and trust him like a brother. Speak to him freely.

I kiss you, kiss you my love. I thank you again for the last days. I am waiting, waiting ardently for more and more of them.

Yours T.

I kiss all of you again. And in spite of all the horror – we knew that it was unavoidable – it is spring, spring... .

The new intermediary, Zimmer, told me that I had to change quarters and I was moved into a flat shared by three young girls. They had helped many a fugitive to cross the frontier and would look after me well.

It was a great relief: I could throw off the disguise and breathe fresh air again. With the letter under my pillow I slept peacefully for the first time and woke up in a sheer ecstasy of gaiety. All the accumulated suppressed horror of the last days found this peculiar outlet. I was humming, dancing, talking to myself, flirting with myself, beside myself. But the hysterical outburst did not last. I suddenly became aware that something dark and sinister was descending on me.

The girls knew already. Leviné was arrested on the day he wrote the letter and while making the last preparations for his flight. A certain Matissen, a Doctor of Theology, who had offered his own, very fitting papers for Leviné's escape, betrayed him.

At nine o'clock in the evening the house was surrounded by lorries with a large detachment of soldiers who entered the flat and arrested him.

Leviné saw the lorries. This time, he knew, his demeanour would not save him. They knew who he was even before they entered the house.

He was brought up the same night for interrogation and the next morning the news of his arrest was released in an extra edition.

One of the girls silently gave me the paper... . Out of the mist one thought clearly took shape: I must see him!

We had a lawyer friend who could advise me and he came immediately. He had already seen Leviné in prison and told me, over-whelmed, that he was completely calm and composed.

He held out no hope for us: juridically there was not the slightest basis for a death sentence but a military court would hardly respect civil laws. Leviné was too dangerous to this society. They would not let him go. Much, however, depended on Leviné's own behaviour. He should demean himself a little, should try to appease the Court.

The shooting of the hostages was, in fact, the only incriminating point. He should resolutely condemn it.

Our friend had tried to impress on Leviné that this line of defence was the only way to save his life, but did not believe he had succeeded. There was, however, hope that he might respond to my pleas. If I were permitted to see him, I should try. He promised to let me know when to come out of my retreat.

I was arrested next day, on 14th May. There was a woman spy in the girls' midst. She guessed that something was going on in the flat and sent a police squad to search it. By the time they arrived, my room was already cleared and the police were quite satisfied of my innocence. I personally was only concerned with saving the letter. Hidden casually in a drawer among toilet articles it had so far escaped their attention. I told the spy who I was and begged her to save the letter for me. She was genuinely moved. She was a woman, not only a spy. But she was too committed and gave me away. A commissar reappeared, 'found' the letter and led me away.

I was interogated by the Public Prosecutor who was initially entrusted with Leviné's case. Unfortunately, I do not recall the name of this fine man. He must have been considered too soft-hearted for his role, for he was soon replaced by another prosecutor, Mr Hahn, a man of stronger nerves.

Aware of what was ahead of me he did his utmost to spare me the discomfort of prison. He subtly taught me to avoid incriminating answers and sometimes went so far as formulating them for me himself.

'Of course you can see your husband,' he consoled me, and hastily issued the permit.

There was no case against me, he concluded. He would order my immediate release.

Human charity is indeed indestructible and finds its way even into such places! The final decision, however, no longer rested with him. I was kept in so-called 'protective custody.' But my permit to see my husband was not revoked.

The door of Leviné's cell stood open and I saw him first. He was standing in the middle of the cell adjusting, as I realised later, the chains on his wrists. He did not expect to see me, visibly staggered and grew terribly pale.

When he recovered, he used all his eloquence to console me.

'It could have been far, far worse. How often have I escaped death in the Rhineland and Berlin! And I was saved from the Vorwaerts' débâcle by a sheer miracle. We were given six more months. How fortunate we are! We can see each other, talk.... They might permit you to come again and also a last farewell visit.'

He had no illusions about his fate.

'We must be prepared for the worst. Should we be spared – well, we will accept it as a great, unexpected gift.'

He spoke hastily, trying to cram all he could into the short time allotted to us.

He had sent for his mother – 'For your sake,' he added.

A factory had sent him a parcel of bread. 'Only bread!' crossed my mind.

'How thoughtful and moving! I have friends, I am not forgotten!' he said, putting me to shame as he used to on similar occasions.

A strange unfamiliar sound was creeping in from somewhere. I suddenly noticed the chains.

'Oh, this.' He smiled 'It is my Iron Cross; our enemies think that I well deserve it and honour me in their own way.'

After the massacre of the twenty-one Catholic journeymen, lynching was officially forbidden. But the authorities did their best to provoke some thoughtful man to relieve them of the ticklish task of murdering Leviné legally. He was heavily chained and the door of his cell stood wide open, positively inviting an assault.

On the morning after his arrest a crowd of some fifteen incensed clerks burst screaming, with raises arms, into the cell.

Leviné said, "Gentlemen, I am alone". Impressed by Leviné's composure, one of them suddenly threw himself protectively in front of Leviné and saved him from a terrible death.

The cell was nevertheless still kept open. Soldiers were constantly patrolling the corridors, entering his cell and keeping him in a state of great suspense. With only one warder at his side another more successful incident could be expected at any time.

Many came just to gaze at the bloodthirsty tyrant and could hardly suppress their disappointment.

'Oh!' exclaimed one young soldier. 'Is this all!'

There was also a steady flow of various commissions. Many came under rather flimsy pretexts, obviously also to satisfy their curiosity.

At one of these invasions a young commissar, apparently aware of the sensational value of 'last words,' attempted to profit from the occasion. He rushed back into the cell and asked Leviné to write something in his album.

Leviné saw his cold, greedy eyes and wrote, 'I wish you to choose before long a worthier career than the present one.'

I was also besieged by curious interviewers and Leviné wanted me to repeat every word I said.

He abhorred publicity, and wanted to be sure, that I had not failed him. I had not.

There was, however, a time when I broke my restraint, but this I had to keep to myself: a spokesman of a military commission who visited me asked whether my husband would wish to take leave of his child?

He volunteered to telegraph for me and make the necessary arrangements. But we must hurry, there was not much time left.

To expose the futility of the trial, I asked then how he could be so certain before the court pronounced its verdict.

'This is beyond any doubt,' he answered emphatically.

I told Leviné of the lawyer's advice: an outright condemnation of the hostages case would influence the court very favourably.

'Which would amount to joining the victors in kicking the prostrated Munich proletariat,' he smiled.

No, it could not be done. I would not 'plead' and he stroked my hand in appreciation. That was all.

Yes, he slept soundly.

'Of course, I eat. There is plenty of food.'

Food was a hallowed object in the home of his mother. It was tenderly discussed and described.

'You must cook with love,' I had heard his mother saying, and Leviné himself took pleasure in exquisite meals and was a great connoisseur of food. He had taught me to eat some – to me – unknown delicacies and he always chose my meals in restaurants.

But I saw him cheerfully eating up the horrible concoctions of German wartime kitchens, which I could never be persuaded to touch. Neither was he disturbed by the appalling hygienic conditions, smells and not very appetising human environment of which he was quite aware and would describe to me with great humour.

It always puzzled me. Was it a result of an early conditioning to the vagaries of the life of a proletarian leader? It certainly stood him in good stead throughout his Russian wanderings and sustained his physical strength for his last task in Munich.

He was treated well. He nodded in a friendly way to his warder who kept on stealthily mopping his eyes, as he said apologetically:

'You see, we were told that your husband ordered the execution of 10,000 prison warders and policemen. My wife is affectionate and frail, very much like yourself. You will know how she felt.'

This man had not been on duty during the invasion of the lynching crowd but he assured me that my husband was now safe. The entire staff knew that they had been deceived and would protect him to a man.

We had to speak German but the warder never interfered when Leviné lowered his voice to speak of his mood and other intimate subjects. He could even whisper some tender Russian words which he could never bring himself to say in German.

The warders treated Leviné with such overt reverence and sympathy that the authorities grew wary of his influence and found it advisable to keep on changing the warders.

But this did not prevent the staff from demonstrating their sympathy in every way.

During our confinement at the Munich Police Headquarters we could communicate almost freely with each other. The pretty girl with whom I was sharing a cell received generous food parcels and our wardress agreed to take gifts to him.

On my birthday, the 18th May, she brought me his last present a bar of chocolate. The hard, Junoesque woman was quite transfigured with delight.

To make me worthy of Leviné, I was naively endowed with imaginary wealth and titles. I heard many a story of this from fellow political prisoners.

The place became a sort of a sanctuary to us and we were very distressed when we were informed one morning of our transfer to the Stadelheim prison.

We were allowed a few minutes for saying good-bye and I always secretly suspected that we owed this to a daring stratagem of the prison staff itself. This higher authorities were not very forthcoming with permits.

Leviné stormed and bitterly complained to his lawyers that after our transfer to Stadelheim we had to wait for ten long days.

He was initially convinced that in a few days all would be over. When it became evident that he was facing a longer procedure, he started to write a diary for me.

'The copy-book to my wife (several weeks later),

The Spartacus-Programme to my boy.

Please give these pages to my wife, Isa-Rosa Leviné after my execution?'

The first entry carries the date of 16th May and the first sentences are an almost uncanny repetition of a letter from his Russian prison to a certain 'Miss R.'

Police Headquarters, Munich, Friday, 16th May, 9 o'clock a.m.

Dearest!

Will these pages be handed over to you? Perhaps. On this 'perhaps' I am writing to you. Wirting and talking to you and so I feel you close to me in these my last days. I see your eyes and lips, caress your hands and tell you how I feel, what I think in these last days. And when our little boy grows up, he too will read these pages, will know how much his Father loved his Mother, will try to give her much affection and make up for the loss. Do you know, darling, how I always wanted a little girl? Now I am glad that we have a boy. He will stand by you, will support you, advise you, will certainly even as a youth, be of great help to you. It is true many years will have to go by till then. Our poor baby! At present he is little and helpless himself. My heart convulses, but I.... .

There he stopped. He could not go on. He explained it to me at our first meeting: he was preparing for a last battle and was determined to avoid anything which might undermine his strength and break his spirit.

He tried to resume writing next day. The diary registered: '17th May' but he left it at that. He continued to write several days later in his new prison.

Stadelheim

25th May (Sunday) 6 o'clock p.m.

Darling!

9 days have passed since I started writing to you and

I suddenly stopped. You know why, I told you. And then a lot of people kept on coming who disturbed me: representatives of Military Police, of the Voluntary Corps, Oberland, of the County Court, police commissars – an endless coming and going. I was no longer alone with you, I stopped, I could not write. Next day you came yourself. What joy it was! Do you really know, Oslik, *how* glad I was? Was I able to show it to you? Have you felt it, my darling? It was so good that you were permitted to stay so long. I was so happy to hear your voice, to see you, to feel you at my side.

Here he stopped again but he could no longer afford long interruptions. Time was running out.

Ascension Day, 29th May, 7 o'clock p.m.

Dearest, dearest, dearest!

It is getting serious. On Monday the trial begins. This sudden haste is disquieting. It was intended to interrogate innumerable witnesses – but it suddenly seems unnecessary.

And so it is coming to an end, dearest, dearest, dearest! Daily, hourly I am thinking of you. I speak to you, hold you in my arms, console you, Oslik, little Oslik! I could not write all those days. I had a tiny little flame of hope. And to keep my chin up, I artificially fanned it. Lived as if nothing was looming over me. Ate, drank, read. But in these pages I must be honest. Should I continue my self-deception here? No, I could not do it. I was writing to you! To you I could not lie. And had I told you the truth? Then all my laboriously constructed house of cards would have collapsed. And so I gave up writing. And yet I was always with you and waited daily, hourly to see you, yourself. In vain. Shall I see you again? Darling, darling, dearest darling!

I am writing with clenched teeth. When the warder looks through the iron bars, he must not see how I feel. Dearest, dearest, I kiss you!

I am very sad, I am filled with such deep sadness. Death itself does not concern me. A few last minutes, the rattle of the guns, perhaps my last salute to the world revolution. Oh, it is not that. Not death, not dying, but parting with life. But how terrible when life is meaningless and one is only obsessed with the fear of death. No, in spite of my sadness, I am serene and happy. And for this I thank you, dearest.

Without you my life would not be complete. Yes, it was made rich and purposeful through my work, through the privilege of taking part in this struggle. But you have brought fulfilment. Dearest, dearest, dearest. I kiss your forehead, eyes and lips and thank you for everything, everything. Thank you for your gift to me of yourself; thank you for my little boy who will live on as part of me; thank you also for myself whom you have changed and improved. Thank you above all for yourself for you, for you.

Dearest, if you knew what quiet and peaceful happiness it gives me to be able to pour out my heart to you once more.

I read the other day the II part of Faust and some words of the haunted me. Facing execution by her husband, Hélène said: 'Pain I feel, not fear.' These words were spoken out of my own heart. I have been repeating them all these days. For I too felt no fear but pain, pain.

But now I have overcome it. While I am writing I feel a great calm coming over me. I am composed now. I am still sad, but my sadness is interspersed with glimpses of joy when I think of all the happy hours of our life together.

During the first few days I always had before my eyes you and the baby – abandoned and lonely – and could have cried with pain. Darling, even now I must not think of it, nor will I! You are not angry with me? For I am not able to. No, I will conjure up peaceful, gentle images. And you know, in my memory two pictures are fused. You sitting beside me on my plank bed and the boy riding on my knees with the rattling chains. It seems to me that both happened at the same time and I see you both together.

Darling, it is getting dark and I am going to bed. But before falling asleep I shall quietly recall past memories for a while.

Do you remember how I came home for the last time late at night, sitting beside you and telling you all that had happened! And how young and pretty you were and how glad that I said so? And how silly you were to think that it only seemed so to me!.... A tiny, tiny sapling of hope tries to germinate and sprout again. Nonsense, Tjulen! Be sensible! Nothing doing! It is the end!

This foolish little sapling which is trying to make me believe that we shall be reunited once more, be happy... who knows? Perhaps? – Well, that would be an unexpected, great gift. I must, however, come to terms with the other extreme. And I shall be content if tomorrow you get a permit to see me. Heavens, how happy it would make me! Well, Oslinka this little illusion should be permitted to me.

It is almost dark. I am going to sleep, pretending that I shall definitely see you tomorrow. The mere thought of it makes me happy like a child.

Goodnight, Oslinka! Dear, little g.[4]) Oslik.

Friday, 30th May, morning, 8 o'clock

Good morning Oslinka! Good morning, darling!

I can see through the window a fraction of blue skies – outside the sun is surely shining. I am in a very serene mood. Be that as it may. Come what may. Now it is no longer self-deception. Now I am really composed. If I am sentenced to mere hard labour – well and good. Should the other fate befall me – also right. During the last six months I have had to be prepared for this end every day, every hour.

But today, I wish to be happy. The birds are cheerfully twittering away although it is already 8 o'clock – it is May, May, in spite of everything! Perhaps I shall see you today, Oslik, darling! Wouldn't it be fine! And when they take me out for my walk I shall dance the roundelay with you on the small green lawn. And our boy will watch and beg to join us.

Dearest, dearest, if you only knew how much I love you. Oslinka, little, poor, when I am no more – this you must know: I loved you very, very much. I loved you, Oslinka....

And now, child, my lawyer is coming and I must get ready. I kiss your forehead and think of you tenderly.

Morning, 10 o'clock

Good day, Oslik! I am just back from my walk. The sun was burning, the sky was blue – it was really beautiful. There are two broad strips of lawn in the courtyard: they are covered with masses of white daisies, yellow buttercups and blue – I don't know their name – in Russia they are called 'Anjutas' dear Eyes.[5]) A butterfly was straying over them, a bee was buzzing in their midst – how fine it was!

It only hurt to think how much we were looking forward to spending the spring at last – the two of us, I mean the three, with the child – in the country. Perhaps we shall live to do it. And so I sway between hope and despair.

I did not dance the roundelay to the end, Oslik. When I thought of the child who danced with us I was again overcome with grief, oh, and I did not dare to think of it. I have just been reading the *Odyssey*. How I envy the old Greeks! Then men were allowed to weep, even to howl with pain, without losing in dignity and esteem. I, however, must not becaught out by the spying warder, must choke and gulp, clench my teeth so that nobody can say: 'He is scared. He's cries.'

Oslik, Oslenochek, you are not jealous that I am always so overcome when I think of the boy.

The diary is completed with a short note, immediately before his execution:

5th June.
Dearest! I have just seen you. Now comes my last walk. I love you, dearest. I thank you, dearest.
Kiss our boy. T.

He had also written a letter to his mother. I never knew its contents. Neither did her daughter nor any other member of the family. Its first sentences, however, were very often repeated:

Dear Mother! I am very well aware of the great pain I am causing you.... .

Not only the letter, but the diaries of his youth and numberless other scripts and documents were withheld from me. Perhaps they exist in the East Berlin or other archives.

Leviné asked his mother to visit me in prison, for it would give him great relief. She refused. She would come after the trial, not before, and she would come 'unreservedly,' she assured him. 'You know, I don't do anything by halves.'

Leviné repeated her words to me but he had no illusions and was very worried.

At our last meeting he mentioned a family I could always rely on for any help. He again proved his good judgement, but also that he was very preoccupied with the matter. For they were not our close friends. At the same time, he never mentioned his motheror even his sister.

Family affairs, declarations of love, flowers, butterflies and hardly a word of propaganda in his diary or his last conversations with me. Was this consistent with the conduct of a proletarian leader?

A reviewer of a short novel by Slonimsky, a Russian writer, based on the last phase of Leviné's life, contested the accuracy of certain episodes. True, some passages, particularly the description of our farewell meeting, had been rather vulgarised. In their essence, however, they were authentic.

A strong epicurean streak and a sense of humour were always alive in Leviné and he relished any joyous moment life offered him. His peculiar gift of drawing a precise line between his private and political life made it possible for him to keep faith with both.

The Party engaged three lawyers for Leviné's defence, two of them members of the Independent Socialist Party. One, Dr Sauter, was chosen chiefly for his knowledge of the local conditions; the second, Rosenfeld, for his prominence. At the beginning of the revolution he was appointed Minister of Justice during the short-lived coalition government of the two socialist parties and he had very good connections.

The third, Count Pestalozza, was a member of the Catholic Centre Party and belonged to the old Bavarian aristocracy. He at first flatly refused the assignment, but some outlines of Leviné's life which appeared in the newspapers attracted him and he changed his mind. Before long he changed from a professional defender into a touching, compassionate friend. He spared no effort to put Leviné at his ease. It was he who, on his own responsibility, got me out of prison immediately after the execution, took care of me, and made arrangements for reuniting me with my child.

It was entirely due to his intervention and influence that Leviné was allowed a private, to be scare secret burial.[6]

Pestalozza watched jealously over Leviné's good name, and on one occasion was the first, even before the party, to stand up in public in its defence.

Sitting on the other side of the fence Pestalozza was more familiar with the mood of Leviné's judges than his socialist colleagues could ever be. He tacitly agreed with Leviné that in the last analysis it was not so much his offences that would stand trial: the man and his value to the revolution would be sized upon, and they alone would determine the verdict.

He was, therefore, fascinated by Leviné's determination to use the Court as a forum for revolutionary propaganda.

The devout Catholic was perhaps more alive to the spirit of the revolutionary martyr and, unlike his counterparts, understood that efforts to change his mind would be futile. He knew that Leviné's fate was sealed and treated him with the tenderness one might reserve for a dying friend.

'Don't send this man to his death,' he pleaded, 'for should you do so, he would not die, he would start to live again. The life of this man would lie on the conscience of the entire community and his ideas would generate the seed of terrible revenge.'

'Pestalozza is much closer to me than my socialist lawyers,' Leviné said to me in amazement.

He was to leave him a friendly note of thanks which ended with: 'I shake your hand.'

V

The trial was to open on the 2nd June but the Defence Counsel was only permitted to see the documents on the 30th May.

However, this did not shake Rosenfeld's faith in the power of the written code of justice. He visited me in prison and was genuinely astonished to find me in despair.

'A death sentence is quite out of the question,' he said. 'Of course, the danger of an assassination cannot be ruled out but we shall take all precautions to avert it.'

In its dealings with political offences the German law distinguishes (or did so at that time) between acts motivated by honest convictions: 'honourable,' and by personal advantage, greed, lust for power: 'dishonourable motives.' The penalty ranged accordingly between the fortress, the mildest form of punishment reserved for superior convicts, and death. Of course, the final assessment of the 'motives' rested with the Court yet the law offered the defence certain advantages.

Letters testifying to Leviné's integrity were arriving from all sides: from renowned public figures like the Privy Councillor Gotheim, Gustav Radbruch and Alfred Weber, to landladies, housewives, nurses and students.

The elderly aunt of one of Leviné's pupils wrote that she knew him only from hearsay but he had a great beneficial influence on her nephew. She was, therefore, convinced that such a man could not be suspected of ulterior motives.

Leviné heard of the letters and would tell me all the moving stories at our short meetings; but he hardly attached any judicial value to the testimonies. He knew that his fate depended on the balance of power between the two warring camps and at that moment his side of the scales was at the bottom.

He tried to make the most of his last days and was hoping that I would be permitted to attend the trial.

'My hey-day without you?' he smiled.

The lawyers, however, were very much against my presence: too much of a 'foreign' aura, or too much of a strain on Leviné – I never knew. Nor do I know whether the idea was frustrated by the refusal of the authorities or whether Leviné himself was persuaded to drop it.

As a consolation, we were allowed a short meeting in the morning before his departure to the Court.

He looked very elated and happy. The chains had been removed for the occasion. He stretched out his arms to show it but his very tender wrists bore the sinister marks.

'I have to leave you here, but you will be with me all the time. No,' he corrected himself: 'Every minute I can spare... .' To the last moment he could not speak a word to me which was not strictly. true

'There can be no doubt of it,' said the officer, referring to Leviné's execution.

He knew what he was talking about.

On the second day of the trial I was informed that I was to be transferred to another prison. It was intended as a charitable act: I should be spared hearing the shots which would kill my husband.

At that moment I did not grasp the implication of the order, only that I was being torn away from him even before the end.

I asked to see the prison governor.

He was powerless, he said. He must obey orders. He begged me to be reasonable, otherwise they would remove me by force that very day.

Not enough time for a hunger-strike. Perhaps a riot would help.

I started screaming wildly with all the pent-up horror of the last weeks. And indeed, the prison soon resounded with shrieks and doors banging.

I was locked up. The storm soon subsided. What next?

A chance visit of my sister-in-law brought salvation. Her escort, a high-ranking officer must have known the reason for my transfer. He must also have realised what the well meant gesture looked like to me. He hastily left the cell and soon returned to assure me that I could stay on.

We owed two more meetings to his intervention.

The verdict was thus a foregone conclusion but the trial was played out in the grand manner.[1]

The soldiers in attendance were impatient, indignant. Why all this fuss? they grumbled. They were practical men.

Inside, in a hall packed to capacity, Leviné was fighting his great battle.

He was guided by the same considerations which had impelled him to take over the leadership of a movement he knew was doomed from the start. He had aimed to transform a pitiful, confused situation into a moral victory and a treasury for a future revolution. The task demanded great sacrifice, but he found the courage to exhort this, in his own readiness to throw his own life into the balance at any moment.

Now he saw it as his task to defend the Soviet Republic, the defeated workers, and to keep alive in their hearts the grandeur of their recent triumph.

He also thought it necessary to create a symbol to emulate and to inspire to new deeds. It demanded his own life and he took his turn with an unequalled simplicity.

The leaders who confessed to uncommitted crimes or abjured their political convictions, claimed that they did it to preserve themselves in order to serve the revolution.

Many people suggested that Leviné should have tried to follow the same line at his own trial. And he knew very well that by playing on the conceptions and emotions of his judges, he might have saved his life.

Perhaps Leviné could have saved his life. But it would not be the life of a revolutionary leader and he would have been of no more value to his cause.

There is no bargaining in matters of human integrity. A compromising, crawling Leviné would not have achieved in a lifetime what he achieved in the last short days. For the simple reason that he would have been morally dead.

Guided by these considerations, Leviné conducted his own defence. His opening words were a challenge to the legality of the trial:

'The indictment of high treason is only based on the fact that the Soviet Republic has been defeated.... When it succeeds it ceases to be high treason.'

Much the same was said in a leading article of the *Münchener Neueste Nachrichten* which stated that 'only unsuccessful high treason is high treason. If it succeeds it ceases to be high treason. High treason is thus a political, not a legal issue.

Leviné deliberately laid bare the abyss dividing him from his judges:

'I look upon this Court as the representative of my political adversaries. How could I defend myself before my enemies for actions which they must regard as threatening their very existence?'

He did not plead for mercy:

'Had I wished to achieve a more lenient sentence I ought rather to be silent. For my Counsel, who is closer to you both politically and as individuals, could conduct my case far more effectively.'

He rejected any attempt to dispose the Court or even the emotional intelligentsia in his favour. He did not minimise his part in the events. On the contrary, he explicitly accepted full responsibility for his actions, even for those 'I and my friends did not approve of.' This was the only hint of his own attitude to the hostages case.

Over the heads of his judges he was addressing the workers of Munich and beyond them the workers at large, expounding his ideas of a socialist society, the Communist tactics and the limitations of the powers of a revolutionary leader.

The emancipation of the workers can be only achieved by their own efforts.

A socialist society could be created without violence and bloodshed. He quoted the Communist programme:

The proletarian revolution has no need of terror....
It detests and abhors murder. It has no need of these means of struggle, for it fights not individuals but institutions.

It was the propertied class who hitherto always took up arms to defend its threatened privileges:

And because we know it, because we don't live in cloud-cuckoo-land, we were compelled to arm the workers to defend ourselves against the onslaught of the dispossessed capitalists.

Each of his defences included a calculated counter-attack:

The Prosecution has asked how I could possibly justify keeping people away from work for ten days at a time when work was so urgently needed. The German Government had kept millions of proletarians away from work, not for ten, but for many hundreds of days.

The German Government aspired to Baghdad and

Longwy: we wanted Communism. But the means which you did not condemn in their case you should also not condemn in ours just because we pursue other aims."

Well calculated was his account of the further developments:

"Some time later on the Tuesday after Easter, it was proposed to call off the strike in view of its economic effects. I made a counter proposal: Sunday and Monday were Easter holidays. If the workers had gone back to work on Tuesday, it would have created the impression that the strike had fizzled out. I suggested a more dignified conclusion, more consistent with the will of the working class, namely: the workers should continue to strike on Tuesday to make it quite obvious that it rested entirely with the workers whether they wished to return to work or not.

Reminding the workers of their recent triumph he challenged:

The Prosecution will know how this resolution was carried out. The workers, with hundreds of post-office employees, men and women, in their pale blue uniforms in the vanguard, marched to the Wittelsbach Palace to express their solidarity with those who have been portrayed in this Court as the terrorists and enslavers of the Munich proletariat.

The Prosecution was forced to withdraw the indictment of Leviné's guilt in the shooting of the hostages – the only justification for the death penalty. It did, however, insinuate that Leviné was morally responsible for the act.

He answered with one his most daring counter-attacks:

'The guilty are those who in August, 1914 were the first to take hostages, though they were never brought to justice or sentenced to death. If anyone else is to blame, it is the men who sneaked off to Bamberg and from there sent misguided proletarians together with officers' units and Negroes to fight against Munich.'

Leviné's words produced an uproar in the Court and the President threatened to cut off his speech. He must, however, have had second thoughts. The audience did not share in his indignation and was ostensibly on the side of the defendant.

Leviné repeated his charge but claimed that the manner in which it was made was provoked by the accusation of cowardice which the Prosecution had made against him:

One of the gravest accusations that could be levelled against someone who has been engaged for sixteen years in the revolutionary struggle.

It must be assumed that he was not really upset. The accusation of cowardice was the best the Prosecution could think of to substantiate the verdict of the death sentence. Leviné's indignation must rather be regarded as a subtle way of exposing the crude and cynical disregard of justice which distinguished the verdict.

The insult itself he answered with contempt:

'I cannot prevent the Counsel for the Prosecution from making such an accusation. But I may perhaps invite him who demands the death penalty to be present at the execution.'

He ridiculed:

The Prosecution accuses me of insisting on harsh punishment for looting, and at the same time holds me responsible for it. I cannot quite understand it: either I ought not have instructed the tribunal to apply severe measures, in which case I cannot be blamed for looting, or I should be allowed to instruct the tribunal in its duties in the manner I think necessary in the interests of our work and our task in which case I cannot be reproached for the harsh measures. While blaming me for having considered the introduction of the death penalty, the Prosecution is demanding the death penalty for me, for me who have neither looted nor murdered.

Leviné spoke in the name of all dispossessed:

Take a look around! In this very Court are officials who earn only 150 to 180 marks monthly, despite the present cost of living. Take a look at the homes in the so-called 'Spartacist nests' and you will understand that we have not endangered internal peace; we have only revealed that internal peace does not exist. And as long as it does not exist the struggle will go on. And if the struggle assumes military forms and brings in its wake all the ghastly misery and distress which actually prevailed in Munich, during the first few days of May, it is not we who are to blame but those who denied the working class the right to decide its own destiny.

Under the shadow of death, he was trying to make the workers of Munich conscious of their own actions, appealing to them to unite for victory.

When the proletariat is united in its will and purpose, it is invincible.

He concluded:

We Communists are all dead men on leave. Of this I am fully aware. I do not know whether you will extend my leave or whether I shall have to join Karl Liebknecht and Rosa Luxemburg. I await your verdict in any case with composure and inner serenity. For I know that whatever your verdict, the course of events cannot be halted.

And sooner or later other judges will sit in this Hall and then those who have transgressed against the dictatorship of the proletariat will be punished for high treason.

Pronounce your verdict, if you deem it proper. I have only striven to foil the attempt to stain my political activity, the name of the Soviet Republic with which I feel myself so closely bound up, the good name of the workers of Munich. They – and I together with them – we have all of us tried, to the best of our knowledge and conscience, to do our duty towards the International, the Communist world revolution.

The impact of the speech, which is reprinted in full in Appendix V, exceeded all imagination.

The soldiers ordered to guard Leviné crowded around him and, forgetting all discipline, shook his hands and showered questions on him, eager to learn more from the man they were unwittingly helping to silence forever.

An old colonel ran out crying: 'Oh, he is a Christ but he came into this world a thousand years too soon.'

The officer who escorted Leviné back to prison was unable to suppress his emotion which he expressed in a peculiar way:

'I know we cannot possibly let you live. But it was preposterous to deny you honourable motives – very, very unfair'.

The representatives of the Press, the bourgeois Press, assigned to denounce Leviné were unable to keep their balance.

Münchener Neueste Nachrichten wrote:

All that we have seen and heard of Leviné during these days only further strengthens the impression gained already in the weeks of April: a man of rare intelligence, an agitator of outstanding oratorical power, was confronting his judges.

Die Münchner Post, the voice of the Social-Democrats, wrote:

Leviné faced the Court on the second day of the trial with an indifference to the fate hanging over him which alone could shatter the indictment of cowardice by the Public Prosecutor.[2] The *unstudied* posture of the defendant undoubtedly impressed many of those who had not experienced the Leviné of the second Soviet Republic.

Leviné relieved his Counsel of the task of defending him. In his final speech, which put into the shade all the rhetoric of his professional advocates, he resolutely swept aside all the little tricks which his Counsel brought forward in his favour.

Lucid, calm and to the point the speech was more effective than all that had been said in his defence during the long preceding hours. Once again it became evident that he possessed courage *wrongfully denied to him*, that he skilfully remained master of the situation, that he succeeded with a superiority of his own, in crystallising all those points which ensured him his influence on the masses.

...There is not a trace in Leviné of 'the moral collapse of the leader of the Soviet Republic' alleged in the official report and eagerly circulated by the Munich bourgeois forces.

Die Münchner Zeitung tried to shrug off the sentiment which Leviné had inspired, by some spiteful insinuations, but they were too obvious to conceal their immediate response:

Leviné's words 'We Communists are only dead men on leave' evoked a feeling as if the heavy beat of dark wings swept over the Court and it took some moments to realise that the world revolutionary Leviné, had borrowed this metaphor from the conceptual world of militarism.

Indeed the allusion to the military term, very familiar so soon after the war, only deepened the impact of the tragic words.

The report continues:

Many people also dismissed the words: 'Long Live the Revolution:' with which Leviné saluted his death sentence as a histrionic gesture. It seems, however, that those words were not so much histrionic as an outlet for the unperturbed composure and smiling serenity which marked Leviné's conduct throughout the trial. At any rate they dispersed the gloomy atmosphere which hung heavy upon the Court after the pronouncement of this – as of every – death sentence.

They 'dispersed'.... They brought them back to reality: Leviné was not defeated and they 'could not possibly let him live.'

But the scene is described with reverence and even with a touch of warmth, characteristic of the feelings Leviné evoked in those who came into contact with him during those last weeks:

The judges have retired for the final deliberations....
Those who remain in the Hall for fear of losing their comfortable seats are debating – about the plea of the defence and Leviné's own brilliant speech.

Leviné is calmness personified.... An Officer is holding back soldiers who are trying to press forward. Leviné is talking to them, expounding his political ideas. Even at this hour he is the impassioned agitator.

It is six o'clock. Leviné is occasionally looking into a newspaper. From time to time his gaze strays dreamily to the window: into freedom. His lawyer approaches him. Leviné smiles. His smile has grown tired, more mechanical. He remains calm but one feels that the long wait has put a strain even on a man of his nerve.

...The tension is steadily rising: even the onlooker is affected. Leviné is again absorbed in the paper. Suddenly, he moves towards his guard, leans down and begins to speak. At that moment the door of the conference room is flung open. The die is cast.

Leviné's leave was not extended but the words: 'We Communists are only dead men on leave' reverberated far beyond the German frontiers.

I have heard them in Vilno, Paris, Tel-Aviv from people who did not even know his name:

'You know there was a Communist in Germany who said.... '

They were repeated in America and Canada.

Arthur Köstler included them in his book *Darkness at Noon* though wrongly attributing them to Lenin. Isaak Deutscher said that essentially these words made Leviné the legend of his youth, and strangely, so wrote the American, Whittaker Chambers, of Alger Hiss repute.

Leviné's moral victory was so immense that he himself seemed intoxicated by its impact and for a short while believed that they would not dare to carry out the sentence.

At the end of the trial he asked to see me and was granted half an hour.

I was brought to him – as I was convinced – for the final farewell.

Indifferent as Leviné was to his own fate, he knew at once what I was thinking.

'No, no, nothing is going to happen,' he kept on saying. It took me quite a while to understand his words and he was almost in tears.

'I was afraid this would happen,' he said when I had calmed down, 'and explicitly asked the lawyers to prepare you carefully for the meeting. What a terrible blunder!'

He was quite shaken and it looked as if he had forgotten it was he, not I, who was facing a tragic death.

And again: 'I missed you very much but it was perhaps better that way: The strain might have proved too much for you.'

He started talking of the trial and repeated the essential parts of his speech.

It was in a large room packed with people – with warders and policemen of all ranks. The Prison Governor seemed to have gathered all those he could for the occasion.

Everybody thronged forward so as not to miss a single word: a tense, enthralled audience.

Leviné looked for a while at the excited faces and said quietly: 'No, they would not dare.'

But his words sounded like an objective political assessment. The tone carried no hope.

The verdict was pronounced on Tuesday evening, the 3rd of June and, in accordance with the martial law, the sentence was to be carried out within twenty-four hours.

It was, however, the first political execution of the century and the government waited for the reaction of the workers.

In Munich no serious resistance could be expected. As a further precautionary measure, 150 workers had been arrested on the morning after the trial.

Everything depended on the Reich.

Throughout the trial, the Social-Democratic Press did its best to dull the vigilance of the workers. It mocked at the Communists' fears: there was no thought of making martyrs for them by executing their leaders, it claimed.[3]

The Bavarian Prime Minister Hoffmann fled to Switzerland on account of the illness of his wife. He washed his hands of the act by a wire, requesting the *postponement* of the sentence. It arrived 'too late.' Equally 'too late' came a telegram from the Reichs Chancellor, Scheidemann, with a similar request.[4]

When on Thursday morning, the 5th, it became evident that the country was calm. Leviné's fate was sealed.

On the 5th June, the Government issued a proclamation:

The Ministrial Council had found no cause for remitting by an Act of Grace, the death sentence which the Military Court pronounced on Leviné for treason.

The sentence was hurriedly carried out at 1.45 that afternoon.

Leviné was granted his last wish: a full hour from 12 to 1 o'clock for taking leave of me.

The great Russian writers have indulged in the portrayal of heroes accepting their death, not as trembling, tortured creatures being whipped into a dark, gruesome void, but as dignified human beings reaching new spiritual heights.

None of the idealised images could, however, match the unobtrusive, quiet simplicity with which Leviné, in the prime of his life and in full strength, accepted his early death.

He was strangely alert and elated, more sensitive and compassionate than ever before.

When I entered the room he was already waiting for me. He was deadly pale.

The sentence had been read out to him only minutes before and he did not know how to tell me the news. This seemed to be his greatest concern for he was visibly relieved afterwards, and regained his normal colour.

He first tried to prepare me:

'Nothing is going to happen. It has not yet been decided. We don't know for certain.'

Then very softly: 'Yes, Oslik, today, soon. No, I won't tell you what time. It will be better for you not to know.'

He had worked out every detail.

'I am not afraid. You too must not fear. It will be easy now. At one time I would have had to face hostile people. The thought disturbed me, but it is different now. They know that I am not their enemy.

'It will soon be over. It is you who will suffer more. But don't forget: you must not live a joyless life. Not a joyless life.'

He tried to impress it on me, knowing how meaningless the words were to me at that moment.

'You must think of our boy. He must not be burdened with an unhappy mother.'

Our two warders had discreetly retired to the far corner of the room and were unashamedly sobbing.

Leviné was among friends and started speaking Russian. He could never bear the artificiality of speaking to me in another language and at once looked relieved, more like himself.

We were sitting on a plank bed. He was smiling, laughing. The few tears were for my sake!

'Poor Oslik.'

Not a complaint, not even a reflex of sorrow for himself.

He spoke of his love, recalling episodes which used to move or delight him and which he seemed to relish even during those moments.

Somebody entered the room. He was stealing our precious time.

Leviné asked quietly: 'Are you on duty here?' And then: 'No, friend, there is nothing to watch.'

There was no reproach in his words but something in his voice which made the man hide his face and hastily leave.

'What do I wish you to do? Anything you choose. You will find out for yourself. You are paying your share to the revolution now. You will see what more you can do. Don't tie yourself down with promises.

'I am calm and happy. Let me have another look at you, Oslik. A good look at you,' he kept saying as if he were going on an ordinary journey.

Time was running out. The warder cautioned, but Leviné thought that a few minutes would not matter.

It did matter. Precisely at one o'clock an officer opened the door:

'Leviné, get ready!'

Leviné looked at me and it was for my sake that he asked for another five minutes.

'Dearest, it will soon be over. Give me your handkerchief.'

He pressed the tear-soaked handkerchief to his heart.

'I shall take it with me, I shall hold it in my hand.'

I had brought a few flowers from my cell. He chose one and attached it with great care to his jacket.

The Officer reappeared.

It was Leviné who was leading.

I followed blindly in an inhuman effort not to fail him, and in awe of the simplicity of his bearing, common only to children and saints.

We parted.

The corridor was crowded with soldiers. His remarkable gift of drawing a line in a moment between the personal and the political did not fail him.

They must not see him suffer or see him frightened.

He suddenly stiffened and lifted up his head.

I saw him march with firm steps the long, long corridor and disappear into his cell.

He never once turned his head, never gave me another look.

He wrote another message to his lawyer:

'Dear Count, good-bye. Please hand over the little diary to my wife (some weeks after my death.) The Programme of the Communists is for my son.'

And in his diary: 'Now comes my last walk.'

Another little note was written in Russian. There was a word which somehow caught my imagination for its folksy flavour and I had been waiting for it all these years.

It cannot be translated. The nearest is, 'A feast for my eyes.' Exhausting his vocabulary in inventing new words of endearment, he had missed this one.

He found it on the threshold of his death:

To my wife: My dear, my own one, beloved, *Njenagljadnaja!* I hug you, I kiss you. I loved you, you alone. I thank you for all the happiness you have given me. I have just seen you. I go to my death filled with you.

Yours T.

Thank you, thank you!

He was not withering away, his spiritual growth was reaching its heights.

He obliterated himself.

Manifesting the true meaning of 'love thine enemy,' he consoled the warder who was leading him to his execution:

'I know, it is hard on you, an old man, to do this duty.'

He refused to be blindfolded and in the face of the firing squad raised the hand holding my handkerchief and hailed for the last time the true love of his life.

'Long Live the World Revolution.'

Accounts of Leviné's last minutes appeared everywhere, but truth was inevitably freely mixed with fantasy. The most persistent was his request for a cigarette.

'He wanted to meet his death with a cigarette in his mouth,' reported the Munich correspondent of the *Berliner Neue Zeitung*.

Shortly afterwards the warder who accompanied him brought me Leviné's last greetings.

He told me that he did not suffer much. The first salvo hit him straight in the heart. He gave me a minute account of Leviné's conduct. It did not contain that invention.

The workers expressed their feeling by picturing the dying Leviné still waving a white cloth in honour of the revolution. It appeared in innumerable drawings throughout the country and apparently inspired a sculpture which was exhibited in the Mannheim Art Gallery.

I did not hear the shots.

Life is a keen producer of tragi-comedy. My wardress thoughtfully transferred me to another room and brought for comfort the two fellow prisoners she thought fittest for the situation: Frau Kämpfer, who at the trial testified against Leviné, and the wife of Klingelhöfer.

They happened to be good friends and were obviously delighted to have a good chat.

Above all the occasion seemed to enhance their awareness of their own happy marriages, for they were falling over themselves with praise of the care and devotion of their husbands.

The wardress refused to take me back to my cell. I should not be left alone.

I don't know how long it all lasted. Count Pestalozza suddenly came to take me away.

Toller did not spare me either. He gave his own version of my state:

'In a cell of the adjacent women's prison his wife lay screaming, pressing her hands to her ears so as not to hear the shots which killed him.'

This melodramatic scene was presumably supposed to express his compassion. But this was a delayed shock: I read the description many years later.

Unfortunately, life is also a good manufacturer of the grotesque. Count Pestalozza, the faithful executor of Leviné's will, misunderstood his reference to his Jewish origins.

He arranged for an orthodox Jewish burial complete with a sermon by a rabbi at the Israelitches Friedhof.

Leviné's death produced a storm of indignation. The token telegrams of Hoffmann and Scheidemann appeased no one. Telegrams from such figures do not arrive 'too late.'

The liberal *Frankfurter Zeitung* wrote that it was the duty of the Social-Democrats to prevent the execution 'by every means, even at the risk of evoking a cabinet crisis.'

Even papers like the Berlin *Neue Zeitung*, which denounced Leviné as 'the seducer of the Munich proletariat' and as an 'unsympathetic character who deserted the fighting workers and so was unworthy of clemency;' concluded:

Wide circles, from the government down to the non-socialist community, left no doubt that under the prevailing political conditions, which were the background of Leviné's crimes, the application of mercy and political wisdom would be more more appropriate than punishment. Both socialist parties, usually at loggerheads, agreed that this was a case which simply cried out for a reprieve.

The general dismay was enhanced by the realisation that this was a manifest case of judicial murder. It is sufficient to examine the basis on which the sentence was constructed to see with what cynicism the Court abused its authority.

The first Soviet Republic, by any standards an act of treason, was obligingly defined as '*a mere insubordination*' against the constitutional government.

That the latter transferred its seat to Bamberg and explicitly reserved its rights was the flimsy reason for that clemency.

But the Second Soviet Republic had not transgressed against the authority of a constitutional but of an 'unlawful' government, created despite Leviné's resistance.

However, the Court was not called upon to pass political judgement, but to assess the *motives* which dictated the policy of the defendant.

The Court preffered to overlook this ticklish point. Instead, it keenly enumerated Leviné's revolutionary measures 'to transform the entire legal and economic structure into a Communist (or socialist) state,' and declared arbitrarily:

'It stands beyond doubt that a man who meddles in such a way with the destiny of a people is guided by dishonourable motives.'

It was in other words a conclusion that the ideas of a man of Leviné's 'great intellectual powers' ought to correspond to the views of the Prosecution. The failure to share these views was dishonourable and therefore punishable by death.

This was a travesty of justice. 'Class-justice' ceased to be a mere invective used by the Communists and became a manifest reality.

Even the sentences passed on Professor Salz, Leviné's host, Botho Schmidt and the Communist Zimmer bore its ugly marks.

The first two defendants were immediately set free:

The Court found no evidence of aiding and abetting high treason, nor sufficient evidence of an offence of favouring it. They are therefore discharged.

As for Zimmer, there was not sufficient evidence of the crime of aiding and abetting high treason, but the Court regards him as highly suspect on the offence of favouring it.

Zimmer had no part in sheltering Leviné. His crime consisted in helping me and delivering to me a strictly personal letter. Yet he was referred to an ordinary Court and sentenced to two years' imprisonment.

The outraged workers reacted to the execution of Leviné with protest demonstrations and a 24-hour general strike which was observed throughout the country. In the large centres life came to a standstill. An attempt of the speakers of the S.P.D.-dominated trade unions to exempt vital industries was drowned in uproar. In some places it lead to skirmishes.

Die Neue Zeitung reported 'serious riots in Hamburg.'

All this also came 'too late.'

It is impossible to do Leviné full justice without comparing his policy with that of the Bolsheviks, in an event which went down in the history of 1917 as the July Days.

In spite of their disparity – the July Days originated in a spontaneous mass movement with 500,000 armed workers, soldiers and sailors demonstrating in the streets of Petrograd under the Bolshevik slogan: 'All Power to the Soviets,' while the Munich events were only the product of an agreement between a few leaders, without any collaboration from the masses – their identity is unmistakable.[5]

Both movements were regarded by the parties as untimely, both were thrust upon them against their will and their explicit warnings, and both pose the same question:

'What is the duty of the leaders confronted with such a complex situation?'

Leviné's struggle to prevent the creation of the Soviet Republic is in complete keeping with the attempt of the Bolsheviks to stem the July movement.

His arguments for refusing to join the movement were almost identical with those of the great teacher.

Lenin said:

We did not yet have a majority among the workers and soldiers of the two capitals.... We would not have re-retained power... in spite of the fact that at certain moments Petrograd was in our hands, because the workers and soldiers would not have fought and died at that time for the sake of holding Petrograd.... There did not exist such burning hatred, such fury of despair... the Army and the provinces could and would have marched against Petrograd.[6]

Apart from mainly political and strategic reasons, a Soviet Republic can be only proclaimed by Soviets and then only if a majority of Communists stand behind them, the inevitable intervention of the Army and so on. Leviné, to his honour, also spoke, and in almost the same words as Lenin, of the lack of determination of the masses to achieve their ends:

'Where are your shining eyes? Your enthusiasm? Your will to fight and die for the Soviet Republic?'

As to Lenin's reason: "At that time even the Bolsheviks did not have and could not have the conscious determination to treat Tseretelli and Co. as counter-revolutionaries," it is not amiss to mention that at this point the German Party was one ahead of the Bolsheviks. Rosa Luxemburg had no illusions about the German Tseretellis and Leviné foresaw from the start that 'the Eberts will just as readily shoot at fathers and mothers as Wilhelm II.'[7]

But a revolutionary party cannot stand aloof and revel in its cleverness and foresight. It must give a positive answer to the problem: where do we go from here?

The Bolsheviks were drawn into the July movement practically by the scruff of their necks. They could do no less with their entire membership on the streets. But they saw their sole task as giving the movement 'a peaceful, organised character' and used all their authority to prevent any transgressive action, which was in fact only an continuation of holding the masses back.

Was, then, Leviné right to take over under the prevailing circumstances and to give battle?

This the Bolsheviks had refused to do in spite of the inhuman pressure. To be sure, the Bolsheviks *without Lenin*. While accepting unreservedly the responsibility for the policy of the Party: 'A leader is responsible not only for his own actions but also for those of the people he is leading.'

Lenin significantly makes a point of stating that at the onset of those fatal days he was ill and out of town.

The predominantly Menshevik Soviet Executive was naturally even less inclined to take the plunge. The demonstrators, utterly confused and worn out by two days of marching the streets, obeyed the Party order to disperse.

Lenin defended the policy but he did not seem at all happy and kept on returning to the problem. As far as I, at least, can see it is the only subject where certain contradictions and evasions mar his statements.

'At that time Petrograd could not even seize power physically,' he wrote to the Moscow committee, whereas he had argued before that 'We could not have *retained* power... in spite of the fact that at certain moments Petrograd was in our hands.'

Another argument, that 'the Army and the provinces could and would have marched against Petrograd,' is equally invalidated by another statement that:

'The troops will not advance against a government of peace.'[8]

Lenin admitted to errors and spoke of the Party's 'hope,' a word which he thought was quite impermissible as a factor of political calculations... .

...The real error of our Party on July 16–18, as now revealed by events, was only that the Party considered the national situation *less* revolutionary than it proved to be, that the

Party *still* considered possible a peaceful development of political transformations through a change in the policies of the Soviets.... . But this erroneous view, sustained only by the *hope* that events would not develop too fast, could not have been got rid of by our Party in any other way than by participating in the popular movement of July 16–18 with the slogan 'All power to the Soviets,' with the aim of giving the movement a peaceful and organised character.[9]

But an erroneous assessment of the national situation is not conducive to sober judgement, and it turned out that 'a peaceful organised movement' only served the counter-revolution:

'The enemy achieved an easy victory because we did not fight. The Party paid dearly for it.'[10]

Lenin is more outspoken when taking into account the terror to which the Party was submitted despite its restraint (Leviné said: 'We shall in any case have to pay the bloody price,') and arrived at the conclusion, 'If the Bolsheviks made any mistake it was only in declining to take power.'[11]

There is, however, a more direct answer. At the end of August, only a few weeks after the July Days (16–18), anticipating a similar situation in Moscow, Lenin wrote:

...Since the strike, since July 16–18, Moscow is acquiring, or can acquire, the significance of a *centre*. In this tremendous proletarian centre, which is larger than Petrograd, the growth of a movement similar to that of July 16–18 is entirely feasible.

At that time the task in Petrograd was to give the movement a peaceful and organised character. This *was* a correct slogan. The task *now* in Moscow is entirely different. The old slogan would be absolutely incorrect at present. The task now would be for the workers to *seize power* themselves and to declare themselves the government in the name of peace, land to the peasants, etc.... . It is highly important to have 'at the helm' in Moscow persons who, in case the movement rises, will understand the *new* tasks, the *new* slogan of seizing power, the new ways and means leading to it.

This is very similar to the situation in Petrograd prior to July 16–18, 1917. But the difference in the situation is that at that time Petrograd could not even seize power physically,[12] and had it done so physically, it could not have retained it politically.

Now the situation is entirely different. Now, if a *spontaneous* movement flares up in Moscow, the slogan must be nothing but seizure of power. This is why it is highly important, unusually important, that the movement in Moscow be led by persons fit for the task, who have *fully* grasped and thoroughly assimilated this slogan.[13]

The national situation could hardly be regarded as *more* unfavourable for a Bolshevik insurrection. The counter-revolution was stronger than ever, and Trotsky, in his *History of the Russian Revolution*, gives an excruciating picture of the sorry state of the Bolshevik Party, its rapid decline, with apathy, loss of confidence, disappointment and even hostility among the workers.

'The July Days had produced a serious shift of power to the right.... The reaction was on the offensive, the democracy in retreat,' testifies Trotsky.

The Party had only just begun to recover from the heavy blows. Moscow itself became a centre of counter-revolutionary activities and the above-mentioned strike of August was a desperate 24-hour protest against an Assembly regarded by the workers as another challenge and conspiracy of the reactionary forces.

It should be borne in mind that Lenin was obviously speaking of a *spontaneous*, which means a *still untimely, movement* and of a situation 'similar to the pre-July Days.' For when he thought the moment ripe, he did not wait for the workers to come out but himself determined the time for insurrection, and with what passionate urgency!

No, nothing had changed except that Lenin was again in full control of the situation.

His letter must be regarded as a complete renunciation of the July policy and it is in full accord with his repeated warnings against the danger of suppressing accumulated revolutionary energy *once unleashed*, and with Marx's views.

It is also irrelevant whether the Bolsheviks could have at that time *retained* power. Many, even Mensheviks, asserted that it was possible. Lenin defended the Moscow uprising of the 1905 revolution which was to all intents and purposes doomed in advance, against Plechanov's famous: 'One should not have taken up' arms!' and 'A defeat in battle is a source of future victory.'

He regarded a defenceless retreat as the greatest demoralising factor.

The moral defeat in the wake of the July Days was indisputable but even by Trotsky it was balanced against the 'physical' defeat.

'... The victim were counted by tens and not by tens of thousands.... The workers were not bled to death.'

He does not take into account the Petrograd soldiers sent to the trenches, renewed death penalties, etc., and of course does not appreciate that a Menshevik government could not afford such massacres in their own interests: they would have to give too much power to the counter-revolutionary generals, and their fight against Kornilov showed that they did not go so far.

But apart from that the laws of revolution make no distinction between moral and physical defeat. Both are deadly. Sacrifices are, cynically speaking, its overhead expenses. The thousands who risked their freedom and lives and often perished in its service did not expect immediate returns.

'The real fruit of their battle lies not in immediate results but in the ever-expanding union of the workers,' teaches the Communist Manifesto.

'He [Marx] saw in the mass revolutionary movement, although it did not achieve its aims, a historic experiment of gigantic proportions, a certain advance of the world proletarian revolution, a practical step, more important than hundreds of programmes and discussions,' testifies Lenin.[15]

A moral defeat may cost immeasurably more physical destruction in the long run or indefinitely postpone the revolution. And Lenin passionately warned against a defenceless retreat.

Leviné acted in fact in complete keeping with the teachings of the great masters. But it appears that theory alone does not guarantee the appropriate action. Not when it demands decisions involving human – and not least one's own – life.

Leviné had moreover to find his way under almost daily changing circumstances of which history knew no precedents. He himself was destined to add a new chapter to revolutionary theory to prove its validity once more.

The role of the revolutionary leader in history is both over- and underestimated, but its importance cannot be overvalued.

True, the leader cannot create the national conditions which enable him to influence the course of history. On the other hand the most favourable conditions can peter out without the so-called 'personal factor.'

Lenin warned that no difficulty was too complex for the ruling class to tackle and overcome, 'if we let them.' In other words, without a party and a set of well-trained, able leaders, the working class could not achieve its emancipation.

Trotsky, by any standard one of the greatest leaders, goes further: he ascribes the success of the October Revolution to one man only,: not to himself, but to Lenin, and Trotsky could not easity be accused of excessive humility.

Of course there would have been 'a revolution.' But without Lenin's master-mind, his vision, it would have split into a series of uncoordinated uprisings which could be defeated one by one.

Trotsky explains his utterly 'unMarxist' claim that Lenin-alone was capable of creating the national mood and, above all, of the *timely* readjustment of his party's policy to the new conditions and tasks: time being a decisive factor in a revolutionary situation.

The success of a revolutionary leader will therefore largely depend on his ability to absorb Lenin's teaching, his way of thinking, all the specific characteristics which distinguish him from other brilliant, dedicated revolutionaries.

Politics according to Lenin became a science, and 'without revolutionary theory no revolutionary practice.'

A leader of a modern revolution is therefore remote from the image of a daredevil with a mysterious capacity for inspiring blind obedience in 'the mob.'

The leader must be some steps ahead of the people, and thus demands a broad outlook, the ability to draw historic parallels and a thorough acquaintance with world affairs, past and present.

Lenin demanded knowledge of the essential events in history and public life of *every* party member.

As to the leaders, he insisted that to 'beat' their counterparts they must absorb not only political and economic knowledge but the existing bourgeois culture as well.

They can qualify for their role only by making politics their profession to the exclusion of any other striving.

But knowledge, and even oratorical and literary talents must be regarded as mere accessories. The essential feature is dedication to the cause and readiness to pledge one's life to its service.

Suffering and death are an integral part of the struggle and the leaders must be prepared to head the casualty list.

And indeed, in proportion to the rank and file every revolutionary upheaval claimed its heaviest toll among the leaders.

Moreover, the leaders who lived up to these standards regarded their share as a privilege, preferable to all the temptations of a conventional life.

'I tell you,' said Liebknecht at his trial, 'no general ever wore his uniform with the pride with which I shall wear my penitential garb.'

And Leviné spoke of the heavy chains he had to wear in his Munich prison as his 'iron cross.'

Leviné consciously trained himself for his role and succeeded in transforming an essentially artistic, introspective dreamer into a determined, disciplined partisan who never faltered in performing his revolutionary duty.

In his hour of trial he even displayed a certain affinity with Lenin's way of thinking which sometimes found expression in strangely identical words.

Was not Leviné's term 'Adolescent Disorder,' by which he summed up the danger of over-zealous revolutionary fervour, an echo of Lenin's warning against the same phenomenon, which he called 'Left-Wing Communism, and Infantile Disorder?'

Striving to prevent the adventure of a premature Soviet Republic, Leviné was asking, 'Where are our shining eyes? Where is your will to wage an implacable war?'

'Can such imponderables be assessed?' I thought then. 'Are shining eyes indispensable to the proclamation of a Soviet Republic?'

But Leviné was only unwittingly repeating Lenin's words when in an attempt to avert a similarly untimely situation, the famous 'July Days' of 1917, he spoke of want of the same indefinable aspects as 'the fury of despair' and 'the will to fight and die for victory.'

'The soldiers voted against the war' declared Lenin, 'They voted with their feet. They ran away,' he replied to the objection that there had been no vote on the subject.

'Look, this is a *vote of confidence* in our government,' remarked Leviné, pointing out to me a long queue of bourgeois people in front of the War Ministry.

'They did not stir when Toller ordered them to surrender their arms. Now they come. They take us seriously.'

In other words: they 'voted with their feet.'

Adults, not unlike children, express themselves by signs and gestures. A good leader must also be able to understand the mute signs and to translate them into articulate language.

There is a touch of truly Leninist statesmanship in Leviné's instructions for re-elections of new Workers' Councils.

People learn and mature rapidly in times of upheaval and to assess the changing mood of the masses, the Communist Party advocated frequent re-elections of their representative bodies.

On his arrival in Munich Leviné gave this task first priority.

But at that time it was only a matter of customary procedure with the simple slogan: 'Elect Communists into the Councils.'

There was no delving into the personal characteristics of the members.

After the proclamation of the first Soviet Republic, in a clear vision of further development, Leviné set out to create an instrument adequate to meet the new demands.

He instructed: Of the members of the new Revolutionary Workers' Councils other qualities will be required: qualities essential for waging a tenacious revolutionary war. You will have to elect men, capable of making quick decisions and at the same time keeping a sober and open eye on the actual balance of power; capable of audacious revolutionary acts and a circumspect choice of the time for action.

How reminiscent are these instructions of Lenin's 'letter to the Moscow Committee,' urging them in a similar situation to select as members only those who were qualified for the task.

It is highly important to have at the helm in Moscow people... who will understand the new tasks, the new slogans of seizing power, the new ways and means leading to it. (XXI, 108.)

Mercilessly castigating the Social-Democratic and Independent leaders Leviné never fell into the trap of throwing them into the same category. Even at the height of the acute struggle he always made distinctions between the Independents and the Socialists of the Ebert brand, the 'conscious and the unwitting betrayers of the revolution.'

This attitude also found its confirmation in one of Lenin's wittiest articles, an imaginary conversation between a group of Russian Anti-Bolshevik leaders, where he paid meticulous attention to every shade of difference between their ideas and mood.

Attention to detail and precision of terms are is no less important than 'major policy.' In fact, it is the only guarantee of successful 'major' action. It safeguards at least against what Lenin regarded as 'one of the gravest sins against the revolution: the substitution of the abstract for the concrete.'

Keeping in mind the devastating pre-Hitler policy of labelling socialists of all shades 'social fascists' it is easy to appreciate the value of those seemingly minor matters.

In making such daring comparisons I do not forget that Leviné was only the disciple who by straining every nerve succeeded in following in Lenin's footsteps.

Yet the comparison seems relevant, for it shows that leaders destined to perform a similar task – if only in proportion to the trans-formation of Imperial Russia and of a part of Bavaria – must possess some basically similar characteristics. Just as leaders who fulfil other tasks share a similarity of thought, manifested in their style and expressions.

Bolshevism and Menshevism are in no way Russian phenom-ena: they had existed in every party and had an identical style.

Reading the protestations of Kerensky, Eisner, Toller and Bloom one finds that men of different continents, so unlike in traditions, upbringing and age as, for instance, Kerensky of 1917 and Bloom of 1936, spoke the same language.

The style alone might help to detect the fundamental difference between the leaders.

The events of Munich were unquestionably to a great extent shaped by Leviné. But they also transformed him into a man marvelled at by friend and foe.

Leviné, the sensitive romantic, was acclaimed for his 'wild energy', 'cast-iron will,' 'hypnotic powers' and 'the calm with which he faced danger.'

The situation demanded a leader of great political experience but above all a man with the audacity to uphold the cause in the face of deadly peril.

They had all learned their Marx and partly their Lenin. They all knew how passionately they were warned against defenceless retreat. Yet the erudite Marxist, Thalheimer, condoned and even defended Brandler's disastrous unopposed retreat of October 1923.

And Paul Levi who condemned the battle of Munich was allowed to lead the German Party for years.

Lenin's passionate denouncement of Plekhanov's similar view on the abortive Moscow uprising in the 1905 revolution, the famous: 'They should not have taken arms!' was simply overlooked.

Not to mention the capitulation of the German Communist Party to Hitler.

It seems to be very difficult to remember the lessons one has learned, and theory without the courage to live it out in practice remains a dead letter.

Another and perhaps greater difficulty is to grasp the essentials of a given situation, and not to depart from one's own conclusions.

'We looked with admiration to the man who, almost suffocating under the humdrum routine work, never lost sight of the essential political perspectives,' writes Leviné's biographer, Paul Werner.[16]

People spoke excitedly of the way he conducted the Committee sessions, limiting them almost to minutes. He presented the problems with such precision and clarity as to permit decisions to be taken mostly without debate.

'He is growing, growing before our very eyes,' somebody exclaimed.

To assess Leviné's achievement one must bear in mind that he was a complete stranger to the Munich workers. They had their own leaders, Levien, Mühsam, Toller, to admire and follow. He was also foreign in nationality and appearance – a mixture of a saint and a shrewd man of the world.

His first public appearance was to oppose the creation of the Soviet Republic, a movement ostensibly the summit of Communist aims, vaguely desired by the workers and favoured by the other parties.

He was destroying cherished illussions, and rosy day-dreams, in Lenin's words, 'pouring vinegar and bile into the sweetish water' – something people do not like. And what no-one likes at all, he was predicting a hard struggle, bloodshed and was demanding sacrifices.

Only some three weeks after he arrived in Munich, and without a real party he was confronted with an unprecedented situation. Worse still, he had to rid the minds of the handful of available members of a host of chaotic conceptions.

Yet he succeeded in creating a harmonious collaboration with the former set of leaders, to keep down pettiness, jealousy, rivalry, all the manifestations of so-called 'human nature' and to inspire them with a spirit of calm serenity and enthusiasm.

Good leadership must be judged by the radius of influence it is able to extend for its ideas. Within the limits determined by the objective situation Leviné succeeded in uniting and guiding the entire working class of Munich in defiance of the leaders of the Social-Democratic and Independent Social-Democratic Parties.

Scornful of histrionics, he never belonged to the easily *acclaimed* heroes of the masses, not even during the Munich period. Exhausted by overwork he once sighed: 'History seems to be in the habit of creating its darlings and its outcasts. Mine is the thankless role of the "elder brother," to correct the harm incurred by history's pampered pets.'

In his speeches he relied entirely on the logic of his arguments.

A genuine respect for human dignity excluded from the start any tendency to domineering, as well as a taste for adulation.

On the contrary, he regarded it as one of the essential tasks to awaken in the workers a true sense of the equality of men. Condescending baby-talk, attempts to patronise or to impose on the workers the will of the 'clever leaders' infuriated him.

I once witnessed this attitude in practice.

At a meeting, where Leviné was still trying to avert the proclamation of a Soviet Republic Mühsam declared:

'If I thought it necessary to proclaim a Soviet Republic I wouldn't care twopence whether the workers agreed or not.'

I was sitting behind Leviné and could literally *see* his mounting anger.

'Comrades!' he exploded, 'do you realise that Mühsam's words are a slap in the face of the workers?'

They did not. Mühsam's declaration sounded very 'militant' and he was even applauded. But how quickly they understood when it was pointed out to them and how it raised their own dignity and their confidence in Leviné.

Another confirmation of Lenin's idea that class-consciousness must be instilled into the workers from 'outside.'

Complete honesty was another test of his respect for the people. Even during the Communist Soviet Republic, at a time when it was very tempting to sow illusions, he told the workers, 'We do not know whether our first onslaught will suffice and whether we shall be able to hold out to the end. We shall try.'

'He has the natural grace of a born leader,' said the renowned German writer, Leonard Frank.

'Yes, but also the quiet modesty of a disciplined partisan,' retorted a listener.

Leviné had many of the qualities which go into the making of a revolutionary leader: knowledge, selfless devotion to the cause, courage. But his driving power was love, infinite love and care for all those who are deprived and oppressed.

Notes

Chapter I

[1] In 1920 he joined the Communist Party.

[2] The Social Revolutionary Party, founded in 1901, championed individual terror and chiefly represented the peasants. After the February revolution it was the strongest party, but quickly lost its influence when it failed to live up to its own agrarian programme. It soon split into two sections, Right and Left. The Left supported and then entirely united with the Bolsheviks.

[3] 1st March 1908, No. 61.

[4] Professor Fjodor Stepun, 'The Past and the Unforgettable,' from *My Life 1884–1924*, Munich 1947, p. 146.

[5] Karl Jacob Hirsch, *Return to God – Letters to my Son*, Wuppertal, 1967, p. 51.

[6] The Spartacist League had been formed in January, 1916, by those elements in the workers' movement opposed to the Imperialist War. It took its name from Spartacus, the leader of the revolt against Rome in the years 73–71 B.C.

Chapter II

[1] The Ukrainian Soviets had been crushed by the combined forces of the German Army and the reactionary strata from within. A puppet government was set up, but a bitter guerilla struggle was still in progress. The guerillas were heroically supported by the peasantry whom the Germans were sucking dry.

The Bolshevik government was forced by a German ultimatum to conclude an immediate peace treaty with the puppet government. It seemed as though they were siding with the oppressors and this was one of the hardest ultimatums to swallow.

2 Born 13th August 1871, leader and cofounder of the Spartacus League. Lawyer and political writer, member of the Reichstag in 1912. He was the only member of the Social Democratic Party in the Reichstag to vote against war credits. On 1st May 1916 he was arrested in Berlin in connection with an anti-war demonstration and sentenced to two and one-half years' hard labour. In October 1918 he was released and on, 15th January 1919, was murdered by agents of the counter-revolution.

3 Rosa Luxemburg, born in Russian Poland in 1871. Worked actively among Polish Socialists until she went to Germany and married formally a German. Editor and contributor of various Socialist papers. Took part in Russian Revolution of 1905. In 1914 was sentenced to one year's imprisonment, thereafter in protective custody, for anti-war activities. Founder with Liebknecht of Spartacus League. After the Revolution co-editor of *Rote Fahne*. Arrested on January 15th, 1919, she was brutally murdered by army officers on her way to prison.

4 Even before Leviné's arrival, there had been an attempt to bring out a *Rote Fahne*. One or two numbers appeared in February 1919. Then it petered out. The first number issued under Leviné's editorship is dated March 18th. From then on a complete change in the whole of its policy can be traced.

5 The Independent Social-Democratic Party (*Unabhangige sozialdemokratische Pertei Deutschlands* or USPD), or Independents, closely resembled the Independent Labour Party.

6 Neither the K.P.D. nor Karl Radek, to whom I gave a copy in 1931, thought fit to publish a book of an opposition leader. I was unable to preserve my own copy. (R.L.-M.)

7 The Social-Democratic Party of Germany (Sozialdemokratische Partei Deutschlands or SPD), frequently referred to as the Majority Socialists, corresponded more or less to the British Labour Party.

8 Hugo Haase, born in Allenstein, East Prussia, on September 29, 1863. On the outbreak of war in 1914 he was parliamentary leader of the Social-Democratic Party in the Reichstag. Founder of the Independent Social-Democratic Party at Gotha in 1917, he continued to belong to its moderate wing. One of the members of the provisional Government set up after the outbreak of the Revolution, he resigned in protest against the collaboration of the Majority Socialists with the bourgeoisie towards the end of 1918. One of the most genuine personalities of the

German workers' movement, he was bitterly attacked by the reactionaries, despite his moderate policy. Died in 1919 as a result of an attempt on his life.

9 All the subsequent quotations are taken from the Protocol of the Congress. (R.L.-M.)

10 For that purpose procedure demanded a faction of no less than twenty members. The twelve Spartacist delegates could, according to Leviné, easily supplement the number with other left-minded delegates particularly from among the soldiers.

11 Friedrich Ebert, born 1871 in Heidelberg, a saddler by trade. Joining the Social-Democratic Party in 1889, he became its leader during the war of 1914-1918. On November 9, 1918, when the German armies were collapsing on the Western Front and Parliamentary Government in Germany was breaking down, he accepted the Chancellorship from Prince Max of Baden and thereafter assumed what amounted to dictatorial power as head of the Provisional Government, the Council of People's Representatives. On February 11 he was elected President of Germany by the National Assembly which had been elected by popular vote on January 19 and which met at Weimar to elaborate a constitution for the new Republic. Ebert filled the office of President until his death on February 28, 1925. His words, "I hate revolution as I hate sin" secured him an unenviable reputation among the revolutionary workers of Germany.

12 Philipp Scheidemann, born Kassel, July 26, 1865. Entered Reichstag in 1903 as Social-Democrat and leader of his party during war of 1914. Associated with Erzberger in "Peace Resolution" of July 1917, demanding peace without annexation or indemnities. July 1918 Vice-President of Reichstag. October 3 Secretary of State without Portfolio in Prince Max of Baden's cabinet. On November 9 proclaimed German Republic. On November 10 one of three Majority Socialists who joined provisional Government. Elected President of first Republican Ministry by Weimar Assembly on February 8, 1919. Resigned June 20, 1919 as protest against signing of Versailles Treaty and resumed leadership of Majority Socialists.

13 Kaiser Wilhelm II told army recruits that they must be ready to fire on their fathers and mothers if he ordered them to do so.

14 Quoted by Nettl in his book on Rosa Luxemburg.

15 Participation in the election was never regarded as a matter of principle, and it was also very soon taken over by events. On January 19th (election day) Karl Liebknecht and Rosa Luxemburg were dead

and no immunity could protect the Communist delegates from a similar fate.

Nevertheless, Leviné's arguments against participation in the election are very significant. It is true that he was momentarily carried away by the general mood, but he also knew how to learn from these moods. He concluded:

'The fact that our comrades from the Central Committee say that the masses are not yet sufficiently enlightened speaks out against participation. We could possibly explain here to the comrades how one can be against the National Assembly and in favour of participation in the elections, but these comrades would not be capable of making it clear enough to their factory colleagues. It is quite true that the masses think primitively. The moment you say to them, take part in the elections, their instinctive hostility to the National Assembly fades and the centre of gravity shifts from the task of building the workers' Soviets to expecting gains.

'Whether we will or not, the masses will vote for the National Assembly. How can we succeed in winning back the masses afterwards? We are facing the most difficult struggles. But if the workers should first be defeated, then the disappointed masses will not look for salvation in the National Assembly but will say: the Spartacists were right after all when they told us to build up our Soviets.'

[16] This incident occurred during one of the most violent periods of the struggle in Berlin. Among the troops not demobilised was the so-called People's Naval Division. It was quartered in the Palace in Berlin, was for a time able to defy the authority of the Government of People's Representatives and was regarded as the mainstay of the revolution. Ebert managed to obtain assistance of General Gröner to crush the People's Naval Division. As a result of this attrocity the Independents resigned from the Government.

Chapter III

[1] The Central Council was a body elected by the Soldiers', Workers' and Peasants' Councils. The Revolutionary Central Council which functioned under Toller's first Soviet Republic, was elected by the revolutionary workers. The Central Council had all the character of a deliberative assembly, but possessed far more power, and the whole basis of the difference between the Independents and the Communists was

the Communist contention that full power should be given to the Central Council.

2 Kurt Eisner, born May 14, 1867. A member of the SPD, he joined the Independents after the split in the party. On the staff of *Vorwaerts* and later a free-lance journalist. Distinguished himself by his courageous stand against the war, sentenced to imprisonment. Released just before the Revolution, he proclaimed, on November 8, 1918, the Bavarian Republic, of which he was appointed Premier. As Prime Minister he pursued a policy similar to that of Kerenski in Russia, but he made himself very unpopular with the reactionaries on account of his pronounced Francophile tendencies. He was shot by Count Arco on February 21, 1919.

3 A Doctor of Science, he came from a Russo-German family. An excellent speaker, he was the most popular figure in the Bavarian Revolution until the appearance of Leviné. Later became Leviné's closest collaborator as a member of the Executive Council. After the collapse of the Revolution he escaped to Russia, where he devoted himself principally to scientific studies.

4 *Rote Fahne*, 23rd February, 1919.

5 *Rote Fahne*, 19th March, 1919.

6 Karl Liebknecht would have got carried away and overlooked the absence of a basis for the Proclamation of a Soviet Republic. Rosa Luxemburg was too dogmatic and perhaps lacked that indomitable courage to take over a hopeless situation.

'Karl, where is our programme?' were the words with which she admonished him for his attitude during the so-called Spartacus week. (R.L.-M.)

7 It will be remembered that on the formation of the Hoffmann Government on March 17 the Diet had been adjourned sine die. A meeting of the Diet was now called for Tuesday, April 4, at 4.0 p.m. It was the calling of this meeting that brought the events of April 4 to a head. On Thursday April 3 the Workers' and Soldiers' Council of Augsburg called a meeting at which it was decided to send a delegation to Munich to demand of the Central Council the proclamation of a Bavarian Soviet Republic. On April 4 the Munich Central Council held a meeting in the Löwenbräukellar at which it was announced that a Soviet Republic would be proclaimed. Subsequently there followed a conference between certain Majority Socialist Ministers of the Hoffmann Government and the Central Council at the War Office.

8 *Reichswehr* Minister in the Social-Democratic Government of Ger-

many after the Revolution. Notorious for the ruthlessness with which he crushed the workers' movement with the aid of a volunteer force commanded by former professional officers. His activity can be characterised best by his able motto to his book: "*Von piel bis papp*"– "someone has got to be the bloodhound."

⁹ Member of the Bavarian Diet (parliament) and the National Assembly, Chairman of the Bavarian Peasant Association, Dürr was tour commandant at the time of this speech.

¹⁰ Carl Dietrich, born 10th December 1873 in Haugsdarf, joiner, Trade Union Secretary, Delegate from Upper-Silesia in 1919 to the Central People's Council, Member of the National Assembly. Worked in the Communist Soviet Republic in an advisory capacity in the Financial Commission. Escaped to the Soviet Union.

¹¹ Karl Kautsky, born 1854. Economist and writer, he one was of the most important theoreticians of the Second International and of German Social-Democracy. For many years, until the period 1910–1912, he adhered to the left wing of the Social-Democratic Party and had pronounced sympathies with the 1905 Russian Revolution and the Bolsheviks. Later drifted over to the moderates, whom he had previously attacked so virulently. During the war he rejected the idea of revolutionary defeatism and justified himself in the famous dictum: "The International is an instrument of peace and is unfitted for struggle in the midst of war." He became one of the bitterest opponents of the Bolshevik Revolution and its protagonists.

¹² Ernst Toller, born 1893 in Bromberg. Well-known poet and dramatist. Joined the army as a volunteer in 1914, but invalided out and became a convinced Pacifist and Socialist. Collaborated with Eisner in the Bavarian Revolution in 1918 and became at the age of twenty-six Chairman of the Independent Social-Democratic Party. An excellent speaker, he lacked revolutionary experience, accepted dictatorship of the proletariat but assured that he only wanted "dictatorship of love," and rejected the use of violence. Fought as a commander in the Red Army. Was condemned to five years detention in a fortress after the collapse of the Munich Soviet Republic. He lived in England for a short time after Hitler's seizure of power, and later when his sight faded he committed suicide in America in 1939.

¹³ Johannes Hoffmann, born March 7, 1867. Of peasant stock, he became an elementary school teacher, later a journalist. He joined the Social-Democratic Government. After the death of Eisner he became Prime Minister of Bavaria and held that post until March 1920.

The Hoffmann Government withdrew at first to Nuremberg and then to Bamberg, whence it organised resistance to the Munich regime.
[14] Franz Epp, born 1868. In May, 1919, he organised the attack on the Soviet Republic. After 1933 he was District Leader in Bavaria under the Hitler regime.
[15] Die Münchener Tragödie, Paul Herte.
[16] Prof. A. Rosenberg wrote; in *Entstehung und Geschichte der Weimarer Republik*:

'After one week the adventure of the Soviet-Republic had already come to an end and the visionaries who wished to play People's Representatives had been unseated. But then Leviné thought it the duty of the Communists to jump into the breach and to save the honour of the Soviet idea. They organised a new government and tried, supported by a section of Munich workers and soldiers, to give the invading government troops battle.'

This is how the learned gentlemen treat history! What does it matter that 'after one week' not Leviné but Hoffmann's Government thought it their duty 'to jump into the breach' and at a moment when even the sceptical Leviné believed that 'everything will dissolve amicably.' For it was the assault on the first, calm, inert, harmless Soviet Republic that brought everything to a head.

Rosenberg admits, though, that 'Leviné showed at his trial and execution great heroism which gained him enthusiastic sympathy even from the opponents of his policies.'
[17] A Soviet Government was formed of Commissars (or People's Representatives) with Leviné and Levien at its head. The so-called Revolutionary Central Council of the Toller regime was replaced by a Committee of Action of fifteen. An Executive Council of four was established on which were two Independents, a Communist, Levien, and a Moderate, Männer. In this new Government the Commissars represented, very roughly, an inner Cabinet, the Executive Council a Ministry, and the Councils or Soviets a Legislature. The Committee of Action, over which Leviné presided, and which was in almost permanent session formed a direct link with the hierarchy of Workers' and Factory Councils. Thus direct representation was assured, and the will of the masses was constantly expressed. Hence the fundamental difference between the "Soviet" or "Council" system and parliamentary democracy.
[18] Commander of the forces controlling the Munich railway station. One of the leaders of the coup against the Soviet Republic of April 13,

1919. Arrested several members of the Government, including the well-known Anarchist leader, Mühsam.

[19] Leviné predicted: 'They know where to look for their deadliest enemies.' They also desperately hunted throughout the night for Leviné and Levien.

[20] Paul Fröhlich:

' "A medley of problems daily assails the executive council and in most cases that means Leviné," ' writes Leviné's biographer, Paul Werner. "One day there was a big diplomatic reception. Munich's entire diplomatic corps appeared. They demanded letters of safe conduct and immunity from the laws of the proletarian dictatorship. This was granted. The Prussian ambassador appeared... ."

'Leviné wanted to deal with the case himself. The ambassador wanted his confiscated car back and tried to impress the despised Spartacists by claiming his alleged extraterritoriality'. "Extraterritoriality rests on reciprocity," Leviné instructed the diplomat. "Bring us a guarantee that your government will recognise our Republic and the immunity of our diplomatic representatives and you will receive your letters of safe conduct."

'Furious at this unexpected rebuff, the man forgot all his manners and rushed away without taking his leave.'

'We were all filled with serene cheerfulness which was in complete contrast to our stormy life. It was marked by the feeling that even should we be wiped out tomorrow by the flood that rages around us, we were anyway walking in the right direction. Leviné was always able to convey to his friends this feeling and his unshakeable inner calm.'

[21] Tobias Axelrod was sent on a mission to Germany by the Russian Soviet Government and was arrested in Munich. Later he was liberated by the Soviet Republic and continued to lend his services as a technical expert until the entry of the counter-revolutionaries into the town. Sentenced to fifteen years' imprisonment he was later exchanged by the Russian Government.

[22] Social-Democratic worker. Condemned to two years detention in a fortress after the defeat of the Soviet Republic.

[23] One of its members was Rudolf Hess.

[24] Gustav Klingelhofer: member of the Soldier's Council, member of Toller's cabinet, collaborated in the Communist Soviet Republic. Independent Social-Democrat. Sentenced to five and a one-half years detention in a fortress.

[25] Recorded in Trotsky's *Russian Revolution*.

[26] *Ibid.*

[27] German law recognises (or, rather, recognised at the time) a distinction between revolutionary acts dictated by "honourable" and "dishonourable" convictions. The penalty for honourable convictions was confinement in a fortress – the mildest form of imprisonment; for dishonourable convictions death. The decision, of course, rested with the court. One has only to read the judgement of the court to see how lightly it disregarded the need for further evidence of Leviné's "dishonourable convictions."

[28] *Internationale* 1919, 9–10 and 13–14.

[29] Philip Price wrote in his *Germany in Transition*:

'...The majority of Socialists had it in their power to decide whether the Soviet Republic should come into existence or not...' He quotes another contemporary observer who said: 'They at least gave the impression that they would support the Soviet Republic, even if they did not enter it. Although the former War Minister and the Majority Socialist Schneppenhorst subsequently denied it, nevertheless the fact was established by the witness in the trial of Nutt, Independent Socialist editor of the *Neue Zeitung*, that Schneppenhorst verbally declared that he "would guarantee the Soviet Republic in Bavaria with his head"....'

'In the trial of Sauber, the Trade Union Secretary, who was present during the conference at the War Office, Schieffer made the following statement in the witness box: 'Schneppenhorst took the view that having regard to the need for unity among the proletariat, it was impossible to come through without the Soviet Republic.'

Sir George Young, in his *The New Germany*, writes: 'Of course, in this curious *chasser-croiser*, it is open to anyone to regard the Majoritarians as mere governmental *agents provocateurs*, working for a premature proclamation of the *Raterepublik*. This was the view taken by *The Times*....'

Chapter IV

[1] VII, 278.

[2] Lenin, XXI, 128.

[3] *Münchener Neueste Nachrichten*, 14th October 1919.

[4] naked.

[5] pansies.

6 In the Israelitischen Friedhof.

Chapter V

1 'The counter-revolution paid tribute in its peculiar way to the defendant. The law court had been turned into an army camp. Machine-guns and dumps of grenades covered the steps. The limited number of attendants was subjected to three or more painstaking searches. The courtroom was small and narrow and full of uniforms and weapons.'

As his sentence depended on the motives for his policy, honourable or dishonourable, his lawyers summoned many witnesses: 'university professors, public figures, trade unionists and so on, all adversaries of his political views and aims. And they all testified to the purity of his motives, and his revolutionary ideas, his self-sacrifice and his indifference to personal advantages, his kindness and his humanity....'

2 Dishonourable motives, based on his 'cowardice.'

3 *Volksstimme*, Social-Democratic organ for South-West Germany 4th June 1919:

'The Communists and Independents have had undeserved good fortune. One of the murderers of Karl Liebknecht and Rosa Luxemburg, [a man] whom the Court Martial also held partially responsible [for the act] has recently escaped, and on Tuesday the Russian Bolshevik, Dr Eugen Leviné, was condemned to death for high treason by the Court Martial established in Munich in conjunction with the state of siege.

'Now certainly no ministry in the world would be so lacking in common sense as to carry out the death sentence.'

On Wednesday, the 5th of May, the same paper wrote:

'The leaders of the Spartacus adventures ordered the execution of a number of bourgeois hostages in the Luipold High School. The unfortunates were so brutally murdered that three of the victims could not be identified until the Saturday. The corpses were found lying in a heap in the shool yard. Their shoes were missing. The still unidentified female corpse bore the marks of bestial torture. The eyes of the other corpses had been put out, their tongues and hands cut off. At the time of the murder, Leviné, Nissen and Dr Levien were in the cellar of the school.'

Volksstimme published this filthy atrocity story even though they had to add on the very same page:

'The official bulletin strangely insists that the mutilations described in the above communique did not take place.'

4 Philips Price writes in *Germany in Transition*: 'The Majority Socialist Ministers in the Hoffmann Government, most of whom were in some way or other compromised in the events leading up to the creation of the Soviet regime, issued with the rest of the Ministry, twenty-four hours after Leviné's sentence, the statement that they "saw no reason to quash the sentence." Whereupon the *Frankfurter Zeitung*, an honest middle-class organ, remarked that 'some members of the Government, if they were really against the shooting of Leviné, might have carried through their point by a simple majority vote in the Cabinet.' But this the Majority Socialist leaders dared not do. They could not vote, as many of them no doubt wished, for they were prisoners in the hands of the men whom they had called back to power.'

5 Trotsky even compares the July Days with the German 'March Action' of 1921 which was closer to a deliberate Communist Putsch, and the October 1923, meticulously planned, uprising. (He strangely forgot to mention Munich and, more surprisingly, the 'Spartacus Week.')

6 XXI, 225–6. German edition.

7 Leviné's report on the All-German Soviet Congress. See Appendix I.

8 XXI, 278 (*English edition*).

9 XXI, 159.

10 XXI, 159.

11 XXI, 269.

12 We have seen that this was not so. (R.L.-M.).

13 XXI, 108–9 (*English edition*).

14 Trotsky, *The Russian Revolution*, 594.

15 XXI, 178.

16 Pseudonym of Paul Froelich. Born 1889, member of the second Soviet Government in Munich. Member of the Reichstag and editor of works of Rosa Luxemburg. Expelled from the Communist Party in 1929 for his opposition to the party line.

Appendices

I

Eugen Levinés *Report On the First All-German Soviet Congress*

Comrades,
The Soviet Congress came to an end two days ago. You will have read about the proceedings in the papers and I do not wish to bore you with another account of the speeches and discussions, which you certainly know already.

For the time being, I should like to confine myself to making an assessment of the Congress, and the conclusions we must draw from it for our future activities in the Workers' and Soldiers' Soviets.

We did not have very high hopes of the Congress from the start. We knew that we, the Spartacists, would be a tiny minority and we also knew that our neighbours on the right, the Independents, would not have a majority either.

Nevertheless we could never have imagined that it would, in fact, present such a hopeless picture, nor could we have envisaged that the Soviet Congress would be composed, as one colleague has remarked, of Party Secretaries with their numerous "tickets," and zealous Trade Union officials, indifferent to the interests of the workers and concerned only with narrow Party interests; that those would be in the majority who are ready to stake the interests of the working class and the revolution, for the sake of picking up mandates to the National Assembly.

What then were the points of vital and decisive significance upon which the Congress had to decide? Above all, those that were rejected.

The Spartacist delegates proposed that the Congress should declare itself the highest legislative and executive authority. But first, an interesting little detail: this proposal was to be introduced at the very beginning of the Congress. The half-hearted section of the Independents, however, managed to shelve it and so ensure that this demand would not be submitted right at the start, but would be dealt with amidst a host of other proposals; and this facilitated its rejection.

This in itself shows that, in order to consider the fate of the Congress, we must first of all establish the relationship between the Spartacus League and the Independents. For when you read the Congress report you must certainly have wondered what had happened to the Spartacus group.

You knew that some of us were there and you may have asked where were they? Or if you listened to any speeches you might have asked what were the fundamental differences between the Spartacus group and the Independents?

It was only a small matter that actually set the ball rolling. Just as a tiny grain of sand can start off a whole avalanche, so an organisational blunder forced the Spartacus League into a hopeless position. I want to deal with this factional problem first, to show you how this blunder paralysed us and deprived us of all possibility of action.

Prior to the Congress we held a conference for all Spartacists, where Liebknecht asked us what we would do if the Independents failed to submit our proposals. We declared, in that case we will do it ourselves.

At 8 o'clock next morning, we had a meeting with the Independents. After endless debating and devious stratagems they declared: 'Yes, we agree with these proposals, but one can't go at it like a bull at a gate. The proposal that the Congress should declare itself the supreme authority should, therefore, not be submitted at the start of the Congress.'

They dealt with the proposal for an international appeal in the same way. It was agreed that we should immediately demand that Liebknecht and Rosa Luxemburg be invited, but no agreement was reached on the other motions and we could not finish the session, because the Congress was to begin at 10 o'clock. This is what followed:

A working committee had been appointed the day before with Geyer as its secretary – a man who could not make up his mind. In actual fact, the typical middle line knew how to push the interests of the Independents to the fore, so that the Spartacus League sank into insignificance.

Geyer ruled that we could not introduce resolutions that had not previously been debated.

'But you pledged yourselves to introduce the resolutions!'

To which the moderate Independents answered, 'Yes, we

meant to introduce them but they haven't been debated yet, and this is why we can't submit them.'

Under the influence of the Scheidemannites, the resolution to invite Liebknecht and Rosa Luxemburg was rejected. The resolution on an international appeal disappeared. We do not know what became of it. The secretary of the Independents claims to have given it to the secretary of the Congress, a manoeuvre which first became apparent at the next session, when we said; 'The proposal has vanished, we want it renewed,' and the Minister declared: 'This is defiance of the Entente. If the Congress appeals to the workers of the Entente over the heads of their governments, then the Entente might take it as a reason to declare war.'

We observed that it was much more provocative to keep Solf and Erzberger in office. 'In this case you are prepared to countenance it, yet when we want to appeal to the people you stab us in the back.'

In this manner any constructive work with the Independents was made impossible from the start.

The debates amongst the Independents were all determined by the fact that the Right wing trembled lest the Left might go too far.

The proposal to resume relations with the Soviet Republic was left to one Comrade Ziegler, whom I had never set eyes on before. I was at the Pre-conference and do not know what happened. Then one fine day I happen to read in the *Berliner Tageblatt* that Comrade Ziegler had withdrawn his motion for the resumption of relations with the Soviet Republic. Another donation to the government's waste-paper basket.

The motion itself was handled in a very cunning way. Nobody was even told that it was up for debate. When we succeeded in getting the countersignature of the faction, it was too late.

We suggested that Brass should deal with the problem, but his protests were so half-hearted that it was easy for the Congress to reject the motion, which it would naturally have done in any case, since the matter had certainly been decided in advance. This is just one example of the way in which the string-pullers operated behind the scenes.

On the most crucial questions, such as the National Assembly and the declaration of the Congress as the supreme authority we, of course, had no hope at all. We knew that the National Assembly would be passed and that the Congress would also approve the report of the government and the Executive Committee. It was also clear that nothing could come of nationalisation, after the speech by Hilferding, who out of sheer misgivings and fear had literally strangled it.

But all this would not account for the question with which I began – where was the Spartacus League?

By the end of the Congress we had established that the Spartacus group had twelve delegates. To form a faction we needed twenty. We could easily have won over eight of the soldiers, and could then have acted as a faction and been able to send up our own speakers... but this was completely smothered in the chaos of discussions and debates with the Independent faction.

Instead of operating from the Congress platform, we were tied to the Independent faction, which hung round our necks like a millstone, and a very treacherous one at that, which succeeded in interfering with the list of speakers and paralysed our activities at every turn.

What took place behind the scenes of the faction is of the greatest significance. It is quite true that we were in no way able to influence the faction itself. It is another matter when we are dealing with a mass meeting of Independents; there we Spartacists are able to whip them to the left, as we so often say. But parliamentary indifference has made the gentlemen of the faction so thick-skinned that our whip lashes have no effect on them.

Dittmann, who is bent on an amalgamation of the S.P.D., and the Independents, and others, including Luise Zietz, who champion joint tickets for the National Assembly, are quite unyielding to our lashes. On the contrary they find them most unpleasant and so move even further to the Right out of sheer personal resentment.

We must put an end to this unnatural alliance, this marriage of fishes and young lions. We cannot possibly act the part of the whip that drives the independents. How can there be an alliance between a whip and a donkey which digs in its heels and declares 'you can go on whipping me, but I won't budge.' If we continue to ally ourselves with the U.S.P. we shall be the donkeys. I want to show you how we are continually hampered by having to take the Independents into account. While trying to carry them along with us we only lose our hold on the people, and find ourselves drawn to the Right. Is this then the task of the Revolution – to drag a thousand men hither and thither?

For the first time the Independent faction finally pulled itself together and resolved to take no part in the elections to the Central Council. Haase and Dittmann stormed against this decision but the resolution was carried with a large majority. However, even when the left-wing Independents had allowed themselves to be swept along, they lacked the energy to draw the conclusions from their own political decisions. The next day, when we said, 'It stands to reason that if we don't participate in the elections to the Central Council, our people cannot remain in the government,' and tried to press our point, Haase declared, 'I shall only withdraw if the authorised bodies demand it.'

'The authorised bodies' meant party headquarters and the party conference. Since, as you know, a party conference is not going to be convened despite all pressure, and since Haase himself is the party headquarters, we shall be waiting in vain.

They responded with a vehement attack on us. They argued that we Spartacists above all had no right to make such a demand, since we were already half outside the Party, and that a comrade when challenged had replied: 'Yes, I am *still* in the U.S.P.D.'

The main issue was lost sight of: whether we could take part in a government when all the power was put into the hands of the Peoples' Delegates. Instead they concentrated on personal squabbles and accused us of spoiling the fruits of their policies for them.

How, then, was the situation at the Congress affected by the relationship between the Spartacus League and the U.S.P.D.?

The conductor's baton was in the hands of the S.P.D. After some uncertainty, lasting a day and a half, the front-line soldiers were won over by speeches on law and order. They were bamboozled with great finesse. Soldiers' meetings were arranged on the very premises of the Congress.

The bourgeois element, the Democratic Union, stood united behind the S.P.D., but the U.S.P.D., instead of uniting to act against them, wriggled in order to preserve their own Peoples' Delegates, Haase, Dittman and Barth, and the Spartacus League were worn down by every possible delay, standing order. and the like.

Then came catastrophe. The results were as follows:

The motion to declare the Soviet Congress a legislative body: rejected.

The motion to invite Rosa Luxemburg and Karl Liebknecht: submitted twice and rejected.

The motion for an international appeal to the peoples of England and France: first shelved, then submitted anew and rejected.

The motion to resume relations with the Soviet Government: first arbitrarily withdrawn and then after being renewed, rejected.

It was logical. How could it be otherwise! The first point, to declare Germany a united socialist republic is one, to which the S.P.D. is particularly opposed. They don't want a socialist republic.

The demand of the soldiers was more successful, first because they were armed, and second because the conflict with the High Command was becoming critical.

The High Command left an inquiry of the Peoples' Representatives unanswered and the situation became so critical that the Peoples' Representatives needed the armed forces for their own protection.

Then we come to the reception of the deputation. There was an attempt to alter its legitimate demand, for the soldiers wanted the supreme power to belong to the Soldiers' Councils. Then there was more manoeuvring. Of course, the Central Council should be the highest authority and the supreme power. Instead the supreme power was given to the Peoples' Representatives, which means that six men have all the military forces of Germany at their command. The situation remains as it was; before, we had one Kaiser [Wilhelm II], now we have six. Unless the troops are enlightened, these six men have the power to betray dispose of in the same way as before. And we believe that Ebert, at least, is just as prepared to shoot at father and mother as Wilhelm von Hohenzollern was.

This decision is fraught with great danger. But here the tragedy becomes a comedy. The Peoples' Representatives, who dared to deprive the workers' representatives – i.e. the Central Council – of their power, did not dare to take it from Hindenburg and his generals. They had the courage to declare that the supreme power did not belong to the Central Council, but they lacked the courage to say to Hindenburg; – The supreme power belongs to us alone; they said 'in agreement with the High Command.'

This clearly reveals the entire situation. The Peoples' Representatives realise they are suspended in the air and that they must rely either on the working masses, which means on the Central Council, or on the counter-revolution, which means on the High Command. Ebert, Scheidemann and Landsbert have chosen, with the amicable support of Haase, Dittmann and Barth, to build their power, together with the High Command on bayonets directed against the working class. That is one of the most disastrous results of the Congress and is something we must all clearly understand. The small achievement that the local Workers' and Soldiers' Councils are to share the local power with the High Command just vanishes. For the Local Workers' and Soldiers' Councils exercise this local power only with the agreement of the High Command,

and the High Command is not subordinate to the Peoples' Representatives, but well-nigh equal. The essential factor therefore remains the High Command.

Now, up to the National Assembly the Peoples' Representatives have the power to promulgate the laws which will smother that half-dead child, the Soviet system, with the soft pillow of their alleged support for the Soviets. Then people will say; but there aren't any Soviets left, and the National Assembly is naturally the product of the revolution.

So the dangers that threaten the workers' organisations are enormous and the Congress has only sharpened them. It is not the Peoples' Representatives who are at the head of state but Hindenburg and Ebert representatives, who in possession of the entire power can throttle the present Workers' and Soldiers' Soviets as they did in Neukölln. I don't wish to deal with the manoeuvrings of the S.P.D. now, these manoeuvres are only relevant in relation to the Independents. But the whole Congress has thus set its seal on these counter-revolutionary policies. The socialisation question discussed at the end reveals another danger: an attempt to kill it off with the sham socialism. The *Rote Fahne* has recently disclosed this.

In former revolutions the struggle was simple. The counter-revolution fought in the open, on the side of the monarchy, and did not hide its views. Nowadays the struggle is much more difficult because capitalism and imperialism hide behind the mask of the S.P.D. and we have to fight them in disguise.

We are entering not merely an election campaign but the very struggle for existence confronting the workers' organisation, the Soviet system.

I have already tried to give you an idea of the Soviet system in Russia and to compare the achievements of the German Soviets during the revolution.

I have tried to show by the Russian example what should have been done in the early days. Now we are confronted by a changed situation. When I wish to deal with the problem of the German Soviets, I cannot go by the book.

Now we can no longer say, this is the way the Russians acted and this is why we must do the same, because they already had the power.

Take the example of some Lower Rhine Soviet, established purely as a result of an agreement between the S.P.D. and the U.S.P.D.

Our task is to create a Soviet organisation that does not exist solely on paper: such an organisation can be torn to pieces. Our duty in the near future is to build up an organisation from below.

I suggest that in large plants we should follow the Russian example; i.e. we must not elect ten or twelve people direct from the meeting, because the best orators or party leaders would then be chosen again, and not the people. Instead we must first organise a Soviet in every workshop. In the Russian Soviet organisation the basis in large plants was not this workshop Soviet. There people could judge their representatives by deeds and by words, they could confront them at any time, and when they failed they could be recalled immediately and replaced by others. The factory Soviets were built out of the workshop Soviets. For Germany we must first introduce amalgamation of all the workshops and then apply the same principle of recall.

Now the question arises whether outsiders should be allowed in the factory Soviets. I think the elected representatives should certainly continue to be drawn from the works, to prevent the danger of infiltration by Trade Union employees.

Of course we must permit electioneering, which means we must not restrict the electioneering and the speakers to factory members. On the contrary we can also invite speakers to explain to the masses the function of the factory Soviets.

In most factories there will be enough comrades to do this very successfully, but others might not have enough trained speakers.

In such situations we must be allowed to bring in outsiders, and the factory Soviets must also have the right to invite outsiders in in an advisory capacity. But when an important question arises, why shouldn't we be allowed to invite Rosa Luxemburg and Liebknecht. And if the S.P.D. is heavily represented in the factory Soviets, for God's sake, let Ebert speak, so that the factory council may get acquainted with all the intentions of this man.

The battle ahead of us can only be won if we have the support of the masses *amalgamated in a strong organisation*. So we must develop the organisation of factory Soviets and where they have not been properly elected, hold new elections, even at the risk of the S.P.D. and the Christian centre being elected, in order to clarify the meaning of the Soviet system. That is, workshop Soviets and factory Soviets built only on factory members – but absolute freedom in election propaganda and the *unconditonal recall* of any delegate.

That is the essential feature distinguishing us from the Social-

Democrats: that we must always be able to recall a delegate if he does not fulfil our aspirations. This must be the basis for our propaganda in factory Soviets.

We must also undertake the extension of factory control, and our leading comrades present, the Spartacists, must explain that socialisation means that the factory becomes not their private property, but public property. Then we can proceed. The Workers' and Soldiers' Soviets have become at best only control bodies. The factory Soviets are the source of our strength, with which we shall fight the revolutionary counter-attack. The first task is to get our people into the factory Soviets. We must have at least one comrade in every Soviet to lead it is our aims.

Once we have achieved this, we can proceed to our next task: to convene conferences of factory Soviets, district by district as well as industry by industry. This is of the greatest importance. When we have succeeded in creating such organisations, the National Assembly will hold no terrors for us. It may then confer as much as it likes, the workers' Soviets will do their job.

We must ask, what should the Workers' Soviets be doing in the local organisations now? That must depend on who has the majority. If a workers' council can and will start the struggle, well and good. We know that we cannot count on a respite and we know we are facing a débâcle. We have therefore no reason to speak of peaceful developments, which it is claimed will solve our problems.

We would in no way advocate an armed struggle in this situation, because that would lead to a fight between the workers themselves. We would, however, suggest that the workers' Soviets should defend their rights with all their might. If a workers' council is dropped, then try to elect a new one from the factory Soviets. It was our weakness that our workers' and soldiers' soviets were not rooted in the masses.

Haase and Ebert assigned to the Soldiers' Soviets only advisory status. Where Soviets had merely been appointed the Army units capitulated. Units with elected Soviets, however, did not give a damn for the Haase and Ebert decrees. When a Workers' Council is really elected by the factory soviets, it will fight. For this reason, we must try to get our Spartacists into the factory soviets. Our men, that is, but not 'our' Independents.

There has been much talk about socialisation, but we have never moved an inch towards it. The appointed commission on socialisation should have consisted of people convinced that socialisation was both possible and necessary, who would try to work out the means of implementing it.

Instead, the chosen commission discussed *whether* socialisation should be introduced. It included representatives of capitalism and professors, among them Lederer, who declared that he believed socialisation to be hardly possible at present.

People appear at the Soviet Congress who tell us that in Hamburg a man advocated the socialisation of steam trawlers, but knew absolutely nothing about them. Yes. None of us here have any idea about steam trawlers, but nevertheless we can still say that steam trawlers too must be socialised.

We have profitable factories which are very well provided for, and factories which run at a loss. We have seen some factory owners attempt to hand over their unprofitable factories to the workers. That is another danger, and a very real one.

We welcome workers' control, but in cases where this control is exercised not in the public interest but in the interest of a given factory, the following situation could arise: there is a shortage of raw materials but a small factory has a very active comrade on the council, who declares 'my first concern is to get our factory going and keep my colleagues in work.' He uses all his powers and succeeds in getting more coal for this little factory than does a factory with ten times more workers.

This is factory patriotism, which makes a fair distribution of raw materials impossible. A distribution *per capita* would also be wrong; for a factory with a hundred workers and one with ten thousand stand in a ratio of one to a hundred.

There is no need to provide the small factory with proportionally less coal; it is much more profitable to shut it down and transfer the hundred workers to the larger plant.

There is a danger that backward workers might confuse the idea of workers' control with a primitive non-socialist factory patriotism. This danger is particularly acute where a factory council is able to influence the distribution of raw materials and work. Should we then give up the whole idea of factory soviets? Of course not!

The situation in Russia was different for the following reasons: During the period of factory control the October Revolution took place and turned the factory soviets into different organisations. For the moment the proletariat came to power the soviets were no longer the driving force of the revolution, but became a sort of administrative-organisational apparatus, a kind of governmental support with the task of safeguarding the distribution of raw materials, together with the government. The question of control became secondary, for with public ownership the Soviets could themselves determine the choice of factories and did not have to leave this to the owners. The most profitable were the first to be nationalised. In this new situation, the factory soviets were of great value in the internal structure of the factories but not in the overall amalgamation which took place in industry.

organisational apparatus, a kind of governmental support with the task of safeguarding the distribution of raw materials, together with the government. The question of control became secondary, for with public ownership the Soviets could themselves determine the choice of factories and did not have to leave this to the owners. The most profitable were the first to be nationalised. In this new question, the factories were ... were of great value in the internal structure of the factories but not in the overall arrangement of which took place in industry.

II

Draft of the Organisation of the K.P.D.

(This draft was accepted in the session of the Executive Committee of 10 March 1919.)

Fundamental Prerequisites for the New Organisation

The Munich section of the K.P.D. is a direct product of the revolutionary process of transformation of the proletariat, which began with the November revolution at the end of the war.

Expanding and organizing the party were particularly difficult and inevitably suffered many infantile disorders. Munich and Bavaria in general lacked a revolutionary tradition. Even during the war there was no revolutionary proletarian fighting organisation.

The feeble beginnings before the war which grew in opposition to the old reformist party machine had been almost completely uprooted by the 4th of August. Nothing was left but the personal reminiscences of individual members of this movement.

The U.S.P. which arose in 1917 out of the discontent with the ruling military dictatorship bore none of the traits of the revolutionary proletariat. It was inspired and guided by the moral indignation and pacifist tendencies of Eisner, Schroeder, Unterleitner, etc. It aimed at beauty and harmony.

The U.S.P. was not a revolutionary fighting party. It was unable to prepare the proletarians for a fight with the counter-revolution, a fight carried out with all the methods of political infamy, the terror of a brutal, unbridled soldiery and the pressure of an unscrupulous bureaucracy struggling for its survival.

A new strong instrument for struggle had to be forged for this task during the revolution itself – the K.P.D., which literally grew up in a few weeks from the soil of Munich and Bavaria.

Revolution, however, is not a form of organic development, but a forcible upheaval of political feelings, thoughts and actions. It is an interplay of forces, passions and ideas which increases daily. The process is bound to include illusions and errors. It requires daily adaptation to new situations and requirements. What has been built up through weeks of work must be knocked down again in a few days. There are no final and ideal faultless forms during the process of the revolution.

Revolution does not follow a straight line of development, because the revolution as such does not dictate situations and methods. In most cases it is the counter-revolution which acts as a complete and organised power.

Revolutionary power must aim never to slacken its energies from finding new forms, by drawing on the proletariat's immence reserves of strength and by powerfully expanding the organisational apparatus to meet the new requirements.

The expression of revolutionary will is not found in bewailing of faults, inadequacies and errors, but in building a new revolutionary organisation with new methods and forms.

III

Proclamations of the Government

1.

To the Bavarian People!

Bavarian troops under the command of General Möhl and Reichswehr troops under the command of Lieutenant-General von Oven have encircled Munich. The task of these troops is to liberate Munich and its surroundings harassed by the Spartacists, from the terror of a minority. Soldiers, workers, citizens and peasants of Munich!

Listen to the voice of reason. Avoid the streets and open places to prevent shedding the blood of the innocent. The troops of the government are mercilessly breaking down all armed restistance to bring an end to the sufferings of all. Food, coal, raw materials are waiting to be sent to Munich.

(Signed) Hoffmann, Prime Minister.

2.

To The Population of Munich,

The hopes of the Communist and semi-Communist enthusiasts, who in their bombastic fanaticism promised the proclamation of a Soviet Republic as the dawn of an era of social freedom and justice, have been promptly and cruelly dashed. In the place of unselfish, noble men, brutal and criminal individuals assumed the leading positions in the government. Countless households were looted and considerable sums vanished, never to be seen again. Indiscriminate arrests were made.

Food supplies to the community were recklessly interfered with. The existence of whole sections of small men was jeopardised, and Munich was cut off from the rest of the world.

Food supplies to the town stopped. Infants, the sick and the infirm were exposed to danger. The poor man's kitchen ran out of coal. For over three weeks a heavy weight oppressed the economic and spiritual life of Munich. Every free word against the shameful misrule of an alien clique was punished by the revolutionary tribunal. Hostages were bestially murdered.

The saviours are here. Government troops, troops of the Socialist Government – not White Guards – have marched into Munich to put an end to the terror at long last, to establish freedom for all, to reunite the capital, which had been forcibly cut off from the rest of Bavaria, and thus to restore supplies of goods and normal economic conditions.

There will be no suppression of freedom of opinion, and stern measures will be taken against any violent interference with of public order and the welfare of the community.

The political struggle will be decided not by brute force of arms but by honest spiritual wrestling. To restore peace and order everyone must see to it that arms are surrendered immediately. The whole population of Munich is called upon to collaborate honestly, confidently and actively.

For right and justice! For freedom and Socialism!

Vollhals, Police Commissioner
Schilling, Military Governor

3.

The Action Committee of the Social-Democratic Party asserted: 'The troops of Hoffmann's socialist government come not as enemies of the working class, not as "White Guards", but as protectors of public safety and order. *Comrade Hoffmann is no reactionary or counter-revolutionary, but a radical champion of the socialist movement.* His aides are Social-Democrats like yourselves.

Workers, assist the soldiers in their hard task, without which construction on a socialist basis is impossible. Don't let mistrust create dangerous frictions which in this tense atmosphere could lead to incalculable results. If peace is to be restored in Munich, it is essential that only the soldier and policeman should carry weapons, for they alone are responsible to the government at any time for using them.

Obey, therefore, the orders of the military commanders to surrender all weapons. Do not tolerate the outbreak of more disorder, more confusion and more destruction, but help to begin at long last, with creative work and positive progress to a socialist economic order.

The working class must free itself of the tissue of lies that was created by weeks of suppression of the freedom of expression, and by weeks of unscrupulous official Press deception of the Soviet dictators.

The Hoffmann Government does not fight the Soviet principle. On the contrary, it has resolutely championed the extension, safety and establishment of that principle.

What would happen if every leader, every socialist minister, were to be immediately condemned because he failed to fulfill in his first few weeks of office all the expectations of unprincipled agitators?

Workers of Munich, you must now have the courage of confidence. Inhabitants of Munich, give your active support to the Hoffmann Cabinet!'

IV

Proclamation of Martial Law, May 2nd 1919

And all the beautiful words about pure democracy were crowned by a sinister proclamation staring from the walls in large black letters.

Martial law

'1. On April 25th, 1919, the Government of the Free State of Bavaria, in accordance with Article 5 of the Martial Law Enactment, proclaimed martial law throughout those districts of Bavaria situated on the right bank of the Rhine. Until further notice no public meetings may be held out of doors. All gatherings of people in streets and public places are prohibited. Meetings in closed premises may only take place with the consent of the Military Governor, which must be applied for at least twenty-four hours before the commencement of the meeting. In case of consent a permit will be issued.

2. The curfew will begin at 9 p.m. From 10 p.m. all traffic in the streets and public places is prohibited. Persons who for professional reasons must go out at a later hour can obtain a permit from the Military Governor's Offices or from the district Police Station.

3. The affixing of posters and the distribution of leaflets in streets and public places are only permitted with the consent of the Military Governor.

4. All police will proceed immediately to their posts and take up their duties without delay. They must obey the orders issued by the local commanding officers of the forces.

5. Any contravention of these orders will be punished under Martial Law.'

The Bavarian Commander-in-Chief

Moehl

Lieutenant-General and
Commander in Chief von Oven

On behalf of the Bavarian Government

Dr Ewinger

Munich, May 2nd, 1919.

V

Leviné's Last Speech

I find it rather difficult to state my case. Even before my first interrogation I pointed out that the whole of these proceedings – the entire trial – was really only the outcome of a political and not of a legal situation. The indictment of high treason is based only on the fact that the Soviet Republic was defeated. When it succeeds, it ceases to be high treason. Much the same was said in the leading article of the *Münchener Neueste Nachrichten*, which stated that 'only unsuccessful high treason is high treason. If it succeeds, it ceases to be high treason. High treason is thus a political, not a legal issue.'

I look upon this Court as the representatives of that class I have always regarded as my political adversaries. Perhaps I could account for my actions before Communists; but how could I defend myself before my adversaries for actions which they must regard as directed against their very existence?

I found myself in a similar situation in Russia; I refused to plead and was acquitted for lack of evidence. I shall not pursue the same tactics now; I propose to explain my motives.

I am not defending myself because I expect a more lenient sentence from you. Had I wished this I rather ought to be silent. My Counsel, who are closer to you both politically and as individuals could conduct my defence far more effectively. I am addressing the Court now for the same reasons which made me defend myself so resolutely throughout the whole proceedings. Both in the Press and among the public the most monstrous rumours have been spread about the Soviet Republic, about me personally, about the entire course of events, and I do not wish to let the rumours go by unopposed. The Munich workers have known me only for a short time and some of them may be ghawed by doubts as to whether I am really worthy of the confidence they have placed in me. As I am no longer free, I must use this trial to set everything out clearly.

My second reason is that I am a member of the Communist Party, and this is the most hated and most maligned party in Germany. I regard it therefore as my duty to proclaim in public the motives by which the members of the German Communist Party work, wish to work, strive to work. I owe it to the workers on the Executive Committee and to over twelve hundred members of the Factory Councils with whom I have grown close through our day to day collaboration, even if they ultimately repudiated me. I owe it to them, too, to clear their names.

I am defending myself, then, not to obtain a more lenient sentence, but so as not to miss an opportunity of establishing the facts.

The main difference between myself and the Prosecution is that we regard all political and social phenomena, in Germany as well as in the rest of the world, from totally opposite angles. The Prosecuting Counsel overestimates the power and capacity of leaders to act and to influence events. He assumes that the dice of world history would fall differently according to whether they are cast by honest or dishonest leaders. But the leaders themselves emerge from the masses, even if from a different milieu. They become leaders not because they are superior to the masses but only because they are capable of formulating what the masses themselves intuitively desire but cannot express for lack of formal education. You will therefore find in your bourgeois circles a great many people superior to me in erudition, but at a workers' meeting, I, Gentlemen, would carry the day – and not because of my personal superiority, but only because I would be expressing what the masses felt and wanted.

It was the tragedy of the Munich masses that they still had too little political experience. They were well aware that to achieve victory the entire proletariat must act as a body; but they believed that this body could have various programmes and that it was quite sufficient for the Social-Democrats, the Independent Socialists and the Communists to conclude a formal agreement.

This was actually one of the reasons for the defeat of the Munich Soviet Republic. When the proletariat is united in its will and purpose, it is invincible, but not when unity is established in a merely formal organisational way.

This point of view makes my appraisal of all the issues with which I shall deal later quite different from that of the Prosecution. I do not wish to mitigate my sentence; I do not wish to shift the legal responsibility onto the Executive Council. I answer unreservedly for my actions. I was partly the initiator and I first formulated the ideas which the workers only felt instinctively; but I can say that I would never have taken part in a revolution which was thrust upon the workers by the leaders in the way the Prosecution has described.

When I went as a young student to Russia, I already realised that the activity of a political agitator consists only in formulating the historical will of the masses, not in forcing his own will upon them against their will. This principle governed my actions. I appealed to the masses. When they agreed with me, they responded. When they did not, I had unfortunately to play the part I did play and to reap the legal consequences of what others in their folly had sown. I say all this not to explain my personal attitude, but because it expresses the fundamental views of the Communist Party. This party is generally regarded as a group of people who set out to impose minority terror and dictatorship over the proletariat. Yet every line of the party programme testifies that the proletariat alone is destined to achieve its emancipation.

Our whole attitude to the much-debated question of terror and the use of force follows on from this viewpoint that not only a major part of the task but the entire task is assigned to the masses. I have already had the opportunity to expound my attitude to the dicta-torship of the proletariat: that it is only an intermediate stage between the dictatorship of capital and the establishment of complete democracy with only one class of working people. The Communist Party is con-vinced that this programme could very well be realised without violence if the dwindling minority of property owners would not close their minds to historical necessity. The armed struggle of which we are so vehemently accused only begins when this dwindling minority neverthe-less proceeds to defend the privileges of its caste and class by force of arms.

'The Proletarian Revolution has no need of terror for its aims; it detests and abhors murder. It has no need of these means of struggle, for it fights not individuals but institutions.' How then does the struggle arise? Why, having gained power, do we build a Red Army? Because history teaches us that every privileged class has hitherto defended itself by force when its privileges have been endangered. And because we know this; because we do not live in cloud-cuckoo-land; because we cannot believe that conditions in Bavaria are different – that the Bavarian bourgeoisie and the capitalists would allow themselves to be expropriated without a struggle – we were compelled to arm the workers to defend ourselves against the onslaught of the dispossessed capitalists.

This is how it has been in the past and this is how we shall naturally always act in the future, whenever we succeed in attaining power. We did not call on the workers to take up arms out of pleasure in bloodshed. On the contrary, we would be only too happy if the hitherto privileged classes would refrain from embarking upon a hopeless struggle – for one day the struggle will be hopeless. I should like to draw your attention to the fact that the victory of the proletariat in November also passed without bloodshed. In Berlin, for example, the first shots were fired at six o'clock in the evening from the Royal Stables when a group of officers opened fire on defenceless pedestrians out of annoyance at the course of events.

In my view we armed the proletariat to deter the bourgeoisie from an armed counter-attack. The President of the Court or the Public Prosecutor earlier quoted part of an article from the Bulletin of the Executive Council, expressing the apprehension that any gun not surrendered by the bourgeoisie would be used against the proletariat.

While I was initially extremely pessimistic about the situation and did not believe that Bavaria was any different and that the Bavarian Government would not dare to allow the Prussians to march on Munich, I gradually came to hope that we might possibly succeed in holding out until Soviet Republics had been proclaimed in other parts of Germany and that the Hoffmann Government would refrain from attacking us.

We all regard the events of the early days of May not as a proletarian offensive but as an unmotivated bloodbath into which the White Guards plunged the Munich working class.

During the whole time I was in Munich I had the great joy of working hand in hand with my Communist friends. There was always complete unanimity between us and I therefore felt that I was not a stranger but could identify myself with these Communist workers, and through them with the entire Munich working class. I was therefore entitled, at least for that period, to speak in their name.

A second point which also follows from my whole outlook is the recall and dismissal at any time of each and every functionary. The cornerstone of a Soviet Republic is the factory council. The workers are not organised regionally, but in the factories, where they are together every day, where they can get to know each other in the course of their daily work, and where elections of the functionaries are held on totally different principles. There the workers know whether their representative is a mere babbler or a man who can stand his ground.

That is why we accepted this form of organisation as natural and normal – all the more so since the new state was to include only working people. Every representative would hold office only as long as his electors wished. It was therefore not an empty gesture when I repeatedly offered to return my mandate to the Factory Councils. Hence I can say that I and my friends – I may call them my friends – of the Action Committee, all thirty-five of us who resigned on 27th April, were prepared to do so at any time. Not one of us clung to his mandate. And I can assure you that the life we led had no great attraction for any of us, nor for the workers among us, weary after their daily work.

All of us remained in office only out of a sense of duty and regarded it as a heavy burden. I repudiate any suggestion that any single one of us craved for or was drunk with power. Not a single one of us wrested power by force. We received it from the workers of Munich. In the course of two weeks they compelled us three times to keep our mandates. I therefore also reject the allegations that only a triumvirate – Levien, Leviné and Axelrod – or an alien clique, determined the policy. None of these three was a member of the Revolutionary Tribunal or the Committee for Combating the Counter-Revolution.

I should also like personally to reject a reproach which, it is true, was raised from outside the Court but was partly also levelled at me by the Prosecution – namely, that we are aliens. I know very well that I am of Russian origin. I am a Jew, I am not Bavarian. How then could I presume to accept a post which, according to my Counsel corresponded to that of Prime Minister? To understand this you must project yourself into the minds of the working class.

Our ideal is a future German Soviet Republic which one day will be merged into an International Soviet Republic. As long, however, as that was not achieved, Soviet Republics could and can only be affected in separate places, and we were of course convinced that everyone who felt fit for a given post must accept it if no one else was available.

I accepted the post because my previous activity had also given me insight into economic relationships and because I felt justified and indeed morally bound to accept it as no one else was there. And as long as I held the post I had a duty to perform towards the German as well as the International proletariat, and the Communist Revolution.

The Prosecution accuses me of having instigated the ten days' general strike. It is true that it was I who moved the resolution calling for a general strike. It was obvious that to safeguard a proletarian dictatorship the entire proletariat should stand by, and stand by armed.

We had no police, and it was essential to prevent looting and so forth. The Prosecution has asked how I could possibly justify keeping people away from their work for ten days at a time when work was so urgently needed. The German Government kept millions of proletarians away from work, not for ten, but for many hundreds of days. The German Government aspired after Bagdad and Longwy. We wanted Communism. The means, however, which you do not condemn in their case, you should also not condemn in ours just because we pursue other aims.

The Prosecution claims that the workers only struck under the threat of machine-guns. In reality the motion calling for the strike was unanimously adopted by the representatives of all the factories, including the clerical staff; the officials' organisations, the post office workers – all were in favour of the strike.

Where then is the terror? Where the violation by a minority? Why does the Prosecution accept the legends which discredit the workers of Munich? Why will it not admit that they acted in accordance with their own mass-resolutions?

Some time later, on the Tuesday after Easter, it was proposed to call off the strike in view of its economic effects. I made a counter-proposal. Sunday and Monday were Easter holidays. If the workers returned to work on Tuesday, it would have created the impression that the strike had fizzled out. I suggested a more dignified conclusion, more consistent with the will of the working class – namely, to strike on Tuesday, to close all theatres, to stop all trams running so that it was quite clear that it entirely depended on the individual, free decisions of the workers whether they worked or not. This resolution was again accepted unanimously.

The Prosecution will know how it was carried out. The workers, with hundreds of post office employees, men and women, in their pale-blue uniforms in the vanguard, marched to the Wittelsbach Palace to express their solidarity with those who have been portrayed in this Court as terrorists and the enslavers of the Munich proletariat.

In the opening stage of the Soviet Republic we had to prevent the propaganda of the bourgeois Press. We were not in a position to introduce mere censorship and were therefore compelled, it is true, to close down the newspapers.

You say that is terror. Yes, it is terror. The same terror practised by the Hoffmann Government in suppressing the *Rote Fahne*.

The same terror which affords me no other opportunity of justifying myself before my Party comrades than to appeal to the President of this Court to let me state my case.

The Prosecution accuses me of having insisted on harsh sentences and at the same time holds me responsible for the looting in the Soviet Republic. I cannot quite understand it. Either I ought not to have instructed the Tribunal to apply severe measures, as was testified by the witness Kaempfer, in which case I cannot be reproached for the looting; or else I should have been allowed to instruct the Tribunal in its duties in the manner I considered necessary in the interests of our work and our task, and then I cannot be reproached for having done so. While condemning me for even considering the introduction of capital punishment, the Prosecution is demanding in the same breath the death penalty for me – for me who neither looted nor murdered.

The Prosecution has spoken of the internal peace which I have endangered. I did not endanger it, because internal peace does not exist. As long as the word 'socialism' merely heads the notepaper of the various governments there can be no internal peace; and as long as there are shareholders who could double their fortunes in the five years of war without doing a stroke of work, the workers will try to claim their share of that increased wealth and the shareholders will not allow it. And the more the economic conditions deteriorate in the aftermath of the war, when the prisoners of war return to find no work, no homes, no clothes and the little there is cannot be justly distributed because there is no Communist Republic, the internal struggle will continue. And if it assumes forms of which I and my freinds do not approve, the struggle will go on as an inevitable phenomenon against which there is no appeal.

Take a look round! In this very Court are officials who earn monthly only 150 to 180 marks under the present cost of living. Take a look at the homes of the so-called 'Spartacist nests', and you will understand that we have not endangered the internal peace; we have only revealed that internal peace does not exist. And so long as it does not exist this struggle will go on. And if it assumes military forms and carries in its wake all the ghastly misery and distress that actually prevailed in Munich during the first days of May, it is not we who are to blame but those who deny the working class the right to decide its own destiny.

The Prosecution has claimed that I am morally guilty of shooting the hostages. I emphatically repudiate this charge. The guilty are those who in August 1914 were the first to take hostages, though they were never brought to justice or sentenced to death. If anyone else is to blame it is the men who sneaked off to Bamberg and from there sent misguided proletarians together with Officers' Units and Negroes to fight against Munich.

[Uproar and indignation among the judges. The President intervenes and tries to stop Leviné from proceeding].

Mr President, I know very well what I may bring on myself by this statement. But I must say that I have been provoked by the Prosecuting Counsel as never before in my whole political career. To justify his demand for the death sentence the Prosecution charged me with dishonourable motives, and based this charge above all on an accusation of cowardice – one of the gravest accusations that can be levelled against a man who has been engaged for sixteen years in the revolutionary struggle.

I am prepared to let that pass and will only say that if the Prosecution reprimands me for not having joined the Red Army after I withdrew from the government and had no more duties to fulfill, I must refer to the statement already made by my Counsel – namely, that I am guided by the code of honour prevailing among my own friends.

On the last evening we held a meeting, attended by workers, members of the Red Army and others, at which it was unanimously decided that members of the Red Army were to remain at their posts, while former members of the government were to 'disappear'.

I disappeared. I disappeared, I 'sneaked away' in agreement with my Communist friends. But not to save my skin.

Gentlemen, you were very indignant about one of my remarks. I shall not speak about the manner in which I made that remark, but in substance it is nevertheless true. I have read myself in the newspapers that among the troops which marched on Munich there were Negroes. Moreover the Hoffmann Government had not shrunk from certain other measures. Everyone must admit that the blockade of Munich, the closing of the railways and the stoppage of food supplies as practised in this 'free state', were nothing more than a repetition of the English blockade which was regarded as morally so objectionable.

As to the charge of cowardice, I cannot prevent the Prosecuting Counsel from making such accusations. But I may perhaps invite him, who demands the death penalty, to be present at the execution.

He may then also admit that it is a misconception to assume that only those who fight in the front lines of the Red Army risk their lives. You know the poem which appeared in *Vorwaerts* after the Berlin January Days:

A hundred proletarian corpses all in a row;
Karl, Rosa and Company, none on show!
None on show!

Three days later Karl Liebknecht and Rosa Luxemburg were murdered, and the 'Company', my friends Werner Müller and Wolfgang Fernbach were also killed. Not one of them was a member of the Red Army.

Gentlemen, I have twice been accused by representatives of the Bavarian Government of cowardice. The first time by Schneppenhorst for not approving of the establishment of a Soviet Republic; the second time by the present Prosecution for fighting not by force of arms but in my own way, according to my own judgement, and for my absence from the battlefield as agreed with the Communist Party.

I am coming to a close. During the last six months I have no longer been able to live with my family. Occasionally my wife could not even visit me. I could not see my three-year-old boy because the police have kept a vigilant warch on us.

Such was my life and it is not compatible with lust for power or with cowardice. When Toller, who tried to persuade me to proclaim the Soviet Republic, in his turn accused me of cowardice, I said to him: 'What do you want? The Social Democrats start, then run away and betray us; the Independents fall for the bait, join us, and later let us down, and we Communists are stood up against the wall.

We Communists are all dead men on leave. Of this I am fully aware. I do not know if you will extend my leave or whether I shall have to join Karl Liebknecht and Rosa Luxemburg. In any case I await your verdict with composure and inner serenity. For I know that, whatever your verdict, events cannot be stopped. The Prosecuting Counsel believes that the leaders incited the masses. But just as leaders could not prevent the mistakes of the masses under the pseudo-Soviet Republic, so the disappearance of one or other of the leaders will under no circumstances hold up the movement.

And yet I know, sooner or later other judges will sit in this Hall and then those will be punished for high treason who have transgressed against the dictatorship of the proletariat.

Pronounce your verdict if you deem it proper. I have only

striven to foil your attempt to stain my political activity, the name of the Soviet Republic with which I feel myself so closely bound up, and the good name of the workers of Munich. They – and I together with them – we have all of us tried to the best of our knowledge and conscience to do our duty towards the International, the Communist World Revolution.

VI

Leviné's Death Sentence

Eugene Leviné has been condemned to death for the crime of high treason.

Grounds: From April 4th to 5th the Revolutionary Central Council met in order to overthrow the legal constitution and to proclaim a Soviet Republic despite Leviné's opposition. The Hoffmann Ministry transferred its seat to Bamberg, while explicitly reserving its rights. The Diet was not dissolved. The proclamation of the Soviet Government was not founded as a State power. It was merely an act of insubordination against the existing constitutional government.

On the night of April 13th to 14th a part of the Munich garrison sought to help the legal government to re-establish its power.

On this date began Leviné's positive activity aimed at changing by force the Bavarian constitution. He brought about the proclamation of the second Soviet-Republic and the dictatorship of the proletariat. On his initiative an Executive Council and a Committee of Action were set up under his presidency. He ordered the immediate proclamation of a general strike to mobilise the masses for his purposes. The proletariat was armed, a Red Army organised to fight against the government forces. Leviné repeatedly called for the most resolute resistance. A Judicial Commission was appointed to combat the counter-revolution, that is to persecute and suppress the supporters of the lawful government.

The Revolutionary Tribunal, which was taken over from the first Soviet Republic, was to serve the same ends. Numerous actions were carried out by the Red Army to extend the Communist rule by force of arms beyond the borders of Munich. All these measures were designed to transform the entire legal and economical structure into a Communist or Socialist State.

Leviné explicitly accepted full responsibility for all this.

Such conduct warrants a charge of high treason.

Leviné was an alien intruder in Bavaria and he was not in the least concerned with the nature of its constitution.

A man of great intellectual powers, he was fully aware of the implications of his actions. It stands beyond doubt that a man who meddles in such a way with the destiny of a people is guided by dishonourable convictions. For this reason the defendant is denied mitigating circumstances. The Court regards moreover severest punishment as an imperative command of justice.

In accordance with Article 3 of Martial Law the Court therefore pronounces the death sentence.

Index